THE COEXISTENCE OF RACE AND RACISM

Can They Become Extinct Together?

Janis Faye Hutchinson

University Press of America,® Inc.
Lanham · Boulder · New York · Toronto · Oxford

Copyright © 2005 by
University Press of America,® Inc.
4501 Forbes Boulevard
Suite 200
Lanham, Maryland 20706
UPA Acquisitions Department (301) 459-3366

PO Box 317
Oxford
OX2 9RU, UK

Library of Congress Control Number: 2005924846
ISBN 0-7618-3213-0 (paperback : alk. ppr.)

To Kenneth Turner

TABLE OF CONTENTS

PREFACE

As an African-American female growing up in Birmingham during the civil rights period, I always had a strong consciousness about race and racism. I grew up in a segregated environment in the south that had been the norm since the end of slavery. It was an environment in which race was the most important aspect of a person's existence. All blacks, regardless of class, had to walk to the back to use the colored only restroom, drank from colored only water fountains, attend segregated schools, and eat in the basement at Woolworth. Segregation even divided the downtown area. The black downtown was on Fourth Avenue where there were shoe shops, the Masonic temple, restaurants, two theatres, the Carver and Famous, and a variety of other stores. This downtown was just a few blocks from the white downtown where black people did not go unless they worked there or had to go there.

I witnessed the impact of race on my parents' opportunities. For instance, my mother was a cook at various hotels. Sometimes she came home "fed up" with being passed over for promotions. Often, they wanted her to train a white male to become the chef instead of giving her the position. She would quit, and being a good cook, she would easily find another job. So I saw the limitation that racism imposed on my mother's efforts for upward mobility and her frustration.

In the 1950s my dad was a nurse at the Veteran's Administration Hospital. My father was never optimistic about 'progress' for black people. From the beginning he let us know that we should not expect segregation or inequality to end. According to him, you had to find ways to circumvent the system to make a decent life for yourself. Education, he said, was the key to that circumvention.

While race was an issue in dealing with the larger community, colorism was an issue within the black community. My family is a rainbow in terms of skin color. I often wondered why my brother was very dark and I lighter tone although I knew we had the same mother and father. Blacks thought of and treated light-skinned individuals different from dark-skinned people. Light-skinned blacks were thought to have more opportunity, to be better off economically, and to be physically more attractive. Later, I realized this is internalized racism but at the time it was simply a part of life. This aspect of black life could be detrimental for people trying to live up (or down) to expectations. For instance, a guy in my neighborhood was very light-skinned with straight black hair. If you did not know him or his family, you would think he was white. Because of his appearance, other blacks gave him a hard time since they felt he could "pass" and therefore had more opportunity. He joined a tough group of black guys and was eventually killed in a fight. At the time everyone felt that it was his skin color that killed him.

I wanted to know why I could not go to the Alabama theater to see Cinderella, attend any school I wanted or shop or eat anywhere I pleased. When I was around seven years old, we drove all day, at least it seemed like that, to go to an amusement park. Once we arrived, the white guy very politely told us they did not allow Negroes in the park. He apologized continuously for not allowing us in. What I am saying is that at a very early age I realized that whites treated blacks differently simply because of skin tone, and that blacks treated one another differently based upon the color of their skin. That, I think, began my interest in human biological variation.

People categorize individuals and groups of people along a hierarchy based on their beliefs about beauty, intelligence, economic potential, et cetera. When I became a biological anthropologist I learned how this racial hierarchy developed and was/is sustained. During my graduate training in human variation/genetics, the biological component was always emphasized. For instance, Coon's idea of separate origins for each racial group where Caucasians were the most evolved and had the highest level of civilization (Coon, 1962) was a popular view during my early training in anthropology. While some departments provided opposing perspectives on race such as the interaction of biology and environmental factors and/or the social aspects of race, others taught race as strictly a biological phenomenon. Later in my studies, although the influence of environment on biology was considered in research projects and taught in class the genetic component always had prominence. I began to realize that science reflected lay beliefs rather than being objective endeavors.

As a professor of anthropology, I developed a course on race and anthropology where I looked at the concept of race from an historical perspective. This included an examination of early developments of the race concept in Europe. I began to see stereotypes that were created in the sixteenth century to justify seizure of land and enslavement of people that still exist today. Terminology changed but the story was the same. For instance, entrenched in early European thinking was the idea that culture was a reflection of biology and any difference from the European physical appearance, which was considered the norm and original form, was an indicator of a lower stage of development. This low stage could be noted by simply looking at the individual since physical appearance was an indicator of culture and intelligence. Recently there was a discussion about Ebonics on the Internet in which a woman said that blacks spoke Ebonics because their mouths could not make certain sounds used in the English language. Like the sixteenth century scientists, she assumed biology was the reason for linguistic diversity.

My readings on the history of the race concept, training in biological anthropology, and growing up in the south during the civil rights period provide the context for the present discussion on race. The main thesis of the book is that race and racism are social constructs that shaped and reshaped each other. I show that racism needs race because like "classic race," racism claims that the human species is composed of distinct groups with different biological characteristics (races) and that these groups can be ranked.

ACKNOWLEDGEMENTS

I would like to a number of people who reviewed this book and provided valuable comments on the manuscript. In particular, I would like to thank Faye V. Harrison. Faye read certain chapters a number of times and provided a thorough critique as well as extremely good references and literature that needed to be included. I would also like to thank Steven Mintz, Nancy Krieger, Joseph Kotarba, Rebecca Storey, Leonard Lieberman, Maria Fernandez-Esquer, Terry Tomkins-Walsh, Diane Ballinger, Andrew Gordon, David Williams, and Ida Susser for their comments on this manuscript.

CHAPTER ONE

RACE AND RACISM

Get an education. That's the only way black people are going
to get ahead in this world (James Hutchinson, my father)

In this book, I examine the historical and contemporary connection between
race and racism. It is a critique of the biological concept of race and an examination of the social construction of race. This analysis is also a reflexive investigation in which I use my personal experiences growing up in the south, in the
sixties and seventies, and my training and academic position in biological anthropology to explore the relationship between race and racism. Throughout this
book, I include these experiences and those of friends, family, and colleagues
along with the literature to highlight and provide a context for understanding the
connection between these concepts.

I maintain that racism is constant over time in terms of its goal, the maintenance of the *status quo* and therefore privilege for people of European ancestry.
However, the justification for racism underwent continual change. Two factors
contributed to these changes. First, the rationale for racism changed as the definition and attributes of races were modified to correspond with new developments in biology and genetics. Second, while biological discoveries are one side
of this reconstruction, changing social situations represent the other side. That
is, racism also responded to changing social, political, and economic conditions
that altered its justification. These factors form the context for the link between
race and racism. Definitions of race and racism are provided in the ensuing discussion in order to provide a framework for this connection.

RACE

When someone is asked to define race, he/she cannot do it. Instead, they describe characteristics that they associate with populations while acknowledging that everyone who belongs to that group may not possess those particular characteristics. Although racial classification by the average person is done on an ad hoc basis, the primary trait used is skin color. Based upon this single trait, the average person places individuals into racial categories.

They are using a "classic" approach to racial categories. In "classic" race, human biological variation can be partitioned into discrete categories and ranked. Culture, personality, and mental abilities are considered biologically based and associated with these ranked groups. Since colonial times physicians, natural historians, psychologists, and anthropologists considered physical and cultural differences between populations to be due to biological factors as reflected in racial features.

The following are some examples of the definition of "modern" race among scientists.

> Race differences are genetic differences between Mendelian populations, not between persons. ... Race differences are compounds of individual differences; they are more often relative than absolute; races differ in the frequencies of some genes more often than in that a certain gene is wholly absent in one race and present in every individual of another (Dobzhansky, 1968:78).

> Race is a division of a species that differs from other divisions by the frequency with which certain hereditary traits appear among its members (Brues, 1977:1).

> A race is considered, in common usage, to be a subdivision of a species formed by a group of individuals sharing common biological characteristics that distinguish them from other groups (Cavalli-Sforza and Bodmer, 1971: 698).

> A subspecies is an aggregate of local populations of a species, inhabiting a geographic subdivision of the range of the species, and differing taxonomically from other populations of the species (Mayr, 1982:289).

> There are no races, there are only clines (Livingston, 1964: 47)

> "Race" is a term for a problem, which is created by social factors, and by social factors alone; it is, therefore, entirely a social problem (Montagu, 1961:102).

> Race should not be seen as something tangible that exists in the
> outside world, which has to be discovered, described, and de-
> fined, but as a cultural creation, a product of human invention
> (Smedley: 1993: 6).

The first four definitions emphasize genetic diversity. For instance, Cavalli-Sforza and Bodmer discuss biological characteristics and include differences in gene frequencies to identify races. With "modern" race, while biological variation is overlapping, subdivisions or aggregates are identified and considered races.

The definitions by Brues (1971), Cavalli-Sforza and Bodmer (1971) and Mayr (1982) also suggest that the human species can be partitioned into categories, subspecies (races). In this subspecies view of human diversity, populations adapted to differing geographical environments that resulted in differing gene frequencies and biological and behavioral characteristics. Human variation, then, is the product of natural selection. Scientists who believe that races exist, classifiers, associate gene frequencies with certain health, psychological, and behavioral outcomes in contemporary, historical or pre-historical populations. For them, biological makeup is the explanation for differing health outcomes and behaviors.

Livingstone, on the other hand, argues that discrete categories called races do not exist, only overlapping gradients, clines (see Figure 1.1). Clinalists, like Livingstone, identify overlapping gradients without boundaries between populations. For them individual variability overwhelms group differences. Because boundaries between populations cannot be discerned, discrete groups, biological races, are nonexistent (Livingstone, 1962, 1964; Brace, 1964, 1982; Goodman, 1995, 2001; Armelagos, 1995; Goodman and Armelagos, 1996).

These "classifiers," believe there are boundaries between populations (Dobzhansky, 1968; Mayr, 1982; Glass, 1968; Brues, 1971; Cavalli-Sforza and Bodmer, 1971; Shipman, 1994; Harpending, 1995; Wolpoff et al., 1994). Overlapping gradients represent intergradations between populations (see Figure 1.1). While human diversity represents overlapping distributions, biological anthropologists disagree on how to interpret this variation.

Smedley (1993) and Montagu (1961) acknowledge a social component to the race concept. For them, race is fabricated by society and has non-biological meanings. Race is culturally constructed. These scientists investigate race as a social construct in relation to history, social, political, and economic factors. Likewise, I define race as the partitioning of human variability into categories for historical, social, political, and economic reasons. In this sense, race is a social, and not a biological phenomenon.

From this discussion it is apparent that there are two schools of thought on the race issue: 1) no-biological-race and 2) races exist (classifiers). In the no-biological-race camp there are two perspectives. First, among cultural anthropologists and some physical anthropologists race is a social construct. Individuals decide, for instance, that skin color is more important than ear shape in determining the criteria for races. Also, the idea of race is promoted because of historical and socio-politico-economic factors. In other words, the dominant group has a personal stake in the maintenance of racial classifications. Clinalists represent the second perspective. For them boundaries cannot be identified between overlapping distributions. Therefore, human variation cannot be partitioned into discrete categories and races are nonexistent.

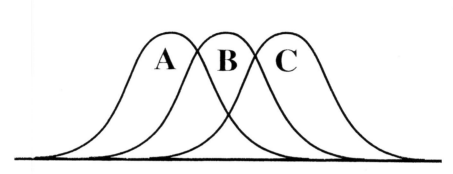

Figure 1.1. Overlapping Distributions

In the races exist group, classifiers can be divided into two groups: "classic" and "modern" race. Division into "classic" and "modern" race does not mean that scientists as early as the 1700s did not recognize that human variation represent overlapping distributions. For example, in *On the Natural Variety of Mankind* (1795) Johann Friedrich Blumenbach stated that "innumerable varieties of mankind run into one another by insensible degrees" (Blumenbach, 1795 [1969]: 264). However, he and craniometrists such as George Samuel Morton and Paul Broca contended that such variation could be partitioned into discrete categories, "classic" race. Craniometrists computed head and body measurements and all types of indices in an effort to reveal the "right" criteria to classify races. Today, the average person considers skin color to be the "right" criteria for defining "classic" race.

For contemporary classifiers, human distributions represent "modern" race. These classifiers contend that there are boundaries between populations although the distributions overlap. Race is not discrete but represents higher frequencies or combinations of characteristics in one population as opposed to another. In the chapter on scientific statements on race and the concluding chapter, I examine the inception and ramifications of the division between cultural and physical anthropologists and the division among physical anthropologists, i.e. clinalists versus classifiers, on the subject of race.

ETHNICITY AND MINORITIES

Ethnicity and race are often used interchangeably. But many scientists make a clear distinction between the terms. While race is usually based on biology, ethnicity is defined by culture. Race and ethnicity share a common descent through collective history, but ethnicity represents psychological and cultural factors. Diop (1991) identified three components of ethnicity: historical, linguistic and psychological. These factors connote the historical origins and cultural component of ethnic groups. However, Barth (1969) argued that boundaries and not cultural differences distinguish ethnic groups. For him, social interaction is the foundation of ethnicity.

Mullings (1978) distinguished between ethnicity as the cognitive (shared cultural norms, values and symbols) and the social structural (the behavioral or social organizational level). All groups exhibit the cognitive component of shared norms, values and symbols. However, ethnic groups differ at the social organizational level because there is a ... "history of unequal constraints".... For instance, slavery and racism relegated African Americans to lower living standards (e.g. housing, occupation, food, health) while Euroethnics with voluntary migration achieved economic parity with the dominant white population (Mullings, 1978). Because of differences at the structural level, ethnicity does not have the same meaning or social consequences for all ethnic groups.

Vincent (1974) emphasized boundaries as the structural aspect of ethnicity while the cultural is the situational element. In terms of the former, a crucial structural element of ethnicity is the recognition of "us versus them" by the group and by others. This "us versus them" perspective derives from the association of ethnicity with nationals in other countries. In terms of the cultural element, individuals can decide if they want to belong to an ethnic group and they can decide if they want to identify as an ethnic. For instance, in the United States an individual may identify as Greek American during a cultural celebration but identify as white American in other situations. In other words, ethnicity is a "purposive group" that exists to deal with particular issues. The cultural element of ethnicity operates in particular situations related to confrontation, ritual and crisis. Therefore, ethnic identification is an *option* open to people in a specific time and place based upon "interrelationships of these individuals with others who are similarly operating within specific ranges of options" (Vincent, 1974:377). Ethnicity, then, is fluid and changeable.

The term minority is also used in relation to ethnicity. Wagley and Harris (1958) provided a definition of minorities that is still relevant today. Minorities are

...a social group whose members are subject to disabilities in
the form of prejudice, discrimination, segregation, or persecution (or a combination of these) at the hands of ... the majority
(1958: 4).

Minorities are subordinates with specific physical or cultural features that are
considered inferior by the dominant group (Wagley and Harris, 1958; Vincent,
1974; Vander Zanden, 1983).

Mullings (1978) distinguished between cultural and oppressed minorities.
Cultural minorities are unorganized as a group and have only the cognitive part
of ethnicity. In figure 1.2, population D may be a cultural minority (ethnic
group), such as Italian Americans, and part of a larger group, population C with
similar physical characteristics. Classifiers may lump the physical appearance of
population D with population C to form a single racial group. Population D may
participate in certain cultural activities such as festivals or holidays as an ethnic
group but racially, as well as politically, socially and economically be part of
the dominant group, C. Cultural minorities, like cognitive ethnics, are fluid.

Oppressed minorities are confined to the lowest levels of stratification of society in terms of labor and allocation of resources.

Often products of capture, conquest, or neo-colonialism, such a
group is also characterized by ethnicity---shared cultural symbolic phenomena; however, in this case ethnicity is utilized by
the dominant group to rationalize the continued structured oppressed status that defines this category (Mullings, 1978:19).

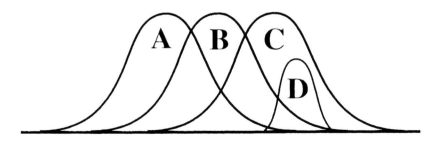

Figure 1.2. Distributions Representing Ethnic Groups

Population A in figure 1.2 can represent an ethnic group, racial group, and
oppressed minority. Physical difference, history, and the persistence of racism
make it impossible for this population to blend into populations B or C. Unlike

cognitive ethnics or cultural minorities, oppressed minority status is static and related to structured inequality.

Although Mullings (1978) used the term minority for both groups (oppressed and cultural), others consider minorities to be only oppressed minorities. In the United States, minority status is not related to population size or the cognitive component of ethnicity. It is based upon power. In this regard, economic discrimination is the cornerstone of majority/minority distinctions (Vincent, 1974). The reason the majority group is dominant is not because of population size but due to its greater power to control economic, political and social mechanisms in society (Wagley and Harris, 1958). Therefore, social subordination and disadvantage are crucial elements in distinguishing a minority from a majority group (Vander Zanden, 1983).

There are historical reasons for differences between minorities and ethnics. For instance, historically, the majority of the working class was people of color, minorities (Brodkin, 2001). While southern and eastern Europeans were part of the working class, because of the structural component of ethnicity they had the opportunity to move out of the minority category and to be or not to be an ethnic. For instance, U.S. federal statistics are collected by race: Black/African American, White (non-Hispanic); and ethnicity such as Hispanic (Wagley and Harris, 1958; Vincent, 1974) and more recently the census bureau categorized various Asian American groups. However, data are not collected, on, for example, German Americans, French Americans, or Italian Americans. On a social level, these Americans can decide whether to be an ethnic or not. The other groups are minorities as reflected in their pre-assigned static statuses. It is evident that minority status has economic and political implications related to the history of inequality in America. As Vincent (1974) stated, "all are ethnics" but all are not minorities. The difference is related to "structured inequality" (Vincent, 1974).

RACISM

Racist ideology is the belief that biological diversity among human groups is the basis for sociocultural differences. Racism emerges when racist ideology is used to claim that biological differences are a legitimate reason for differential treatment of human populations (Metress, 1993). As you will learn from reading this volume, racism is intricately related to the "classic" race concept although it has adapted to "modern" race. In this conception, "modern" races, human diversity, are still ranked. This ranking of populations gives rise to prejudice, stereotypes, ethnocentrism, discrimination, and racism. In order to understand the various manifestations of racism, the other four concepts must be examined.

Prejudice is a prejudgment, attitude, about a person or group without verification or examination of the merits of the judgment (Vander Zanden, 1983). When I was in graduate school, a professor told me that if I missed an A by two points he would give me the points. I had just arrived on campus and was meeting with him because he was the graduate advisor. He did not know me and I was stunned that he assumed I could not make an A in his course without assistance. This was a prejudgment about my ability without the opportunity to evaluate my capabilities or the inclination to withhold judgement until my abilities could be assessed. Such prejudgments can exist about minorities regardless of lack of evidence or evidence to the contrary.

Stereotypes are unreliable and unscientific generalizations that people make about other individuals or groups (Vander Zanden, 1983). They are oversimplifications that "can be" supported with anecdotal evidence. Stereotypes can be positive or negative but the main point is that stereotypes are unreliable generalizations. The graduate advisor assumed that I would be unable to achieve an A in his class because I think he assumed that blacks have lowered abilities. I feel confident in making this statement because my college transcript indicated that I was accomplished and in talking to my white graduate colleagues, none of them had this experience with him. He generalized about me, a stereotype, because of prejudgment, prejudice.

Sumner and Keller (1906:13) defined ethnocentrism as "this view of things in which one's own group is the center of everything, and all others are scaled and rated with reference to it." Put another way, ethnocentrism is an odd "egocentric" thinking where individuals use their own group as a standard for other groups and one's own group is considered superior to others. I would argue that that professor considers other groups, i.e. blacks, inferior to his own group. In his thinking, I could not conform to the standards of his group in terms of mental ability because I was not a member of his group. His thinking was based on my outward physical appearance and not on my achieved mental abilities. Based on my physical appearance I was a member of the outgroup with inferior qualities.

Discrimination is an overt action where members of a racial or ethnic group are treated unequally by members and institutions of the dominant group (Vander Zanden, 1983). While the three previous concepts are attitudes and beliefs about individuals and groups, the latter is a behavior. Discrimination is prejudice and negative stereotypes in action. The action in the case of the professor was that I got a B in the course. I made an 88 on every examination that I took with him. While in the course I compared my answers to others in the class and found that they were virtually the same. One day, I went to his office to talk about my grade and I asked him what was wrong with my answers. He said, "I just didn't like it." I still remember that response. From the look on his face, I knew he was waiting for me to ask for two points. I never did and I did not enroll in another course with him during my graduate training.

Prejudice, negative stereotypes, ethnocentrism and discrimination can be incorporated into individual racism, the negative attitudes and behaviors expressed by members of the dominant group toward the minority group (Vander Zanden, 1983). With this type of racism individuals believe that other groups are inferior to them because of their physical traits; and that biological traits are determinants of morality, intellectual qualities and social behavior. Ultimately, individual racists assume that this inferiority is a legitimate basis for unequal social treatment of groups of people (Jones, 1972) or individuals. When I thought about examples of individual racism and discussed this with friends their examples were endless. For instance, an employee at an airline company was called the N word by a manager who said "haven't you been called an N before so it shouldn't be a big deal." Numerous friends discussed going to department stores and being ignored because the salesperson assumed they could not afford to buy anything. They often said they would "not be acknowledged." From the example of the professor prejudice, negative stereotypes, and ethnocentrism worked together to create a negative attitude toward me. Prejudice, negative stereotypes and ethnocentrism also produced a behavior, discrimination that resulted in my receiving a low grade in the course.

Individual racism can operate as unaware or subtle racism when individuals of the dominant group unknowingly or without intent express prejudice and discrimination against subordinate groups. Although the intent may be friendly and well meaning, the result is still racial prejudice and discrimination. I cannot say if the professor operated at an aware or unaware level in his interaction with me. However, I believe a colleague in a different discipline provides an example of unaware racism. Whenever I see this individual (a white male), that is often because we are in the same building, he talks to me about black music, dance, art, or Africa. It is always about black people or something related to black people. He asks my opinion as if I can speak for all black people or that all black people think or behave in the same way. I have known this individual for at least ten years and would say that he is not a mean person. I am sure he votes for liberal candidates and he speaks out against racial discrimination on campus. Nevertheless, when interacting with me or other blacks, students or colleagues, he reduces the conversation to issues concerning our ancestry. This, to me, is also racism because it suggests that our biology is the most important factor for us and for him.

In the previous examples I discussed two educated people, professors with PhDs. Although educated people appear to be more tolerant of diversity they may oppose structures designed to promote equality. McClelland and Auster (1990) believe this contradiction relates to symbolic racism, a type of individual racism (Pettigrew, 1985). In this type of racism, there is a negative perception and treatment of, for instance, blacks but it is not expressed directly as with "traditional" racism. "Traditional" racists believe, for example, that interracial marriage is wrong and that whites are smarter than blacks. Symbolic racists would disagree with these statements but oppose programs such as busing or affirmative action that seek to improve the status of minorities. Their opposition is based on the grounds that cherished values of meritocracy and free choice are violated. In opposing programs that promote equal rights over individual rights, attention shifts away from present-day inequalities between groups. Instead, individual rights are paramount resulting in those in the best position to exercise these rights, members of the dominant group, maintaining an advantage (McClelland and Auster, 1990).

Another form of racism is collective racism, which involves shared culture. Individuals within a society share culture that is composed of beliefs, attitudes, values, material objects, and behaviors (Ferraro et al., 1994; Kottak, 2000). Since individuals learn and share culture, beliefs and attitudes concerning racial prejudice, members of a society also learn stereotypes and discrimination. Racism and discrimination are learned along with other cultural beliefs and behaviors. This shared understanding can be expressed as collective racism or discrimination that result from shared norms and values that operate within a society to legitimize oppression. The experiences that I had in graduate school (I gave only one example) are not unique to me. Other black and Latino colleagues have told similar stories that include instances of not being called on in class, being ignored by their advisor, shunned by faculty members, or passed over for research opportunities.

Robert Alvarez (1994) provides another perspective on collective racism. He described his experiences as a minority recruit in anthropology. Recruitment of minorities at predominantly white universities is symbolic of fulfilling institutional goals and requirements to diversify the faculty population. However, in efforts to recruit minorities universities operate in "…secrecy, manipulation, misused power, and reasserted hierarchy" (1994:260). In the recruitment process, Alvarez experienced an effort to recruit him but not to hire him. Sometimes specific members of an anthropology department were opposed to the hire because they believed the position should be available to all candidates and not just minorities (ignoring biases due to the "old boy" system). At other times members stated they already had one Chicano in their department and they did not need to hire another one. Also, recruitment of minorities into anthropology does not result in the inclusion of new perspectives and knowledge from such persons and knowledge is not incorporated into the discipline, only minority bodies to show that the department is diverse, (Alvarez, 1994). Such collective attitudes and behaviors flow from learned and shared understandings about minorities. In this collectivism, shared norms and values legitimize exclusion in recruitment and hiring practices. According to Jones (1972:172) racism results from the transformation of race prejudice and/or ethnocentrism through the exercise of power against a racial group defined as inferior, by individuals and institutions with the intentional or unintentional support of the entire (race or) culture.

Collective racism involves support from the group. For example, a friend at a telephone company described a Halloween contest at her company where a white male was dressed as a pimp in black face with a white female that was dressed as a prostitute. A large percentage of the employees (mainly white) did not see anything wrong or racist about his costume. There was no condemnation of the costume by employees or supervisors. As a matter of fact, they liked it so much that he won first prize. Afterward, a black female filed charges with equal employment opportunity and won.

Collective racism can also be expressed as cultural racism. The latter is:

...the belief in the inferiority of the implements, handicrafts, agriculture, economics, music, art, religious beliefs, traditions, language and story of African (Hispanic, Asian, and Indian) peoples; . . . [and the belief that] Black (and other non-White) Americans have no distinctive implements, handicrafts, agriculture, economics, music, art, religious beliefs, traditions, language or story apart from those of mainstream white America (Jones, 1972:148).

Cultural racism is also learned behavior that is shared by members of a society. People of European heritage put forth the notion that Euro-American philosophy, music, art, religion, beauty, and values are superior to those of 84% of the rest of the world's populations. As long as white American standards are used, visible racial groups assume inferior status unless they adopt the cultural ways of whites. For example, black American culture is viewed as inferior because of their African past and their adaptations are considered lower class, urban ghetto, and underclass. The notion of cultural deprivation attests to a disregard for Hispanic culture and black culture (Carter and Goodwin, 1994). In cultural racism oppressed minorities can only be a 'credit to their race' by distancing themselves both psychologically and culturally from their group and assimilating within white society (Helms, 1990; Jones and Wilson, 1996).

Cultural racism may be a factor in internalized racism which is the destructive patterns of behaviors and feelings experienced by victims of racism that are turned upon themselves and each other. The issue that most blacks immediately think of in terms of internalized racism is colorism within the black community. My best friend in elementary school was a very dark-skinned girl who refused to take school pictures because they were in black and white. She said the pictures made her look "too" dark. Lighter-skinned blacks may be viewed as physically more attractive and thought to have more education and money. I think this perspective may be a legacy of slavery where the masters' children were fairer skinned, educated, and some inherited property and other resources. These individuals may have become the leaders of the black community since they had more money and education.

Individual, collective and cultural racism produce institutional racism which

> ...consists of those established laws, customs, and practices, which systematically reflect and produce racial inequalities in American society . . . whether or not the individuals maintaining those practices have racist intentions (Jones, 1972:131).

Carmichael and Hamilton (1967) stated that institutional racism is when one or more of the institutions of a society functions to impose more burdens on and give less benefits to the members of one racial or ethnic group than another on an ongoing basis. Bowser and Hunt (1996) stated that racism is an expression of "institutionalized patterns of white power and social control that were rooted in the very structures of society" (p. xiii).

In terms of institutional racism, a number of friends discussed being followed in stores as they shopped. Not only was one friend followed but also different security people followed her mother and her sister while they shopped together. Whites in the store were not followed. It seems that the store had a policy that blacks must be followed while whites are not. Another example of institutional racism took place in Houston where a black officer in the Sheriff's County Department was called a monkey by a supervisor. The supervisor initially received a three-day suspension but authorities at the Sheriff's Department overturned the suspension. Evidently, they supported his behavior. Examples of institutional racism also include racial profiling, predatory lending, and channeling of people of color into curriculums that lead to low-level jobs.

Racial discrimination in the workplace provides numerous examples of institutional racism. For instance, Georgia Power in Atlanta, a Fortune 500 Company, is being sued by over 2400 former and current black employees for race discrimination in pay and promotion and a hostile work environment. They describe use of the N word by supervisors and that for decades Hangman's nooses hung at all eight plants. Workers cited numerous examples of being passed over for promotions although they had seniority and skills commensurate with the position. One woman said she worked there for twenty years and earned $4,000 less than a white woman that she trained who is doing the same job. A black female who worked there for 16 years was given the title of senior but not the money that went along with the title. A black supervisor analyst earned $37,000 but another analyst, white female, with the same rank made $67,000 and a Project analyst, a rank below her position and white, earned $42,000. A study of wages at Georgia Power showed that blacks formed the bottom of the pay scale and earned 20% less than whites (Dateline NBC, August 21, 2001).

Institutional racism is a function of collective racism. That is, collective racism operates on shared norms and behaviors. Institutional racism is the implementation and institutionalization of those norms and behaviors to oppress a group.

Another type of racism, scientific racism, is the continuation of the aforementioned forms of racism to the realm of science. It is the belief that science proves the existence of permanent innate group differences and legitimates the assertion of racial ranking (Cravens, 1996). Likewise, according to Metress (1993), scientific racism is an attempt to use scientific techniques and language to support theories that some races or populations are biologically superior to others. Research questions, data collection methods and interpretation of findings can take the form of "a priori" conclusions formulated to support inferiority of a group. Hyde (1996) asserted that the theoretical orientation or set of assumptions scientists begin with affects the outcome of the research. Racial bias enters, for example, if the scientist selects an elitist research topic, gives the illusion of objectivity (especially with the positivist approach), uses person-blame explanation and/or begins the research with a biased theoretical model (Jayaratne and Stewart, 1991; Hyde, 1996).

An example of a biased theoretical orientation and set of assumptions can be found in the research of J. Philippe. He assumes that people of color have higher fertility than whites because natural selection operates to produce such genetic differences that are associated with an array of personality traits (1985, 1999). For instance, he argues that those with lowered fertility have higher intelligence, are more altruistic, and have a lower sex drive than those with higher fertility. Even if these personality traits are genetically based, there is no reason to assume that altruism, intelligence, pair bonding, and the like are more prevalent in one group than in another.

One could argue that Rushton began his research with his findings. That is, he knew what he wanted to conclude, presented an illusion of objectivity, and collected data that would support his "a priori" conclusion while excluding other sources of data and explanations. His research, while criticized, has wide support within science as indicated by numerous publications in respected journals.

The popularity of Rushton's work suggests the acceptance of the assumptions that he makes. These assumptions include the existence of racial ranking in nature. Examination of the history of this assumption suggests that whenever races were redefined based on new biological discoveries, forms of racism, including scientific racism, also changed their justification. For instance, in the 1800s measurements were used to distinguish between groups and outward features were the focus of racism. Today races are defined using gene frequencies where they are related to, for instance, social behavior and used to rank groups. Scientific racism can use "classic" or "modern" race to form hierarchies and oppress minorities.

Two factors are important in understanding racism: it is learned and shared by members of a society. Racism is learned as part of the enculturation process (the process of learning ones' culture) (Kottak, 2000). While culture does not determine behavior and individuals have free will, it does condition people to think and behave in certain ways. Enculturation ensures that the culture of racism (individual, symbolic, cultural, collective, institutional, and scientific) is transmitted from one generation to the next. Because racism is learned behavior, it can be unlearned. Some people unlearn or do not learn racism to the same degree of others. In the final chapter I suggest some ways to unlearn racism.

I experienced many forms of racism during my growing up years, while in college and as a professor in anthropology. These experiences are used in this volume to put a face to those on the receiving side of racism. While much of the ensuing discussion involves historical and contemporary analyses of the race concept in science, my experiences in the discipline are used to provide a human side for those learning about race and racism. The volume mainly focuses on race and racism in the United States although scientists and events in Europe are discussed in relation to the historical interplay between these concepts.

Today, although xenophobia is worldwide, racism is strongly identified with prejudice and discrimination against Africans and people of African ancestry. As discussed in the preface, my experiences with racism that inform this discussion relate to black-white relationships in the United States. While I focus on black-white relations, it is not intended to marginalize the experiences of Native Americans, other groups, or xenophobia in Eastern Europe and other parts of the world. Rather, African Americans, in particular, are a good example of what it means to be the "other." This "otherness" was based on dark-skin color and has been extended to create "otherness" in groups. In this creation of "otherness" not only are certain groups oppressed but the oppressors also suffer. This discussion relates to these groups as well but I will use people of African ancestry as a case study.

CHAPTER TWO

EARLY PREJUDICES

I will count Egypt and Babylon among my friends; Philistine,
Tyrian and Nubian shall be there; and Zion shall be called a
mother in whom men of every race are born (Psalms 87:3-6)

This chapter lays the foundation for the connection between racism and race
by examining early evidence of prejudice. For example, religious prejudice, especially against Jews, was a precursor to racial prejudice. In particular, this section examines the crucial shift from prejudice rooted in religious differences to
prejudice rooted in ancestry. It is argued that European concern with race arose
during the Spanish Inquisition with their obsession over *limpieza*, "purity of
blood." The reasons for this shift and a number of explanations for prejudice
against dark-skinned people are examined.

EARLY RACIAL VIEWS

Race was not of primary importance in ancient times. While ancient people
recognized physical differences, appearance was not used to rank or oppress
populations. Egyptians, for instance, recognized physical differences as illustrated by drawings on tombs but did not discriminate based upon physique. As
early as 1350 B.C. they used four colors to represent people: red for Egyptians,
black for sub-Saharan Africa, yellow for the people to the east, and white for
people in the north. The form of prejudice during this period depended on who
was in power. If blacks were in power they called the lighter skinned people the
... "degraded race of Arvad," and when the lighter-skinned people were domi-

nant they referred to the Negroes as ... "the evil race of Ish" (Gossett, 1965:4). Power was the issue. There is no evidence that Egyptians placed any hierarchical social value on facial features or skin color. Pharaohs and slaves in Egypt could be olive, brown, or black with East African or Mediterranean features (Drake, 1987).

Therefore, skin color among ancient people was not used to distinguish the superior from the inferior, but to identify the conquered versus the conqueror. For instance, when the Greeks began to dominate darker people in southwest Asia and Egypt skin tone was a useful marker for themselves and justification of their rule (Bernal, 1997). Also, an emphasis on the moral superiority of light skin color in Egypt was useful to the Persian conquerors as well as the Greeks who played an important role in Egypt (Drake, 1987; Bernal, 1997). Skin color was used as a marker in power relationships.

Another example of the minimal importance of physical appearance in ancient times can be found among the Greeks. Greeks and Romans explained variation in skin color in terms of scientific explanations. For them, people in the south were burned dark by the sun while those in the north lacked sun and people in the middle like Greeks and Romans had the right medium. This is an environmental explanation for dark skin based upon egalitarianism (Devisse, 1976; Jordan, 1977).

Both Greek and Roman cultures portrayed favorable images of blacks. This is evident in the works of Roman and Greek artists, historians, poets, writers, and philosophers (Snowden, 1983). In ancient Greek civilization there was no relationship between slavery and physical features and there was no prejudice against people with black or dark brown skin (Gossett, 1965; Bernal, 1997). Although Greeks divided people into barbarians and Greeks, it was a nonracial division. The Greeks were suspicious of any foreigners, but they treated those who became part of their society, including Africans, in the same way that they treated other Greeks. Interaction and treatment were based on being a member of society rather than physical appearance (Wilson, 1996).

Aristotle's writings, however, were used to support slavery in the United States. In *Politics* he said, "For there is one rule exercised over subjects who are by nature free, another over subjects who are by nature slaves" (Aristotle, 1969:11). But Aristotle maintained that racial differences are due to environmental and climatic factors and that slaves taken in war were often more intelligent than their captors. He did not believe that slaves were less intelligent or less human than others (Wilson, 1996).

> ...nothing comparable to the virulent color prejudice found in modern times existed in the ancient world. This is the view of most scholars who have examined the evidence and who have come to conclusions much as these: the ancients did not fall into the error of biological racism; black skin color was not a

> sign of inferiority, Greeks and Romans did not establish color
> as an obstacle to integration in society; and ancient society was
> one that, for all its faults and failures, never made color the ba-
> sis for judging a man (Snowden, 1983:63).

In ancient times, people were mainly concerned with behavior. Following the customs, speaking the language and worshipping the same god qualified you to be "the people." Invasions occurred over the desire for land, the importance of conquest, the love of battle and the need for economic expansion, not because of beliefs about the biological inferiority of the group being invaded. Ancient people were aware of physical differences but these differences were not used as political and ideological justifications to enslave and oppress others (Diop, 1974; Felder, 1989).

PREJUDICE ROOTED IN RELIGION

Early Christians believed that all people came from the same source. This doctrine was the antithesis of racism. However, promotion of the unity of humankind by the church ended during the Crusades when the church called upon all Christians to take the Holy Land from the infidels. The Crusades provide an early example of religious prejudice because it encouraged and promoted hatred toward non-Christians, mainly Jews and Muslims (Wilson, 1996). For example, on November 26, 1095 A.D. Pope Urban II told his followers to avenge the blood of Christ, to attack opponents of Christianity and to reclaim the Holy Land from the infidels. Six months later Crusaders assaulted Jews and attacked Jewish synagogues and communities along the Rhine Valley (Roth, 1972; Wilson, 1996). This was the beginning of brutal assaults against Jews that continued throughout history (Wilson, 1996).

Christians considered Jews the cursed people and God's murderers rather than the 'Chosen People' (Montagu, 1942). Christians had a number of negative stereotypes about Jews. For instance, Jews were thought to have bad physical, moral and mental characteristics that were biologically inherited. Christians believed that Jews had an unpleasant odor. In addition, it was believed that Jewish children were born with their right hand attached to their heads. To cure their diseases, Jews had to use Christian blood; and this was the basis for their ritual murder of Christian children (Gossett, 1965). These stereotypes were unfounded generalizations about Jews that were believed although there was no evidence to support them. Such stereotypes and religious prejudice provided a rationale for discrimination against Jews that was similar to racial discrimination.

PREJUDICE ROOTED IN ANCESTRY

The earliest evidence of discrimination based upon ancestry is found in the fifteenth century during the Spanish Inquisition. The Inquisition, founded in 1480, excluded from all public offices anyone condemned for Jewish practices and extended this discrimination to their family. The children and grandchildren of those condemned by the Inquisition could not hold positions such as judges, mayors, constables, magistrates, attorneys, secretaries, accountants, surgeons, shopkeepers, brokers, or any other similar public office. Recalcitrant heretics were burned at the stake, lesser offenders were punished, and in 1492 all unconverted Jews were expelled from Spain (Kamen, 1965).

Heretics were forced to wear a garment called *sanbenitos*. In the early sixteenth century, the practice of hanging up the *sanbenitos* of victims after the period for which the garment had to be worn resulted in generational punishment. Generations of whole families were punished for the 'sins' of their ancestors (Kamen, 1965). Through this practice, prejudice was not only against the "guilty," but also against their future descendants. In this way, and exclusion from certain occupations, the Inquisition is the earliest example of prejudice and discrimination based upon ancestry, racism.

Even if Jews converted to Christianity the Inquisition could still punish them. For example, the Marranos of Spain were punished at the time of the Inquisition although the overwhelming majority of Marranos had already converted (Hauben, 1969; Seminario, 1975). The Inquisition was not concerned with the religion of the Marranos. In other words, the aim of the Inquisition was not to eradicate Jewish heresy from the Marranos, but to eradicate the Marranos from the midst of the Spanish people (Hauben, 1969).

The real motivation for the establishment of the Inquisition by Ferdinand V was to confiscate the land and property of Jews. It was to bring their riches, land and businesses into the hands of the Spanish government (Llorente, 1967). "Racial hatred and economic and political considerations were the motivation behind the Inquisition" (Hauben, 1969:43-44).

The basis for negative stereotypes, prejudice, and discrimination against Jews can be found in the social structure of Spain. Throughout the fourteenth century, the basic occupational distinction was that Christians made war and were agriculturists, the Moors were laborers and the Jews formed the middle class (Kamen, 1965). At this time there was a demand for technicians in economic and bureaucratic activities such as accountants, estate managers, secretaries, municipal administrators, et cetera. The fact that converts and Jews dominated the municipal administration irritated the Spanish proletarian masses (Kamen, 1985).

These economic and political considerations spurred the Inquisition and supported collective racism within Spanish society. This collectivism included learned and shared negative stereotypes and prejudices toward Jews and con-verts. Collective racism extended to the royal family of Ferdinand and Isabella who needed to solidify their socioeconomic power. They accomplished this by forging alliances with the feudal nobility against the urban middle class, Jews. This was an attempt by the feudalistic nobility and Old Christians to eliminate Jews who controlled capital and commerce in the towns (Kamen, 1965). In other words, persecution of Jews was not to eliminate Judaism, which was al-ready minimal, but to restructure the economic system in Spanish towns. This restructuring allowed non-Jews to gain access to high-status occupations and in the process provided a base of support for the nobility. Competition for scarce resources and power for the ruling families form the context for discrimination toward anyone of Jewish ancestry.

The Inquisition, then, is an early example of institutional racism. This is demonstrated by the fact that in Spain all prominent institutions in both church and state, led mainly by the Inquisition, discriminated against Jews and conver-sos. In addition, the Inquisition had the support of the average Old Christian citizen, the nobility, and the royal family. Since institutional racism operates through collective racism, the Inquisition was legitimized by shared Spanish norms and beliefs, culture.

Shared norms and values among Old Christians dictated that their heritage could not be shared with Jews and Moors. However, the principal families of Aragon and Castile and maybe the royal family could trace their descent through conversos. With this threat, Old Christians believed that if this contin-ued Spain would collapse. To stop Jewish penetration into the heritage of the Old Christians, in the fifteenth century the Spanish began to stress racial purity and there was a rise of the cult of *limpieza de sangre* — purity of blood (Kamen, 1965).

With *limpieza* and decrees of the Inquisition, it became necessary to prove that you were descended only from Old Christians to gain public employment. If it could be proved that an ancestor had been made to do penance by the Inquisi-tion or was a Moor or Jew, his descendant was considered impure and unable to attain any public office. All applicants for positions had to draw up genealogical proofs of the purity of their lineage. Even in academic life and higher profes-sions, conversos were excluded. For example, a decree of the Inquisition in 1522 forbade universities from granting degrees to descendants of Jews (Kamen, 1965).

Encouraged by the Inquisition, followers of *limpieza* attempted to maintain the *status quo* by preventing Jews from attaining nobility status and therefore access to the politico-economic process. *Limpieza* was not a defensive mecha-nism against heresy. It was openly racist. Jews, like free blacks in the southern United States, were prevented from attaining a higher education and relegated to low-status occupations. For Jews and blacks, prejudice and discrimination were based on ancestry.

While *limpieza* owed its strength to the Inquisition, its decline was due to the same body. The tribunal cleansed Spain of heretical conversos by the beginning of the eighteenth century so the Jewish question ceased for all practical purposes. Jews were a rarity in Spain in the second half of the eighteenth century. Antisemitism then degenerated into an irrational prejudice with no roots in reality. More than reforming ministers were needed to abolish *limpieza*. It survived the abolition of the Inquisition because it was entrenched in Spanish culture. Official recognition of *limpieza* ceased with a royal order in January 31, 1835 and in May 16, 1865 the last official act was abolishment of proofs of purity for marriages and certain government posts (Kamen, 1965).

Limpieza and the Spanish Inquisition mark the shift from religious to racial prejudice that was initiated by economic and sociopolitical factors within Spain. Throughout this volume, it is argued that sociopolitical and economic concerns continue to be factors in the maintenance of racism and support for the race concept.

PREJUDICE ROOTED IN SKIN COLOR

Why and when did physical appearance become a justification for black slavery and oppression? In Spain, as early as the thirteenth century Africans from Morocco, Algiers and other countries were enslaved. Initially, black slaves in Spain were a rarity and were prized. Later, when they were more common, they were considered inferior but this was not because of their ancestry. It was related to their status, slaves, and their religion, Moslem. Unlike slavery in the United States and Caribbean, blacks in Spain could gain their independence over time by buying their freedom, receiving it upon their master's death, or fleeing to cities where cheap labor was needed. Their numbers were always small but there were always some free blacks in Spain. Gradually, blacks in Spain assimilated through intermarriage and ceased to exist as a distinguishable group based upon skin color (Seminario, 1975). Their early bondage was not due to their skin color. Rather, they were enslaved as other groups were enslaved. Their assimilation into the Spanish population suggests that prejudice against them was not rooted in skin color or ancestry but their status, slave.

We must still ask the question what caused the change in attitude toward dark skin and Africans? There must be other explanations for this shift in attitude and behavior toward dark-skinned people. The following are possible explanations for this shift.

Biological Relationship between Africans and Apes

One explanation is that prejudice against blacks appeared among the English because they were introduced to apes and Africans in the same place and at the same time. They immediately discerned similarities between "the man-like beasts and the beast-like men of Africa" (Jordan, 1977: 32). As far as Europeans were concerned, Africans could be another form of ape, with similar moral and mental patterns (Stepan, 1982).

White Americans often described Africans as beasts or bestial and discussed cannibalism, warfare, and diet that seemed to place Africans with beasts. It was also thought that apes and blacks copulated. Sexual union proved a close biological relationship, 'affinity,' and gave credence to English ideas that blacks were lascivious, lewd, and libidinous (Jordan, 1977). Prejudice was rooted in irrational beliefs concerning the biological relationship between Africans and apes.

The Bible

Another explanation for prejudice toward dark-skinned people relates to the story of Ham in the Bible. For the Christian world, the Bible has always been viewed as the word of God. Some interpret the Bible literally, while others have a broader interpretation of its teachings. Whichever, it is seen as a book of morals or rules of faith which teach us how to live our lives. "There is evidence that passages in the Bible were interpreted to justify hierarchical racial classification, enslavement, and oppression of Africans and other people of color" (Felder, 1989:38). The most popular passage used to rationalize black slavery is the so-called curse of Ham in Genesis 9:18-27:

The sons of Noah who came out of the ark were
Shem, Ham and Japheth; Ham was the father of Canaan.
These three were the sons of Noah, and their
descendants spread over the whole earth.
Noah, a man of the soil, began the planting of
vineyards. He drank some of the wine, became drunk and
lay naked inside his tent. When Ham, father of Canaan,
saw his father naked, he told his two brothers outside.
So Shem and Japheth took a cloak, put it on their
shoulders and walked backwards, and so covered their
father's naked body; their faces were turned the other
way, so that they did not see their father naked. When Noah woke
from his drunken sleep, he learnt what his
youngest son had done to him, and said:

Cursed be Canaan,

> slave of slaves
> shall he be to his brothers.
> Blessed, O Lord,
> the tents of Shem;
> may Canaan be his slave.
> May God extend Japheths bounds,
> let him dwell in the tents of Shem,
> may Canaan be their slave.

There are numerous problems in interpreting this passage. For instance, Noah cursed his youngest son. According to Genesis the youngest son is Japheth (Shem, Ham, and Japheth) but Ham is the one cursed. In addition, Ham sees Noah naked but Canaan is punished for the act. The text does not explain why Canaan should be cursed for the wrong of his father (Rice, 1972). In Genesis 10:6 it states that "The sons of Ham: Cush, Mizraim, Put and Canaan" were cursed (Genesis 10:6). But in Christian interpretations of the story of Noah only Canaan was punished and the curse was transferred from Canaan to all Africans who were to have taken the form of ugly blackness and perpetual slavery (Drake, 1987; Bernal, 1997). From these narratives, it is recommended that the Canaanites be subjugated and that Hamites deserve to be "the carriers of wood and drawers of water" (Rice 1972). During the colonial period, this interpretation of the Bible indicated the 'rightness' of slavery and the 'rightness' of the subjugation of those perceived to be cursed by God.

When examining the bible, it is clear that diversity is presented in positive, not negative ways. For instance, in Genesis 10 it is pointed out that the multiplicity and diversity of peoples is the fulfillment of God's command to Noah and his sons. In Genesis 10 God rejoices in mankind in all its manifestations. Westermann stated:

> The whole of humankind takes its origin from them [Shem, Ham, Japheth] . . .humanity is conceived here as a unity, in a way different from the creation; humanity in all its variety across the earth, takes its origin from these three who survived the flood. The purpose of the contrast is to underscore the amazing fact that humanity scattered in all its variety throughout the world comes from one family (1984:486).

Once the unity of humankind is established in Genesis 2:18-23, a rationale for differences in the destinies of certain groups is provided. This is a way to inject both culture and history into theology (Rice, 1972). However, ambiguity in the bible provided an opportunity for interpreters to justify their particular culture, history, and racial ranking by developing self-serving theological constructs. In other words, cultural and historical phenomena were recast as theological truths that held the personal stakes of certain groups (Felder, 1989).

For instance, the Table of Nations (Genesis 10) along with the much later genealogical listing of 1 Chronicles 1:1-2:55 provide an opportunity for racist interpretations. In these listings, there is a tendency to provide a hierarchical arrangement of different groups. For example, the table ends with the descendants of Shem and is stylized to accentuate the importance of his descendants. From the earlier Old Testament version (Jahwist) to the later version (Priestly), Genesis 10 was edited in order to establish the priority of the descendants of Shem. Noah's other descendants, not related to Shem, became increasingly insignificant. This genealogy has erroneously been taken as a reliable source of ancient ethnography (Felder, 1989). "Rather than an objective historical account of genealogies, the table of nations in Genesis 10 is a secularly motivated catalog of people" (Felder, 1989:41).

Contrary to these interpretations, there are numerous examples of blacks being held in high esteem. These narratives, however, were not highlighted like the story of Ham. For instance, in Psalm 87 Zion is the spiritual mother of all humans including Africans who are explicitly mentioned (Rice 1972).

> The Lord loves the gates of Zion
> more than all the dwellings of Jacobs;
> her foundations are laid upon holy hills,
> and he has made her his home (Psalms 87: 1-3).

Aaron's grandson, also the ancestor of the Zadokite priesthood, and one of the sons of Eli was given the Egyptian name, Phinehas, which means the Nubian (Rice, 1972). In Exodus 6:25 it states "Eleazar son of Aaron married one of the daughters of Putiel, and she bore him Phinehas" and "There Eli's two sons, Hophni and Phinehas, were priests of the LORD" (1 Samuel 1:3).

Simon, from North Africa, carried Jesus' cross:

> And as they led Him away, they laid hold on a certain man,
> Simon a Cyrenian, who was coming out of the country, and on
> him they laid the cross that he might bear it after Jesus (Luke
> 23:26).

The portrait of blacks in the Old Testament is that of a wealthy people (Job 28:19) who will soon be converted (Psalms 68:31; Isaiah 11:11). In Zephaniah, "Zephaniah the son of Cush" is referenced and may indicate that one of the Old Testament books was authored by a Black African (Copher, 1986).

The Bible does not support the idea that people of African descent were under a curse. Instead, evidence indicates that they were regarded without prejudice and on an equal basis with other people (Bennett, 1971). The distinction in the Old Testament is not racial but based on national identity and ethnic tribes.

Those who did not meet the criteria for salvation in terms of ethnic (behavior) or national 'in-groups' were relegated to inferior status.

Sophisticated theories about race are the by-products of the post-biblical era (Felder, 1989). Charles (1928) and Perbal (1940) dated the modern development of this interpretation of Genesis 9:20-27 at 1677. At this time J.L. Hannemann published *Curious Inquiry into the Blackness of the Children of Ham*. Hannemann, a Lutheran, claimed that Luther used his position within the church to advocate a racist interpretation of Genesis 9. Intellectuals within the Church preached racism to their flocks and provided Christian Europeans with a rationale for the colonial expansion of Europe and a justification for enslaving Africans. During the era of colonization, all black people were considered descendents of Ham and/or Canaan and were therefore condemned to perpetual servitude (Rice, 1972).

During Napoleon's invasion of Egypt in the late eighteenth century, the curse changed. Scholars brought to Egypt by Napoleon concluded that black Egyptians and not Romans and Greeks were the founders of Western civilization. Following the Egyptian expeditions, a large number of publications in Europe dealing with Egypt and Egyptians argued that Egyptians were not Negroes. The new interpretation was that Egyptians were the descendants of Ham's son Mizraim and it was only Ham's son Canaan that was cursed. The new interpretation defined Hamites as an African population that was distinguished by its race, Caucasian, and anything of value in Africa was brought there by these Hamites, the descendents of Mizraim (Sanders, 1969).

Racist interpretations of the Bible continue today in such versions as *Dake's Annotated Reference Bible*. In Genesis 9:18-27 a racial prophesy is foretold.

> All colors and types of men came into existence after the flood. All men were white up to this point, for there was only one family line of Christ, being mentioned in Luke 3:36 with his son Shem. ...Prophecy that Japheth would be the father of the great and enlarged races. Government, Science and Art are mainly Japhethic. . . . His descendants constitute the leading nations of civilization (Dake, 1981).

Rabbinic Writings

About thirty years ago, based upon readings of ancient and medieval Rabbinic literature, some academics claimed that these texts reflected racism toward blacks and that such attitudes were later adopted by Christians and Moslems. According to them, racism against blacks in western civilization was due to Rabbinic literature (Goldenberg, 1997). For example, Graves and Patai (1964), Sanders (1969), Rice (1972), and Jordan (1977) cite the Bereshith Rabbah as the earliest evidence of a racist interpretation of Genesis. It is a commentary on

Genesis using the work of Rabbis from the second to the fifth centuries (Sanders, 1969; Rice, 1972). Alluding to a tradition that Ham castrated Noah, Rabbi Joseph has Noah say to Ham:

> You have prevented me from doing something in the dark (cohabitation), therefore your seed will be ugly and dark-skinned. The descendants of Ham through Canaan therefore have red eyes, because Ham looked upon the nakedness of his father; they have miss shapen lips, because Ham spoke with his lips to his brothers about the unseemly condition of his father; they have twisted curly hair, because Ham turned and twisted his head round to see the nakedness of his father; and they go about naked, because Ham did not cover the nakedness of his father (Ginzberg, 1925:169).

According to Goldenberg (1997), this passage was mistranslated in the publication by Robert Graves' and Raphael Patai's (1964) book entitled *Hebrew Myths: The Book of Genesis*. The mistranslation continued in citations of this work among subsequent authors. An exact translation of the Tanhuma, a medieval collection of legends and Rabbinic exegeses, is different:

> Ham's eyes turned red, since he looked at his father's nakedness; his lips became crooked, since he spoke with his mouth; the hair of his head and beard became singed, since he turned his face around; and since he did not cover [his father's] nakedness, he went naked and his foreskin was extended (Noah, section 13) (Goldenberg, 1997:28-29).

It can be questioned if this is an anti-black statement or if it speaks of blacks at all. It is an enigmatic text. It may not be depicting any known people but imagination or it may be part of some literary genre that depicts sub-Saharan Africans as strange. It is not unusual to combine literary genre with biblical genealogy. In this passage, Ham is not connected with blackness and there is no connection between the curse of Ham/Canaan and skin color (Goldenberg, 1997).

Some academic scholars argue that Rabbinic writings associated dark skin color with savagery and slavery. In particular, it was stated that the Talmud records a folktale by Rabbis in the third century CE where God forbade Noah and the other creatures on the ark from having sex during the flood. Three animals violated this prohibition: the raven, the dog and Ham, son of Noah, so they were punished. Ham was punished with blackness. In Midrash, Genesis Rabbah 36.7 and elaborated in Genesis 9 it states that Ham saw Noah naked and in retaliation Noah punished Ham by making his progeny black and ugly. These are etiology myths (found around the world) that explain differences and reflect attitudes of society. This passage is in line with pagan, Christian and Islamic views of blacks before the Tanhuma in the eighth to the tenth centuries (Goldenberg, 1997).

Another example of an etiology myth is the story of the Tower of Babel. The punishment for human sinfulness was the introduction of a variety of languages. This answered the question of why there is variation in languages. It is another etiology myth with divine punishment. The reason for divine punishment in such etiologies is to explain differences that go along with worldviews. (Goldenberg, 1997).

The curse of Ham is based on the connection between slavery and blackness but such linkage is not found in early Jewish literature. The two Rabbinic folktales about the origin of dark-skinned people are not within the context of Noah's curse of slavery. These stories discuss blackness but not slavery. Slavery and dark skin are independent etiological myths (Goldenberg, 1997).

European Ideas about Blackness

A more popular explanation for prejudice against dark-skinned people is that Europeans encountered Africans in the fifteen hundreds with preconceived ideas about blackness. In the Oxford English Dictionary of the sixteenth century black was defined as deeply stained with dirt, soiled, dirty, foul, deadly, sinister, horrible, and wicked. It was the opposite of whiteness, which was purity, virginity, virtue, beauty, and beneficence (Jordan, 1977). In European culture, black was the color of sin and death (Banton and Harwood, 1975) and black Africans were considered ugly because of their color, wooly hair, and large lips and nose. Part of the impact of color upon Englishmen was due to the suddenness of their interactions with Africans. Unlike other Europeans like the Spanish and Portuguese who had close contact with North Africa for centuries, the British did not go to West Africa until after 1550 (Jordan, 1977).

Stepan (1982) argued that this view of dark skin created a long-standing prejudice concerning the mental, moral and physical nature of Africans. St. Claire Drake described this perspective as "Modern Manichaean" because it resembles the ancient religious cult of Mani. In Mani people believed there was an eternal struggle between Darkness and Light (Drake, 1987).

Situational Factors

Drake (1987) contended that even if research shows that people interpret "blackness" in abstract symbolism as more negative than positive, its impact depends on the type of social situations and social institutions in which it is found. In other words, situational factors as well as idiosyncratic psychological factors affected the operation of negative psychological cues about blackness.

According to Drake (1987) color symbolism and group stereotypes vary with the type of society. For instance, in the Middle East Africans were traditionally incorporated into Arab communities under the system of domestic slavery. Blacks were not used in a commercial way as primary laborers in fields and white slaves were used in similar ways. Freedom was possible for both slave groups. Race relations in the Middle East was different from those in the Caribbean or in the United States where black slavery was important in economic life and white free labor competed with black slave labor. While slavery existed in all of these situations, racial slavery and institutional racism were present only in the United States and the Caribbean. According to Drake (1987), in an environment of commercial slavery, negative psychological cues about blackness may have helped to justify and rationalize racism and discrimination toward people with dark skin.

UPDATE: BLACKS AND JEWS TODAY

African American and Jewish American relationships have always vacillated between alliance and conflict. Historically, the alliance was due to shared experiences. Both groups experienced slavery, oppression, and minority status in predominately Christian and white societies (Weiss, 1997; Goldenberg, 1997; Carson, 1998; West, 1998; Diner, 1998). Because of these experiences, both groups subscribe to egalitarian ideals of liberalism (Carson, 1998; Diner, 1998). In particular, in the early 1900s Jews advocated equal rights according to law rather than religious or ethnic traditions (Bermer, 1998) and the eradication of distinctions between Americans based upon ancestry (Diner, 1998).

The initial alliance between blacks and Jews occurred in the early 1900s during mass immigration of eastern and southern Europeans to America (West, 1998; Bermer, 1998). With concern about the inferiority of these immigrants, a new pattern of discrimination intensified against Jews. There were restrictions in various areas such as hotel and social clubs as well as employment, education, and housing (Weiss, 1997). Jews and blacks, as well as Asians and some other ethnics were prevented from renting or buying real estate in certain neighborhoods where there was a "restrictive covenant" (Greenberg, 1997).

It was under these circumstances that in the early 1900s Jews aided blacks in founding both the NAACP and the National Urban League (Greenberg, 1997; Bermer, 1998; Weiss, 1997). For instance, Jews worked with the National Urban league to find jobs and provide social services for blacks in cities. This is exactly what German Jews were providing for eastern European Jews through immigrant aid societies (Weiss, 1997). Jewish work with the NAACP and the National Urban League fit with their commitment to social betterment (Weiss, 1997) and this early alliance led many blacks to characterize Jews as allies (Greenberg, 1997).

The mid-century was the heyday for Jewish/black alliance. Jewish organizations such as the Anti-Defamation League, American Jewish Committee, and the American Jewish Congress, who had fought restrictive housing covenants against Jews, helped the NAACP fight for blacks in Supreme Court cases (Greenberg, 1997). Jews were less than 3% of the American population but most of the money for the civil right organizations came from Jews like Joel Spingarn. This collaboration, however, was spotty with a small group of lawyers and not a large involvement from the Jewish or black populations. It was mainly a relationship between the top lawyers of the American Jewish Committee and those of the NAACP (Bermer, 1998; Carson, 1998).

While there was a connection between the groups because of shared experiences, Jews gained a foothold in America by conforming to negative stereotypes about blacks (West, 1998). That is, Jews as white Americans conformed, to some degree, to racial attitudes that supported segregation and discrimination in the early 1900s (Weiss, 1997; West, 1998). For instance, while Jews started businesses in black communities because they were prevented from doing so in other sectors of the city, often, Jewish storekeepers overcharged and underpaid black customers and employees (Hacker, 1998). Sometimes Jewish storeowners sold to but might not employ blacks and those who employed blacks hired them in low wage jobs (Weiss, 1997). Because of daily encounters and conformity to mainstream society, Jews could be hostile to blacks (Bermer, 1998).

Class difference was the core of the early divides between Jews and blacks. Most immigrant Jews came from urban areas with job skills that rural agricultural working blacks did not have. Jews as white ethnics could shift to the white race because rewards and opportunities in the United States are based upon race not ethnicity or religion. Better skills and less discrimination increased class differences between blacks and Jews (Greenberg, 1997).

By the mid-1960s relations between blacks and Jews had soured (West, 1998; Carson, 1998). One reason for this was criticisms of the assimilationist leadership of the civil rights movement. At this time, Jews sought a color-blind America and assimilation rather than cultural pluralism. Black and Jewish civil rights activists advocated assimilation (Bermer, 1998; Carson, 1998).

The Black Power movement broke with this approach. It created a sense of group identity, sense of nationhood and shared religious tradition. Adherents of the movement advocated the creation and institutionalization of group-oriented politics and identity (Martin, 1997). Jews and other whites perceived Black Power as anti-white and racist.

In addition, pressures from grass-roots leaders and black nationalists like Malcolm X forced traditional black activist to connect with group goals rather than assimilation. In post-1965 there were more black grass-roots movements with little black-Jewish connections. Simultaneously, local black leadership expressed resentment of Jewish political and economic power especially as shown in the black communities (Carson, 1998).

There was also a Third World and pan-African consciousness that shifted black support from Israel and Zionism to support for Palestine and Arabs. Stokely Carmichael personified this shift. Israel, he said, was created by the forced removal of Palestinians from their homeland. For him and participants in the Black Power Movement Israel was a "white and European power" occupying land rightfully belonging to Palestinians (Hacker, 1998; Martin, 1997). Israel's First World identification was symbolized by their lack of aid to newly independent black African countries except for apartheid-ridden South Africa. With a Third World perspective, blacks rallied around the idea of a global revolution by the colonized and nonwhites against the colonizers (Bermer, 1998).

While blacks shifted toward Third Worldism, there was a resurgence of Zionism and Jewish consciousness following the Arab-Israeli wars of 1967 and 1973. Jewish support for black movements also dwindled after the 1967 Arab-Israeli war when blacks moved toward racial separation and Jews moved toward increased group consciousness (Martin, 1997). For Jews, they were fleeing evil Europe and the Arab world. For them, blacks should understand that Israel is the "minority civil rights movement of the Middle East" (Bermer, 1998). Jews considered black resistance to Israel as a rejection of Jewish right to survive as a group. Even today, blacks do not understand Jewish attachment to Israel and Zionism as manifested in the state of Israel. Rather, they perceive Jewish defense of Israel as group interest and abandonment of liberal and moral approaches to equality (West, 1998).

Black Nationalism today continues to fuel conflict between Jews and blacks. Black nationalists like Louis Farrakhan and Leonard Jeffries are concerned about Jewish influence and power (West, 1998). For instance, in 1993 in a speech by Khalid Abdul Muhammad, assistant to Minister Louis Farrakhan, at Keane College in New Jersey he discussed "The Secret Relationship Between Blacks and Jews." Muhammad portrayed a Jewish conspiracy against black leaders such as Jesus, Marcus Garvey and now Farrakhan. According to him, Jews conspired in the slave trade and the movies to denigrate blacks, Jewish doctors infected blacks with AIDS, and there are Jewish efforts to miseducate black children in the public school system (Bermer, 1998). Also, Farrakhan used the idea that African Americans are the real Hebrews of the Bible as portrayed in biblical epics of slavery and atonement is meant for blacks, not whites. Farrakhan and other blacks reinvented themselves as the equivalent of the traditional chosen people. So for blacks, Jews stole their identity (Martin, 1997).

Black anti-Semitism was also related to anti-whitism meaning Jews collaborate in white racism (West, 1998). Jews are white and their relationship with blacks has never been an equal one. It has always been as storeowners, landlords, and leaders in the civil rights while there were no similar roles for blacks in Jewish organizations (Shaw, 1997). While the postindustrial global economy intensified the disadvantage of working class Americans, especially blacks, this economy provided privilege and wealth for upper class Americans such as Jews. Such differences suggest that while Jews are a minority, they are a privileged minority (Katz-Fishman and Scott, 1998).

There is also an ideological conflict between Jews and blacks. Jews have always stressed economic and political goals while blacks stressed civil rights (Carson, 1998). Civil rights have been more important to African American politics than those of Jews because blacks are more affected by discrimination than Jews. In other words, anti-Jewish sentiment in the United States has never been comparable to institutional discrimination among African Americans. Jews never needed constitutional legislation for citizenship and never mobilized as a group to ensure better treatment because they can use their economic power and influence to protect their group interests. Anti-Semitism does not affect the life chances of individual Jews. As a result, the success of the civil rights movement impacted black lives more than those of Jews (Carson, 1998).

In addition, attacks by Jews against affirmative action continue to negatively affect Jewish/black relations (West, 1998; Bermer, 1998). Since the 1920s, Jews related their success in gaining jobs in city services to passing competitive exams. Because of this, they want to preserve the merit system (Hacker, 1998) and eliminate quotas. Quotas were used to exclude qualified Jews and have always meant the ceiling to Jewish enrollment and employment. Without quotas Jews experienced upward mobility in education, occupation and economic. They are now upwardly mobile and part of the elite and do not need affirmative action since they are beneficiaries of white privilege (Shaw, 1997).

While quotas were used to keep Jews out, for blacks it lets them in (Chanes, 1997). This shows the different experiences of blacks and Jews. Merit works for Jews but racism has made upward mobility difficult for blacks. Regardless of merit and qualifications, race affects opportunity for blacks (Shaw, 1997). Consequently, the two groups have had different strategies for group progress and differ on where their interests coincide (Carson, 1998).

CHAPTER THREE

RACE, RACISM AND SLAVERY IN THE UNITED STATES

> However cruelly whites exploited blacks, their fates were intricately intertwined. However much masters treated their slaves as chattels, the humanity of their property could not be ignored or evaded. However total the masters' exercise of power, negotiation and compromise were necessary to make slavery function. However sincerely planter patriarchs stressed mutuality and reciprocity, their authority ultimately rested on force. However sentimentally and benevolently some late-eighteenth-century masters viewed slaves, their relentless denial of rights to bondmen increasingly placed slaves outside society. However unequivocally daily existence brought blacks and whites together, growing race consciousness and class distinctions thrust them apart (P.D. Morgan, 1998:257).

INTRODUCTION

American slavery was instrumental in shaping modern perspectives on race and racism. This is apparent among my students who discuss slavery and colonialism as pivotal events in the construction of racism. In their essays they often write that modern racism is a legacy of slavery. Scholars too date modern racism to the period of U.S. slavery. For example, Marvin Harris (1964) maintained that racism arose as an ideological justification for the exploitation of black labor by European nations. In addition, Arnold Rose (1951) dated racial prejudice at 1793 when the invention of the cotton gin gave cotton planters a new interest in slaveholding. On the other hand, Oliver C. Cox (1948) was convinced that modern racism began in the years 1493-94 when Spanish and Portuguese economic power dominated the New World. According to Cox, access to resources in the New World and capitalism defined race relations. Bernal (1997) posited that modern racism began when Portuguese ships out-competed Islamic powers, kidnapped people on the coast of West Africa and brought them back to Portugal to sell as slaves. Since they were taken as prisoners of a just war (any war against non-Christians qualified as a just war) their enslavement was justified.

All of these explanations relate modern racism to the African slave trade and African slavery. This historical period is still a source of embarrassment and shame for many white Americans. When the movie Roots was first televised in the 1970s it was a daily topic of discussion among my friends. I was an undergraduate at the University of Alabama at the time and one of my professors, a white female, said she did not watch it because it made her feel bad. She did not want to think about slavery. She did not want to think about what white people did to black people. For some white Americans, slavery in the United States was a shameful event in U.S. history that they would rather forget or, at least, not be reminded of it. More recently, I have heard whites say that slavery is in the past. They do not feel there is a reason to discuss slavery since they are "color-blind." For some white Americans civil rights legislation ended racism and created an era of equal opportunity for everyone. Therefore, current race relations are not a legacy of slavery (we live in a color-blind society).

While the focus of this chapter is slavery in the United States, it is not a comprehensive examination. There are numerous books about slavery and variation in slavery among regions and populations in the United States, the Caribbean and South America. Rather, I want to provide a critique of the social environment in which race and racism were constructed in the United States. In this critique, slavery is the critical factor creating, promoting and maintaining racism. Three lines of analyses are used to demonstrate the importance of slavery in the development of race and racism. First, I examine the importance of slavery or subordinates in maintaining the social order. Along this line, the naturalness of slavery and inequality are examined. In addition, the use of negative stereotypes about people of African descent is reviewed to provide a context for the *creation of a natural social order*.

Second, it is argued that the construction of race and racism are related to the creation of racial identities and racial hierarchies by slaveholding and non-slaveholding whites. It is proposed that racial classification schemes and racial ranking are a consequence of the creation of racial identities by those in power, i.e. white males (Comaroff and Comaroff, 1991; Omi and Winant, 1994). That is, racial identity developed with the convergence of skin color prejudice, slavery and the power associated with this process in the New World (Drake 1987, 1990). In that context, it emerged as a social category derived from the antagonistic relation of black oppression and white supremacy (Krieger and Bassett, 1986).

According to Ruth Frankenberg (1993), during colonialism whites constructed whiteness in terms of power gained through exploitation of blacks as a resource. In this construction of racial identities, free whites created their identity in opposition to that of black slaves. In other words, whiteness only has meaning in opposition to others. During the antebellum, self-identity among whites was constructed by separating themselves from black slaves. That is, whatever slaves were perceived to be mentally, emotionally or behaviorally, whites were not. Self-identity and well-being among whites centered on contrasts with black slaves. Consequently, the social construction of mental and behavioral differences between blacks and whites and subsequent ranking of those differences were a part of the early construction of white racial identity and was an early manifestation of racism in America.

This examination is not an attempt to determine how white Americans create their identities today. The creation and maintenance of racial identities today are discussed in the final chapter. This chapter provides examples of ways that racial identities may have been created during slavery in terms of what Ruth Frankenberg describes as a "colonial discourse."

Lastly, I argue that race and racism were an integral part of U.S. institutions that functioned to legitimize inequality in the distribution of resources in this country. Race was a political tool used to establish laws that made blacks property without rights and thereby legalize and institutionalize slavery. Institutions at the local, state, and national level enforced certain behaviors and laws to make blacks and their descendants perpetual human property, chattel. It is argued that the creation of slave property was beneficial to a capitalist system that needed a large cheap labor pool. The legalization and maintenance of this permanent cheap labor force was provided by institutional racism, as a function of collective racism.

In this section, I contend that slavery was a pivotal period in U.S. history because it determined how the dominant group interacted with "others." That is, developments during slavery affected the use of power by the state and those with capital. While the title of this chapter indicates a focus on slavery, it is really about the institutionalization of power by the dominant group. This chapter is about the acquisition and maintenance of power and the legalization of that process.

NATURAL SOCIAL ORDER

When considering how slavery affected our current conceptualization of race, we must consider why slavery was acceptable. During the Enlightenment, the golden years for slavery, a rationale for racial ranking was provided by philosophers such as Hobbes and Locke who showed that slavery could be reconciled with beliefs in abstract natural law and natural rights. People such as Voltaire said that slavery was as ancient as war and that war was a part of human nature. Negro slavery was considered an important and a necessary link in the 'great chain of causes and events.' For if slavery were abolished there would be a whole in the nature of things. Most philosophers followed Aquinas who argued that "...if equality was the first intention of nature, inequality was natural in a secondary sense of being necessary for the order and well-being of society" (Davis, 1966:393).

European nobility also used this argument to justify class differences. Subordinates were a part of the *natural social order*. They argued that if peasants were not forced to work they would be drunken, idle and dangerous. Similarly it was believed that tropical climates caused slaves to be unwilling to work unless they were punished. Coercion was necessary to make people work in the tropics and there was a nice balance where the master's self interest and slave's desire for happiness were harmonized. European nobility also contended that government had no right to interfere in the relation between peasant and lord, and that peasants would be content if not for outside agitation. The relation between slave and master was similar to that between peasant and lord except slaves 'lived in luxurious abundance' compared to peasants and workers in Europe (Davis, 1966).

The idea of an organic social hierarchy was embodied in early eighteenth-century American patriarchalism. Using the Great Chain of Being as science, slaveholders argued that societies of men could not exist without subordinates or there would be a defect in the scale of order (Davis, 1966). Masters believed they had a natural right to rule (Berlin, 1998). From this viewpoint, patriarchy was a natural social system. It was based on the protection that the powerful masters offered the weak slaves just as monarchs defined a political system where royal power defended peasants (Morgan, 1998). Reciprocal duties and obligations between slave and master (like lord and peasant) were the essence of patriarchalism (Morgan, 1998).

Patriarchalism was reformulated during the late eighteenth century. Slaveholders discussed duties and obligations less and individual rights, such as property rights, more. Slaves were defined as people without rights and were said to enhance their owners' independence (freedom) since they were viewed increasingly as property (Morgan, 1998). African slavery became not just one form of subordination, but also the foundation of the social order (Berlin, 1998).

Negative Stereotypes

The naturalness of inequality was supported by negative stereotypes of slaves. That is, to distance themselves from black status and justify slavery there were a number of myths about blacks. For example, it was believed that blacks were brought to the South to perform labor that Europeans could not do. It was believed that whites could never raise cotton or a sugar crop in the United States because of the swamps where whites died, but blacks thrived. Actually, whites performed much of the South's heavy agricultural labor but black slaves, unlike free whites, were forced to till the soil in the rice swamps despite the ill effect upon their health. In essence, the belief at that time was that God created Africans to meet the labor needs of the South (Stampp, 1961).

Europeans wondered if African languages were languages at all and their customs and appearance were so different that they believed Africans could not be created in God's image (Stepan, 1982). From the beginning the English stressed differences between themselves and Africans in terms of color, religion, lifestyle, animality and sexuality (Jordan, 1977). Because of these differences, Europeans questioned whether or not Africans were human. The biology of Africans was seen as an indicator of their subhumaness and closeness to lower forms of animals. For instance, in *The History of Jamaica* (1774) Edward Long, a Jamaican planter, linked blacks to the animal world and assigned them to a position intermediate between Europeans and orangutans. He related blacks to beasts by writing of their smell and affirmed that their children, like other animals, matured faster than those of whites. This paved the way for Europeans to interpret differences in terms of a hierarchy.

Critics and defenders of slavery believed in the innate inferiority of blacks. Whatever the cause, the inferior status of blacks was said to manifest itself in laziness, limited intellectual capacity, a childlike simplicity, docility, sensuousness, and tempestuousness (Fogel and Engerman, 1974). In *Notes on the State of Virginia* (1781-1782) Jefferson had doubts about the inherent mental ability of blacks and their fitness for freedom. He thought that blacks were not only physically different but that nature made them mentally and temperamentally different. Morally blacks were equal to whites but not intellectually. Defenders of slavery argued that bondage had a beneficial effect on blacks. It pushed them to the upper limits of their potential (Fogel and Engerman, 1974). This was similar to beliefs about peasants and their relationship to their lord.

Another myth was that Africans were barbarians who needed to be subjected to severe controls and rigid discipline. Blacks were thought to need special laws to restrain them from inhumanity, rape, and disorders to which they were naturally inclined (Stampp, 1961). It was believed that interaction with whites made house servants more like whites, intellectually and culturally, than field hands

(Fogel and Engerman, 1974). Blacks needed to be civilized by acquiring and transmitting the white patterns of social behavior (Stampp, 1961).

The image of the happy-go-lucky black existing on benign plantations was a standard image until the end of WWII. This conformed to an accommodationist interpretation of the ways blacks allegedly adjusted to the realities of slavery. According to this view, blacks accepted slavery because the system was not so bad and because blacks had a 'friendly' nature. This view legitimized the slave system for plantation owners and others (Franklin, 1991).

Slavery also generated images that functioned to perpetuate the system. For instance, the *Sambo* is the stereotypical childlike slave with shuffling feet, downcast eyes and soft voice. Williamson (1986) proposed that blacks used this role to survive and that whites needed the *Sambo* image to feed their egos and mask their fear of slave revolts. The *Sambo* image functioned to reinforce white views of themselves as civilized and Christian and their view of the slave as happy and childlike. On the other hand, Africans were savages. African savages had unrestrained passions, uncontrollable rage, were cannibals, and brutal beast. *Sambos* could become savages if freed from the civilizing influence of slavery (Wilson, 1996).

With these negative stereotypes entrenched in white culture, slave inferiority and the necessity for bondage legitimized the social order. They were not worthy or ready for freedom. Moreover, these stereotypes provided a rationale for the legalization of their bondage.

SLAVERY AND THE FORMATION OF RACIAL IDENTITIES

During colonialism European Americans increasingly made distinctions between themselves and those in bondage, black slaves and Native Americans. These distinctions were the beginnings of the construction of identities, how you think about yourself. Identities based upon physical appearance and perceived associated characteristics were created for European Americans and by European Americans for black slaves and American Indians. In other words, those in power constructed racial identities in colonial America for themselves and all others. These ways of thinking about themselves and all others were incorporated into the dominant culture.

Examination of the construction of racial identities in this section is based upon research by Ruth Frankenberg (1993). She concluded that whiteness is based on a 'colonial discourse' where white racial identity was constructed in terms of power gained through colonialism and slavery. In this discourse, white identity only has meaning in opposition to 'Others.' To be white is to be dominant, superior, culturally neutral, and powerful. Other groups, for example, those of African ancestry, are subordinate, inferior, culture-oriented and powerless. Those in power, i.e. white males, constructed blackness as the opposite of whiteness and consequently constructed race and racial hierarchies along with racism. Power and its political and economic use is central to the creation of races and racism. Others such as Omi and Winant (1994), Smedley (1993, 1998), Winant (1984), Harrison (1995, 1997, 1998a, 1998b), Hutchinson (1997), and Baker, (1998a, 1998b) also contend that power relationships are inherent in the race concept. The following aspects of slavery are discussed in terms of the creation of racial identities by those in power.

Freedom versus Slavery

Characteristics associated with freedom versus slavery were the foundation of the formation of racial identities and racial ranking by the dominant white population. A basic component in this dichotomy concerns ideas about freedom and property. For instance, by the 1500s the British had strong beliefs in absolute ownership of private property. A thing could belong exclusively to an individual. For example, the enclosure movement in Britain in the fifteenth century transformed what were once communal lands (forests and meadows) into private property enclosed by hedges. Now there was absolute possession of land by owners who used their property to earn more profit (Smedley, 1993). Smedley stated that:

> when the English learned to fence in parcels of land and the use of titles became widespread, the sense of exclusive private use of natural resources expanded and matured. Some became very wealthy as the value of these lands increased, while others, those dispersed or dislocated by the privatization of land, were reduced to abject poverty (Smedley, 1993:46-47).

Not only could an individual own things outside of himself but also he could own himself and become property. MacPherson (1962) characterized English society during this period as based on the concept of "possessive individualism." ...that man is free and human by virtue of his sole proprietorship of his own person... (MacPherson, 1962:270).

Freedom was equated with rights in property and property was defined as the basic right that any man had in his own body, labor and capacities. A man could sell his labor property to another man. So a man had property rights in his own selfhood (MacPherson, 1962). In other words you could own yourself and sell your labor, both of which are property. Freedom meant that you had property: land, yourself, your labor. European culture could incorporate African slavery into its society because there was already an accepted idea that one could own their own body and labor and also the labor and body of others.

In America, ideas about property and freedom can be identified in the writings of Thomas Jefferson. For Jefferson, governments did not bestow freedom to its citizens. Rather, freedom came from being independent and independence meant being without debt. According to Jefferson, debt allowed a person to be controlled by others. A debtor is not independent and therefore not free. Consequently, Jefferson contended that he could not free his slaves as long as he was in debt. In *Notes on the State of Virginia,* Jefferson said he needed slaves because he was in debt. Profit from the labor of slaves allowed him to pay his debt and remain free. Owning and using the labor of others without payment, slavery, was a way to avoid debt and loss of property and thereby remain free. Slave property, then, enhanced the freedom of their owner.

This early construction of whiteness involved a commitment to freedom and property. White racial identity (free) was in opposition to black racial identity (slave property). Institutionalization of these racial identities is demonstrated by political strategies advocated in the south. For example, southerners adhered to either a Herrenvolk or aristocracy platform. Herrenvolk democracy meant that democracy was for whites only and blacks were slaves. Herrenvolk values justified equal citizenship for all whites but provided perpetual servitude for all blacks. It was a way to maintain inter-class solidarity between white planters and white non-slaveholders within the South and at the same time create a link between insecure and often 'Negrophobic' lower class whites and southern slaveholding elite (Fredrickson, 1981). Andrew Jackson epitomized the Herrenvolk democracy when he wanted democracy in which Native Americans were exiled, blacks subjugated, white males had political freedom and the slave aristocracy accumulated wealth (Wilson, 1996).

Not all white southerners were content with the Herrenvolk approach. Some elite slaveholders denied the idea of equality more comprehensively and moved toward the idea of aristocracy. Slave aristocracy opposed any form of democracy in favor of a racial caste system of superior white masters, classes other than slaves, and inferior slaves at the bottom (Fredrickson, 1981). John Calhoun typified the slave aristocracy. He opposed democracy altogether and wanted the ruling white planter class to govern with other whites in the middle and blacks subordinated to the bottom. However, all white men were potential aristocrats (Wilson, 1996).

Both value systems functioned to reinforce freedom for whites and perpetual slavery for blacks. Both value systems, then, facilitated the construction of white identity (free) in opposition to black identity (slave).

Social/Family Life

Another aspect of slavery that contributed to the formation of racial identities by those in power concerns social life. In particular, it relates to control of one's social and economic life; they were intricately intertwined. White racial identity was constructed not necessarily in opposition to slave identity but with different social patterns. Although social patterns in both groups were partly a consequence of the system of slavery, such patterns were considered 'natural.'

White men, for instance, were the primary breadwinners and being a breadwinner was synonymous with manhood. As such, only white men competed for political appointment to law enforcement, church, and judicial commission and only white males influenced the economy (Stevenson, 1996). While white men's manhood was demonstrated by their economic and political power, black male slaves lacked power and were robbed of their manhood, breadwinners for the family.

White men, even poor ones, had control of their domestic and, to some extent, their economic lives and the people in them because they were patriarchs. Slaves, on the other hand, had to be obedient to slaveholders because they were the fathers of the plantation and slaves were permanently children (Berlin, 1998). Control isolated white males from black men and all women who had little control over any aspect of their private or public lives (Stevenson, 1996).

Whites were in control of their own family life and as patriarchs, they tried to control the family life of slaves. For instance, an act in 1662 mandated that children of black females be automatically assigned the status of their mother. In other words, slaveholders identified parentage solely with the mother and denied the fathers' role biologically, emotionally, socially or materially (Kulikoff, 1978). Therefore, the white community did not recognize slave fathers as parents of their own children.

White male patriarchs, on the other hand, believed it was their responsibility to take care of slave children (Kulikoff, 1978; Stevenson, 1996). White males controlled their children and slave children while not recognizing the parentage of or social role of slave men. In doing so, to some degree family life of slaves was controlled by white males rather than slave parents. Moreover, in the construction of white identity, white males were the fathers of all children, white and black. Identities were constructed in opposition in terms of control, power, and status.

For whites, patriarchal privilege and monogamous marriage were the foundation of southern white families across cultural, class, and ethnic lines. There was a social ideal that everyone should marry and have and rear children (Stevenson, 1996). However, white patriarchy often determined when and who slaves married (Kulikoff, 1978) and the prevalence of monogamous couples among slaves varied because of the system of slavery. For example, one factor affecting the ability to maintain a monogamous relationship among slaves was the size of the plantation. Small slave owners might be more willing to buy the mate of a slave because co-residential slave couples could increase their property through childbearing. Large slaveholders, on the other hand, might not buy a mate, or sell or rent them out. At the same time, with more slaves on larger plantations, formation of families was possible. Even on larger plantations, however, maintaining monogamous couples was difficult because of a number of factors such as involuntary movement of slaves. For instance, slaves were moved to areas because of changes in the life cycle of owners, business interests, being given as dowry in marriage, or because slaves were employed at several farms that could be spread over great distances even to the Caribbean. In addition, upon the death of a slaveholder slaves might be sold to pay off debts or to make an equitable distribution of capital among heirs (Stevenson, 1996; Jones, 1992; Berlin, 1998).

Consequently, "abroad" marriages (spouses residing on different plantations) were common among slaves (Kulikoff, 1978). As a result, slaves had a variety of household types such as nuclear, nuclear extended, single-parent (mother) families, same-sex single adolescent groupings and single or widowed older people who lived with the slaveholders' family (Stevenson, 1996). Abroad marriages and the 1662 mandate provided the legal background for matrifocal kinship among slaves (Kulikoff, 1978). While white families were patriarchal and nuclear/extended with relatives residing on the plantation, matrifocal families and extended kin networks crossing plantations were common among slaves (Kulikoff, 1978; Stevenson, 1996).

Because of slavery, family life for blacks and whites were different. Whites had marriages with nuclear/extended families where white males were the head of the households. Slaves could marry and could have nuclear families but family members were scattered on various plantations. Lastly, because white males were patriarchs and parentage of black male slaves was not recognized, white males not only controlled their own children but slave children as well. Because of the system of slavery, there were different types of family life for whites versus their slaves that were considered to be due to nature.

Gender Roles

Slavery also affected gender role expectations for whites and blacks. White southerners believed in God-ordained differences between the sexes such as white women were weak, dependent, and emotional while white men were strong, aggressive, and intelligent. But survivorship for slave women and their children necessitated characteristics such as self-reliance and self-determination. These were important attributes for slave women, but among white women these characteristics were considered unfeminine (Stevenson, 1996).

The home, for blacks and whites, was the woman's sphere but white men dominated it. That is, upper class white women did not have domestic power independent of their husbands. The main duty of white women was to give control to white men and the men's primary act was to control their dependents: all children, black slaves and white women (Stevenson, 1996). Black slave men had none of the privileges of the white male patriarch.

However, it must be noted that husbands of white working women in urban or rural areas did not have control over their labor, compensation or home environment. Poor folk could not embrace the behaviors of the upper class (Stevenson, 1996). While white women have worked for wages since colonial times, their numbers have been low until the last few decades. Work was a threat to the femininity of white women as defined by their culture (Brodkin, 2001). In order to protect the femininity of white female workers, they were segregated from men and female slaves. Segregation and the myth that white women were not supposed to work for wages helped to define white femininity. On the other hand, black women were expected to work (Brodkin, 1997).

Women of color worked beside men in the fields, factories and as domestic workers and because they worked they were considered unfeminine. In addition, because black female slaves worked they were considered immoral. Therefore, sexual harassment was "asked for" by these women and their immorality confirmed that they "asked for it" (Brodkin, 2001). Consequently, black female slaves were considered supersexual while white females were thought to be uninterested in sex. Black and white femininity were partly based upon these characteristics and set in opposition to one another.

Southern white women also differed from black women because the former controlled their sexual behavior, although they had to relinquish to their husbands. But, since black women were property they had no control of their sexual organs. There were no rights of sexual exclusivity that they could relinquish to their husbands (Stevenson, 1996). White men's lust for black women removed their possibility of exclusivity to a slave mate (Blassingame, 1975). Whiteness was expressed by white male sexual dominion over both black and white female sexual expression and exclusivity (Stevenson, 1996).

"Gender and racial separation of white women and men, each in their separate and racially white niches, then confirms the naturalness of whiteness and its attributes" (Brodkin, 2001:373). It seems that real Americans are white, where whiteness means privileges that include social respectability, residential freedom, and respectable families and work (Morrison, 1993; Frankenberg, 1993; Williams, 1996; Brodkin, 2001).

Slave Resistance

In the construction of racial identities white slaveholders also had to respond to black slave resistance. That is, while differing social and familial patterns were dictated by the system of slavery, slaves found ways to maintain social and family life. Black slaves created cultural forms that reduced oppression, promoted group solidarity, provided ways to verbalize aggression, sustained hope, built self-esteem, and often represented areas of life free from the control of whites. For example, the social organization of slave quarters was the primary environment that gave them ethical rules and fostered cooperation, mutual assistance, and black solidarity. The work arena was the secondary environment and was far less important in determining personality. Slave culture and way of life defined roles and behavioral patterns, determined the norms of conduct, and provided a network of individual and group relationships that molded personality in the quarters (Blassingame, 1972).

The construction of white and black racial identities by the dominant group was complicated by the reality of their lives. The fact that slaves were not animals was apparent on plantations. Consequently, slaveholders needed to find continual evidence to justify their relationship with and attitudes toward slaves. On an individual and group level, there had to be a continual process of re-evaluation of identities in terms of self and the 'other.'

Internalized Racism

Resistance and the construction of racial identities by white slaveholding males were also complicated by internalized racism among free blacks in the south. For instance, in the eighteenth century, and later, some people of African descent such as those of mixed racial origins and those born in America who were free, tried to integrate into European-American society. They imitated European Americans in terms of speech, dress and deportment. These free blacks were slave owners as economic convenience and in an attempt to break with their slave past (Berlin, 1998).

In the south, free blacks did not adopt the language of the Declaration of Independence like those in the North, but appealed for a place in society and in the process abandoned plantation slaves. Brown people separated themselves from black slaves and from white free people. For example, free blacks developed the Brown Fellowship Society that assisted other free blacks and provided cemeteries and small annuities to widows and children. Instead of bringing blacks together like African-American associations in the North, the Brown Fellowship Society excluded slaves and dark-skinned blacks that organized another association, the Humane Brotherhood. In the lower south there were white, black and brown identities among free people (Berlin, 1998).

Conclusions

Differences in gender, marriage, family and slave resistance and accommodation provide important examples of the social construction of black and white racial identities during slavery. In this construction identities are in opposition or at least differ. Other examples of oppositions in social life include the education of white children, ability of white males to vote, amount of clothing worn, freedom of movement among whites, and labor. In terms of labor, lack of au-

thority over labor activities by black slaves exemplified the creation of work activities and schedules in opposition to that of free people. In addition, physical
differences between blacks and whites included not only skin color but also
identifiers of slave and free persons. For instance, slaves were branded on
cheeks and legs, sometimes hands, chained by their feet and wrists or necks
(Blassingame, 1975; Stevenson, 1996). These insignias of slavery were physical
identifiers of those enslaved while their absence among whites indicated freedom.

The previous discussion examined the construction of whiteness in opposition to blackness during U.S. slavery. In the "colonial discourse" whites constructed whiteness in terms of power gained through exploitation of blacks as a
resource. In this exploitation the inferior "other," people of African descent,
were created where being nonwhite meant lack of power and lack of freedom.
Whiteness, on the other hand, meant power and freedom (Frankenberg, 1993).
With certain beliefs about who should be a slave and why ingrained in the
dominant culture, racial identities were also created and races were defined.

INSTITUTIONAL RACISM

With ideas of freedom and equality written into the Declaration of Independence, there needed to be a justification and legalization of the institution of slavery and simultaneously a way to legitimize racism, especially institutional racism. The concept of race was needed to make blacks property without rights. In
order to mesh slavery with ideas about freedom, negative stereotypes about
black slaves became part of white culture, collective racism. For instance, while
different familial patterns were a consequence of slavery, such patterns were
perceived as biologically based or natural. Perceived mental and behavioral
traits, besides physical characteristics, became ideological justifications for racial categories that were used to institutionalize and legalize slavery. Collective
racism was the mechanism that made institutional racism possible. In other
words, institutional racism is a function of collective racism.

Slave Codes

Race was used to institute legal bondage, distinguish slave from free, and
slave codes were created to formalize and institutionalize the behavior of free
whites and slave blacks. For instance, slave movement and possessions were restricted. Slaves could not leave their plantation without written permission of
masters and slaves were forbade from having firearms, from congregating with
other slaves without the presence of a white supervisor, and from selling and
buying goods. Slaves could not own property, sue or be sued, or have rights and
duties of free people (Flanigan, 1974; Schafer, 1987). Slaves' property be-

longed to their master and they could not testify against whites nor could they enter contracts (Schafer, 1987).

Slave status was as property and person. As personal property, chattel, they could be sold, willed, insured, seized in payment of debt or mortgaged. However, the law considered slaves responsible individuals in criminal law (Flanigan, 1974). For instance, besides striking the master, other capital offenses included arson, conspiracy to rebel and rape of a white woman (Wilson, 1996). The death sentence was reserved for any act that wounded, maimed, bruised or disabled a white person (Morgan, 1998). Slaves could be burned alive for alleged crimes (Fede, 1985). On the other hand free people could not be executed for killing a slave (Morgan, 1998) and masters could legitimately inflict violence on their slaves (Fede, 1985). Although slaves were considered legally responsible for crimes (like whites), unlike whites they did not receive benefits of a procedural system that was designed to protect the innocent as well as to punish the guilty. As a matter of fact, often slaves were punished more severely than whites for similar crimes (Flanigan, 1974).

To protect the institution of slavery, slave codes also dictated white behavior. Whites, including slave owners, were prohibited from teaching slaves to read or from freeing their own slaves unless the slave left the state. Interracial marriage was forbidden (Wilson, 1996). In the 1830s anyone was prohibited from selling, distributing, or possessing abolitionist literature. The 1849 Virginia law prohibited people from saying that the planter class had no right to own slaves as property (Stampp, 1961).

Slave codes were enforced by slave patrols composed of poor whites. These patrols were not illegal vigilante groups, but an integral part of the state militia and an important component of southern society. They were more than policemen since they could exercise the power of punishment as well as arrest (Flanigan, 1974). Slave patrols had power over free and enslaved blacks and whites suspected of violating the codes. They broke up groups of blacks, enforced the prohibition of abolitionist literature, and were authorized to kill slaves who were away from their plantation without proper papers and who resisted arrest. Southern society had a military designed to maintain a system of race control, prevent slave revolts and keep blacks in a subordinate position (Williamson, 1986; Wilson, 1996). These codes and the slave patrol represent a culture in which perceived inferiority of black slaves was the norm. These perceptions legitimized individual and collective racism, which, in turn, resulted in institutional racism. It was (is) a vicious cycle.

The U.S. Constitution

White cultural practices institutionalized the system of slavery, but discriminatory laws formalized and legitimized the subordination of people of African descent. For instance, the Naturalization Act of 1790 established whiteness as a criterion for citizenship. That is, eighteenth-century white identity provided the basis for the incorporation of European immigrants, such as the Irish, into U.S. society. While Anglo Saxons were in control, Irish and Celtic could avoid permanent oppression and inferiority by virtue of being able to become white. Irish miners in Pennsylvania, for instance, despite their own exploitation, declared that they would never accept blacks as brethren because it was only as whites that they could gain opportunity in the United States (Kushnick, 1996). The incorporation of whites into the category "real American", regardless of ethnicity, was central in ensuring the domination of racism and preventing the coalescing of races along class lines. Whites of various ethnicities fused into a single white identity where physical appearance and beliefs about the inferiority of blacks was a factor that united them.

Institutionalization of the distinction between black and white, citizen and non-citizen were outlined at the Constitutional Convention of 1787 where slavery was incorporated into the structure of the new political system (Kushnick, 1996). Many people are unaware that slavery was written into the constitution. They do not know that certain articles in the constitution directly sanctioned slavery and legalized racial distinctions. For instance, Article I, Section 2, Paragraph 3 stated that 'other Persons' [terms such as slaves, blacks, and Negroes were not used in the Constitution because they were offensive to Northerners] were three-fifths of a person. Article I, Section 9, Paragraph 1 prohibited states from banning importation of slaves in any of the existing states before 1808. Therefore, Congress could not end the African slave trade prior to 1808 but Congress also was not required to ban it after that date. Article I, Section 2, Paragraph 3 was the fugitive slave clause which prevented free states from freeing fugitive slaves that reached their borders and required that such slaves be returned to their owner (Finkelman, 1996).

The three-fifths clause gave the South political strength in the House of Representatives and in the Electoral College since three-fifths of slaves would be counted although they could not vote. Based on congressional representation, another clause provided for the indirect election of the president through that same Electoral College. This gave whites in the south a disproportionate influence in the election of the president. The entire structure of the Constitution ensured there would not be emancipation of slaves by the new federal government (Finkelman, 1996). Today, the President is still chosen by the Electoral College and not elected by the "people." This system may have been created to maintain slavery in America but why is the Electoral College rather than a direct vote used to select the President today?

One of the first spin-offs of the proslavery Constitution was the Fugitive Slave Law in 1793 (Finkelman, 1981). The Fugitive slave clause provided that:

> No person held to Service or Labour in one State, under the
> Laws thereof, escaping into another, shall, in Consequence of
> any Law or Regulation therein, be discharged from such Ser-
> vice or Labour, but shall be delivered up on Claim of the Party
> to whom such Service or Labour may be due (Finkelman,
> 1996:81).

This law helped southerners retrieve their human property (Finkelman,
1981). But the strictest fugitive slave measure was enacted in 1850. This law
expanded the power of slavery to touch any state to retrieve those accused of
fleeing slavery. It stated that commissioners of federal circuit courts or those
acting under the authority of the federal courts in territories could issue warrants
to hold fugitive slaves and turn them over to any claimant who could provide
convincing proof that the fugitive was a runaway slave. Slaveholders might present an affidavit from a court in his home state that gave a physical description
of the runaway. If the description fit the free black, the federal commissioner released the individual into the custody of the claimant who could then take his
human property out of the state. The law also included stiff fines and imprisonment for those who obstructed the application of the law (Horton and Horton,
1997).

The Fugitive Slave Law of 1793 gave slaveholders the right to recover their
property anywhere in the country, but states could protect the freedom of accused slaves. The 1850 law overrode those state efforts (Finkelman, 1981).
Now, no place was beyond proslavery reach. People of color, even free ones,
were vulnerable to kidnapping by slave catchers. Any citizen could become a
slave catcher and slave catching could be a profitable activity. Southerners
could depend on the federal government to ignore or abolish the rights of free
blacks (Horton and Horton, 1997).

The constitution was a victory for slaveholders because it sanctioned and legitimized slave property (Finkelman, 1981). The constitution allowed southerners to monopolize offices and policies of the federal government and to use this
leverage to support slavery. It gave slaveholders distinct privileges and protection for their human property in return for specific commercial concessions to
the North. Also, almost all American presidents and their cabinet officers protected slavery in domestic and foreign politics (Finkelman, 1996).

In the United States white identity was constructed and reinforced by race-
based slavery. Behavioral characteristics, as well as physical traits, were associated with racial identities and races were carved out of these associations. Only
with a concept of race could constitutional laws sanction black slaves as property. Without race the demarcation between free versus slave, property versus
non-property and citizen versus non-citizen was blurred. The constitution defined the rights of free whites and the lack of rights for slave blacks.

Race, Class, and Capital

Historically, the majority of the working class was people of color while most of the white native-born workers were centralized in marginal industries such as farming (not agribusiness), timber, and ranching. In the United States the labor force between the 1880s and the 1930s was largely composed of southern and eastern European immigrants (Brodkin, 2001). The dominant group treated groups such as southern and eastern European immigrants, Africans and their descendants, Latinos, and Asians as inferior although they were the core of the industrial working class. The working class was constructed as ... "alien, dangerous, and unfit for inclusion in the national fabric" (Brodkin, 2001:373).

The powerful, those with resources, assets and wealth (capital), constructed race as a central part of shaping the working class (DuBois, 1935; Brodkin, 1997, 2001). Those with capital controlled political policy and defined the unskilled working class as inferior to whites. They continually created people classified as white and not-white and determined these categories by who was at the core of the working class at the time. Those at the core were not-white.

> We can think of the system as having a historic anchor, in constructing African Americans as the core of not-whiteness against which whiteness and a more fluid range of peoples whose changing class locations as more or less white and not-white have been constructed (Brodkin, 1997:473).

In other words, races were ranked along with their work. Southern and eastern Europeans were "not-quite-white" and formed the intermediate group between blacks and native-born whites. However, eventually these groups became skilled laborers and blended into the white category. Today, Asians and Latinos form the intermediate groups between whites and blacks.

So, the organization of labor is central to defining race and race is important in shaping the way that work is arranged (Brodkin, 1997). Labor was organized one way for free whites and another way for people of color. Moreover, their non-whiteness legitimized the reorganization of their work to be less than that of whites. Those who did unskilled labor were constructed by political practices, economic structures, and hegemonic cultural systems as inferior to whites (Brodkin, 2001).

This reorganization was apparent during the postbellum period when unskilled former slaves and not-quite-whites (southern and eastern Europeans) were mobilized to do the most dangerous and disagreeable jobs in extractive industries such as iron and coal mining.

> Southern employees in the extractive sector found it nearly impossible to purchase a home, take advantage of competitive

prices for food and consumer goods, acquire skills or formal
education, and, in increasing numbers over the years, even quit
their jobs (Jones, 1992:130).

The south's extractive industry was a kind of colonial economy where workers supplied raw materials for industrial revolutions in other areas; profits left
the community and kept them in poverty (Jones, 1992).

This means that those who do deskilled and degraded jobs become classified as not-white or not-bright-white racially. It also
means that not-whites and not-bright-whites have their jobs organized in a deskilled and intensely supervised manner and
have dibbies on degraded and degradable jobs (Brodkin, 1997:
474).

Whites avoided undesirable jobs that blacks were left with. For instance, the
Georgia state agricultural commissioner in 1901 stated that "We have [cotton
seed] oil mills and a guano factory; but of course, that is not very pleasant work
for whites, and they do not like it" (Jones, 1992:140). These mills in the south
employed blacks in all position with small numbers of whites as supervisors.
Blacks never supervised whites. Blacks performed the worst jobs with pockets
of whites doing the same. For instance, in lumber camps in the south, black men
did the heaviest work and in the mills they stacked lumber while whites handled
the machines (Jones, 1992).

Blacks were concentrated in the lowest-status jobs and were unable to secure
better positions even if they had the aptitude and seniority. For instance, in 1910
in the Texas lumber industry blacks were underrepresented in the more skilled
positions. And in the coal mines of Birmingham, Alabama employers instituted
policies aimed at discrimination against black workers: less pay for equal work
and job assignment that was based on ethnicity and race. Former slaves were at
the bottom of the job-status hierarchy after eastern and southern European immigrants and native-born whites (Jones, 1992).

From this discussion it is evident that race equals class. A friend who discussed buying a car suggested this association. He said that if a black person is
not dressed a certain way, for instance, in a suit, salespeople will not ask if they
need help finding a car. They assume that the black person does not have
money. Whites, on the other hand, can dress in any attire and it is assumed that
they are potential car buyers. Blacks have to prove their status while whites do
not. It is assumed that race reflects class, ability to pay.

The reason for this relationship is that the state collaborated with capital to
construct racial and gender categories. Laws affecting immigration, marriage,
welfare, census categories, and the constitution that promote and enforce resource segregation illustrate this. In doing so, the state also shaped the dominant

culture and its norms and behaviors that govern society. Since laws create and enforce categories and boundaries, these categories link the cultural with the economic. The state and those with capital then defined the working class as unskilled, non-white, non-feminine and savage (Brodkin, 1997).

CONCLUSIONS

Power, its acquisition and maintenance, is the focus of this chapter. Throughout this chapter, I examined the institutionalization of power by the dominant group. This process involved the creation of racial identities, legalization of slave versus free people, and the use of race to define the working class. In this way, the state and those with capital legitimized structured inequality in America.

While this chapter focused on slavery and power gained by the dominant group, this investigation is not intended to shame, pass blame, or provide a holistic explanation for current race relations. Rather, such examination may reveal long-term effects of slavery. For instance, the idea that blacks are physically constituted for manual labor or that white men have manhood while black men do not may be legacies of slavery. In the black community people often discuss black manhood and how it has been tarnished, unsupported, or considered lacking. Blacks often invoke slavery as an explanation for current views about black men. When one considers these stereotypes as a byproduct of slavery it helps us to understand how such views originated. Understanding history can bring about understanding of why people think the way they do today because stereotypes, ways of thinking and views about "our" group and "other" groups, are transmitted from generation to generation.

After discussing the history of the race concept in class, a white student said she did not think about herself and others in the same way anymore. Now, she stopped to think about her assumptions about the "other." A black student said she did not hate white people anymore because she understands how they came to believe certain things about blacks. It helped her to understand the lack of familiarity and understanding between blacks and whites. The previous discussion on the formation of racial distinctions is intended to provide a starting point for discussions about slavery and its consequences. In that way we can began to make connections between what took place and why during slavery and what are the enduring ramifications of slavery that relate to race and racism in the United States today.

UPDATE: THE REPARATION MOVEMENT

Reparations for slavery have grown as a social movement among African Americans since the passage of legislation approving reparations for Japanese

Americans incarcerated during WWII. A bill to study if descendants of African slaves should receive compensation has been introduced into the House Judiciary Committee each year, but the bill has never reached the floor of Congress (Oliver and Shapiro, 1999).

Like Japanese Americans, black Americans (some or many) believe they should be compensated for the atrocities committed against their ancestors and also for the legacies of slavery. For instance, African Americans often blame slavery for their current problems, i.e. living conditions and opportunities, or lack of opportunities. According to the argument, slavery ended but oppression did not. Similarly, Oliver and Shapiro (1999) assert that monetary reparations are an appropriate way to address racial inequity because the legacy of black labor, accumulation of wealth among white Americans, was denied African Americans by law and social custom during slavery and postemancipation.

Evidence for this position is suggested by the continuation of the planter class in powerful economic and political positions after the civil war. For instance, Cell (1982), argued that the planter class not only survived the war and reconstruction but by the end of the nineteenth century emerged as a powerful class. While emancipation resulted in significant loss of property and investment for planters, it did not cause the end of this class (Cell, 1982; Wilson, 1996). In the late nineteenth century, most of the new industrialists of the South were former slave owners (Mitchell and Mitchell, 1930).

The new approach in the Reparation Movement is to sue companies that profited from slavery. For example, there is evidence that notable names in the banking, finance, insurance, railroads, transportation, publishing, and other industries benefited from slavery. Activists in this movement argue that major corporations possess wealth that was either created by slaves or at their expense. For instance, insurance policies name masters as beneficiaries, railroads used slave labor, ships were insured that brought slaves from Africa to America, and many of the original benefactors of the top universities in the country were slave owners. While the connection between today's corporations and slavery are tenuous, there are records that show the extent to which companies depended on slave   labor   or   profited   from   the   sale   of   slaves (www.usatoday.com/usatonline/2002).

Advocates of reparations argue that the descendants of slave owners continued a legal slavery. For example, the ancestors of African Americans never received land, mules, and plows, were not allowed to be part of the political process and were relegated to low- status occupations. Black Americans argue that as descendants of slaves they are still at the mercy of the descendants of former slave owners who gained privilege because of slavery. Proponents of the argument cite continued manifestations of individual and collective racism as a rationalization for former slave owners and their descendants to maintain a racial caste system with people of African ancestry at the bottom. Inequities between blacks and whites ... "intensified each generation because of the 'artificial head start' accorded to practically all whites" (Oliver and Shapiro, 1999:535) that was reinforced by state policies. African Americans are part of a system that, rather than abolishing slavery, actually transformed it into a racial caste system (institutional racism) with the socioeconomic conditions of slavery. Because of these factors, reparations have become popular among African Americans and controversial.

CHAPTER FOUR

RACE, RACISM, AND SCIENCE I

> Scientific racism helped generate a hierarchy, underpinned by forces beyond the reach of humanity, that justified the superiority of the ruling class, both at home and abroad. It proclaimed the fitness of the capitalist class to rule over the working class and of the white race to rule over the black. And it did so not in the name of divine will or aristocratic reaction but of science and progress (Malik, 1996:100).

In this chapter, I examine the use of science to legitimize racial groups, racial hierarchies, and qualitative differences between groups. In other words, we will examine the origin of scientific racism, the belief that science proves the existence of permanent innate group differences and that racial ranking is valid. The heyday for scientific racism in America was from the 1870s to the 1920s. During this period scientists sought to prove that all group differences were fundamentally biological in origin and that culture was the product of nature, not nurture (Cravens, 1996).

Scientific racism helped to justify individual, collective and institutional racism because science confirmed the idea that human diversity can be partitioned into racial groups where some races are inferior while others are superior. However, scientific endeavors do not occur in isolation but within a social, political and economic context. It is the context of the scientific construction of races and the scientific justification of racism in the late nineteenth and early twentieth centuries that are the focus of this chapter.

THE SOCIAL CONTEXT FOR SCIENTIFIC RACISM

In order to understand how race science was generated during this time period, we must examine the social environment of that era. We need to systematically examine the relationship between society and science in terms of internal relations and economic, political, legal and other associations (Milic, 1984). Along this line, it is apparent that scientific racism in America emerged during the post-slavery era. That 1870 marks an upsurge in scientific activity designed to prove the inferiority of non-Europeans, especially blacks, suggests that such scientific enterprises were a response to the abolition of slavery. Evidence for this is indicated by a poorly developed science of race biology during slavery but when slavery was under attack race biology blossomed. In addition, when slavery was abolished in 1865 theories of biological inequality gained in importance (Gossett, 1965; Banton and Harwood, 1975). It is apparent that black and white relationships in slavery and during abolition influenced anthropological and biological theories of human variation (Drescher, 1990).

Why did this time period produce an increase in scientific racism? One possible answer is that during the post-slavery era, white southerners no longer had a labor force under their control and emancipation meant free blacks competed with whites for jobs. Two factors were important during this period: control of the new labor force and maintenance of the *status quo* with blacks at the bottom of the socioeconomic hierarchy. The initial response to both issues was to maintain a neoslavery. For instance, after emancipation the labor system in the south resembled a gang labor system, which was the slave system of labor organization. For example, free black laborers were organized into gangs that were closely supervised by overseers, there was exclusive control of the labor force by the landlord (former slave owner), use of the plantation as the basic unit of production, continued location of slave quarters as housing for free black laborers (Royce, 1985; Wilson, 1996), and continued employment of former slaves by former slaveowners.

These former slaves had to sign an annual labor contract where individuals contracted for a calendar year and planters paid the workers a share of the crop. Unfortunately, workers were not likely to see cash at the end of the year because of indebtedness. For instance, Planters could invoke the "faithful labor" clause in contracts that legitimized withholding payment from workers who were not in the fields more than two or three days at peak season. There was a furnishing system where planters or merchants advanced supplies and credit at the beginning of the year that meant that workers owed their employer in December. Employers also decided the price of the crop and who and when the crop would be marketed (Jones, 1992).

Planter-led industrialization meant that they controlled labor for both the land and the mills. In this way former slave owners tied blacks to the land through a debt peonage system and excluded them from the mills. In debt peonage, individuals are forced to work against their will. In the beginning of the twentieth century, most southern states had a law that made it illegal to leave a plantation without repaying debt. This was considered labor fraud punishable by imprisonment in the convict lease system. Employers, using these laws, were allowed to engage in forced labor (Wilson, 1996). Peonage files of the U.S. Justice Department show that starting in 1901 there was a prevalent use of non-free black labor in rural southern industries (Jones, 1992). Blacks were prevented from working in the mills and tied to the land in order to maintain a cheap, docile and stable labor for the plantations.

To maintain the social hierarchy, southerners implemented the aristocracy political platform. In this hierarchy upper-class whites ruled, other whites were in the middle and blacks were at the bottom. This hierarchy was maintained by former slave owners, now mill owners, controlling white mill workers by giving them special privileges over blacks and by using blacks as a weapon (strike breakers) against white labor. Mill owners created mill jobs for whites, built houses for them, supported their churches, and contributed to their charities. The result was the formation of a stratified society with blacks at the bottom on the land and poor whites above blacks in the mills (Wilson, 1996). In essence, former slaveowners, now mill owners, continued the aristocracy.

By the early 1870s, sharecropping and the tenant system replaced contract labor (Jones, 1992). Sharecroppers provided labor during the life cycle of the crop, used the plantation owner's mule team and purchased insecticide, seed and other items on credit. The landowner managed the sale of the crop and split the income 50-50 with the sharecropper. Purchases on credit and against anticipated income would be deducted from the croppers' portion of the harvest. Usually they earned just enough to pay their debts and sometimes they started the New Year with outstanding debts (Jones, 1992; Wilson, 1996).

Another strategy to maintain the "traditional" social order was the convict lease system that was enacted after the Civil war. Ninety percent of the offenders were young black men in their late teens and early twenties who were picked up in urban areas for offenses ranging from murder to petty theft, bootlegging, loitering and gambling. Youths who went into town could be arrested for minor charges and transported back to the plantation in chains where they were used in the extractive industries and for railroad construction (Jones, 1992). The result of this system, as with contract labor, debt peonage and sharecropping, was continued black servitude.

After emancipation, other aspects of slavery continued such as segregation. For instance, the Plessy v. Ferguson (1886) decision legitimized segregation in the south and legally segregated free blacks from the majority white population. With blacks isolated in certain neighborhoods, segregated from the majority population in public spaces and forced into occupations that they had during slavery, the disenfranchisement of free blacks was similar to black slavery, a neoslavery.

According to Kuschnick (1996), this disenfranchisement allowed capitalists to reinforce racial hatred. In other words, there was legal tolerance for individual discrimination that contributed to the development of a federally supported racial caste system (Wilson, 1996). In this racial caste system, blacks were restricted to low paying jobs, unhealthy neighborhoods, limited educational opportunities, and exclusion from the political process. Formal slavery was replaced by a racial caste system characterized by social, political, and economic oppression of blacks. This is the type of environment that fostered racism and the environment in which scientific racism flourished.

THE ORIGINS OF SCIENTIFIC RACISM

Another way to control the labor force and gain support for such control was to provide scientific justifications for the disenfranchisement of former slaves. To maintain a racial caste system, scientific rationales were needed for the permanent relegation of non-Europeans, such as African Americans, to the bottom of the socioeconomic hierarchy. One way to accomplish this task was by what Kuhn (1962) described as acquisition of tacit knowledge. Tacit knowledge is adherence to a paradigm because it is acquired through exposure to the literature and education without completely understanding why this paradigm is more acceptable in the scientific community. However, acceptability may have been taken for granted because science and folk beliefs were so intricately intertwined. In that way, science confirmed negative stereotypes about blacks. The following is an examination of a number of paradigms adhered to among scientists that promoted biological inequality between groups.

Outside as a Reflection of the Inside

Scientists in the 1800s were exposed to, and adhered to, a long-standing belief that the outside was a reflection of the inside. Scientists drew on earlier works that suggested a connection between physical constitution, emotion, and mental ability. For instance, the humoral qualities provided an early "natural" explanatory model for biological diversity and paved the way for behavior to be viewed as the product of physical structure. This theory used the concept of the four qualities, hot, cold, dry and moist, which were associated with four physiological qualities: blood, phlegm, black bile, and yellow bile (see Table 4.1) (Foster and Anderson, 1978). Linnaeus (1758) used these descriptions of qualities and temperaments from ancient Greece and associated them with racial groups (see Table 1). The reason for the association of specific qualities and temperaments with specific races is unclear in his writings. However, these associations conformed to popular views that a particular personality could be descriptive of or dominate a race; in that sense it codified the existence of 'racial personalities' (Smedley, 1993).

Race	Humors	Quality	Temperament
European	Hot and Moist	Blood	Sanguine
American Indian	Hot and Dry	Yellow Bile	Choleric
Asian	Cold and Dry	Black Bile	Melancholic
African	Cold and Moist	Phlegm	Phlegmatic

Table 4.1 Linnaeus Racial Classification Scheme (1758)

The order of the hierarchy, with Europeans first and Africans last also implied a ranking of races that still exists today. Even in contemporary times, the order of racial categories is usually given in the sequence shown in table 1. This has the psychological effect of a subtle biological ranking of groups.

Through the educational system, scientists were also exposed to physiognomy. In *Physiognomica,* Aristotle divided the body into areas of physiognomical significance using such signs as characteristic facial expressions, growth of hair, voice features, condition of the flesh, movements, gestures of the body, and body build (Shortland, 1985). Johann Gaspar Lavater popularized Physignomy in the 1700s when he taught that by examining features of the face and the form of the body one could judge the character and disposition of the individual (Davies, 1955). It was an early effort to identify outward physical signs of personality that were already part of folk theory. Traditional beliefs were then validated through the development of a discipline, advocates, procedures of observation, and practical application (Parssinen, 1974).

A similar focus is the doctrine of phrenology, "...the study of the faculties of the mind from the conformation of the skull..." (Nassi and Abramowitz, 1976:592). First developed by Franz Joseph Gall (1757-1828), his basic thesis was:

> ...that the brain was the organ of the mind, that the mental powers of man were based on innate faculties, that each had its seat in a definite region of the brain, that the size of each was a measure of the degree to which it formed a constituent element in the character of the individual, and—for practical purposes the most important of all— that the correspondence between the outer surface of the skull and the contour of the brain was

sufficiently close to enable the trained observer to recognize the
relative importance of the faculties (McLaren, 1981:4).

The original subdivisions by Gall were based on his observations of friends, patients and acquaintances that he believed exhibited certain traits and showed protuberances on the head. For example, after examining the heads of some of his most quarrelsome companions, Gall identified the area designated "combativeness" (McCoy, 1985; Parssinen, 1974).

Humoral theory, physiognomy and phrenology were never subjected to true tests. Rather, they were simply believed to be true. In "normal science," there is no contestation concerning the course of research strategies and no debate concerning the worth of the hypotheses. To be scientific ... "is simply to be a member of a community which shares a nest of commitments"... (Kuhn, 1962:100). This seems to be true among scientists discussed in this section. They were committed to the idea that physical differences between groups were significant and a reflection of cultural and intellectual worth.

To understand why claims of the association between physical constitution, intellect and behavior were considered well founded, we must examine the social atmosphere during this time period. Milic (1984) stated that the social functions of knowledge and ideas are related to 1) socio-integrative factors and 2) the formation of worldviews. The socio-integrative function of knowledge is to justify the social order. This can be accomplished on a global level by justifying the entire social order or by justifying social statuses, rights, privileges, the organization of activities and the ways in which activities such as science are conducted. Knowledge can also organize worldviews and self-consciousness (Milic, 1984). The previous and ensuing discussions are examples of beliefs and knowledge constructed to justify the social order and in the process of this justification, knowledge impacted the worldview of scientists.

Great Chain of Being

Exposure to a number of doctrines through the literature and the educational system contributed to scientists' self-consciousness, their worldview, and their commitment to and justification of the social order. One example that contributed to this process is the resurgence of the Great Chain of Being in the 1800s. In this scenario, higher organisms shared, to some degree, the nature of lower organisms. European mental and physical superiority placed them at the top of the Great Chain while the assumed inferiority of Africans made them 'naturally' closer to the ape. Eurocentricity was proved by contemporary science (Stepan, 1982) and the social order was a natural rather than a human-made process.

In Account of the Regular Gradation in Man, and in Different Animals and Vegetables; and from the Former to the Latter (1795) Charles White (1728-1813), an English surgeon, contended that different species were created with distinct characteristics that they retained from lower forms of life. Gradation was a general principle in nature, including humans. He examined numerous physical and physiological differences between populations such as bones, smell, penis size, clitoris shape, and size of cranium in an attempt to prove the Great Chain of Being (this is similar to Phillippe Rushton's research). The use of bones suggested to White that a natural gradation was revealed because ... "the bones, being that part of the system allowed to be least affected by climate, diet, customs"... (White, 1795:56). In this scenario, each gradation was a different species. "The Negro, the American, some of the Asiatic tribes, and the European, seem evidently to be different species" (White 1795:134).

Charles Darwin echoed Whites' assertion of gradation among human populations. In 1871 Darwin wrote ... "the difference in mind between man and the higher animals, great as it is, is certainly one of degree and not of kind" (Darwin, 1871:105) while in 1795 White stated that ... "it is much more probable that instinct and reason are only different degrees of the same principle" (White, 1795:65). Darwin argued that:

> the senses and intuitions, the various emotions and faculties, such as love, memory, attention, curiosity, imitation, reason, of which man boasts, may be found in an incipient, or even sometimes a well-developed condition, in the lower animals (1871:105).

Darwin's understanding of the connection between the environment and physical makeup could not overcome his Victorian bias toward gradation and hierarchy. Documentation of evolution coupled with natural selection was not enough to change his views about human diversity.

Species versus Varieties

Another concept that affected the worldview of scientists was the distinction between species and varieties. This perspective was intertwined with two other opposing theories, monogenesis and polygenesis. Monogenesists (Buffon, Blumenbach, Linnaeus, Darwin) believed races originated from a single source and that races were varieties within the same species. To them, human races degenerated from the original type, Adam and Eve, who were Caucasians. For example, in *Natural History* (1791a,b) George Louis Leclerc Count de Buffon considered races to be variations of the 'norm' (the white race), but not separate species. He believed that

> ...there was originally but one species, who, after multiplying and spreading over the whole surface of the earth, have undergone various changes by the influence of climate, food, mode

of living, epidemic diseases, and the mixture of dissimilar individuals... (Buffon, 1791b:206-207).

Buffon's criterion of a species was that members must be able to interbreed and since "classic" races conformed to this he considered them varieties and not different species. Johann Friedrich Blumenbach (1752-1840) asserted

> ...that animals belong to one and the same species, if they agree so well in form and constitution, that those things in which they do differ may have arisen by degeneration. We say that those, on the other hand, are of different species, whose essential difference is such as cannot be explained by the known sources of degeneration... (Blumenbach, 1795 [1969]: 188).

Degeneration or modification was caused by climate, diet, mode of life and hybridization. Variation among races was due to environmental factors and because of these factors "innumerable varieties of mankind run into one another by insensible degrees" (Blumenbach, 1795 [1969]: 264). Blumenbach recognized the overlapping distribution of traits between populations and favored a single species with varieties among humans. While he believed that racial classification was arbitrary, he divided humankind into five varieties:

> Caucasian
> American (Native American Indian)
> Mongolian
> Malay
> Ethiopian (African)

These categories became widely accepted and are still used today. Although it may not have been his intent, this racial classification pattern reflects a Great Chain of Being way of thinking that was entrenched in the literature, academia, and among scientists.

Charles Darwin also considered races to be varieties, subspecies, because "even the most distinct races of man ... are much more like each other in form"... (1871:215). However, he did not believe that racial characteristics were subject to natural selection. Races were the product of the "nature of the constitution," the physical environment, mode of life and most importantly sexual selection. Sexual selection is the advantage that members of a particular sex have over other members of the same sex in terms of exclusive reproductive relation. In other words, sexual selection favors those characteristics (e.g. strength, speed, physical attractiveness) that allow, for example, certain males to have an advantage over their rivals (Darwin, 1871). In this way, human diversity was created through mating practices.

According to Darwin, natural selection did not operate on *Homo sapiens*. Instead he argued that humans, in particular Europeans, overcame evolution and were already at the top of the evolutionary scale. This way of thinking was indicated in *The Descent of Man and Selection in Relation to Sex* (1871) where Darwin, in one branch of the evolutionary bush, continued the old ranking of races. For Darwin, humans consisted of varieties rather than separate species, but, one variety, European, was at the top of the evolutionary tree.

The minority view, polygenesism, was the doctrine that God created human races separately. Each race was considered a separate species. George Samuel Morton (1799-1851), the father of American physical anthropology and a polygenesist, defined species as "separate origin and distinctness of race, evinced by the constant transmission of some characteristic peculiarity of organization" (1847:40). He contended that species were a "primordial distinction" that were depicted as early as 3,000 years ago in Egyptian monuments. According to Morton the monuments and paintings showed that ancient Egyptians acknowledged different physical features for blacks and whites (Morton, 1844). Such differences were enough to indicate that they were different species.

In *The Races of Men* (1850), Knox argued that designation of varieties or species was irrelevant because they were significantly different in terms of physical makeup. In terms of blacks, he said "the whole shape of the skeleton differs from ours, and so also I find do the forms of almost every muscle of the body" (Knox 1850:152).

> I feel disposed to think that there must be a physical and, consequently, a psychological inferiority in the dark races generally. This may not depend altogether on deficiency in the size of the brain... but rather, perhaps, to specific characters in the quality of the brain itself (Knox, 1850:151).

The debate over whether races represented varieties or species influenced the way people perceived intermixture. In 1847, Morton published an article in which he argued that hybrids go against nature and that they can be the product of different species. For instance, he cited a number of fertile hybrids produced by, for example, a hinny that is the offspring of a horse and female donkey and matings between wolf, dogs and jackals that produced fertile offspring. He stated that hybrids produced from different species may ... "under very favorable circumstances give birth to fertile progeny" (1847:47). However, species were distinct because of the

> ... natural repugnance between individuals of different kinds. This is indeed overcome in the state of domestication, in which the natural propensities cease, in a great measure, to direct the actions (1847:210).

Since humans are the most "domesticated" they tend to intermix. "The fact that races can interbreed and produce fertile offspring is not proof of the unity of humankind" (1847:212).

White had a different view of intermixture. According to him, mulattoes were like mules, barren. They were less prolific than whites or blacks suggesting that they were two separate species. These distinctions, noted White, showed that humanity was composed of different species, the ability to interbreed and produce fertile offspring was irrelevant, and the idea that climate influenced distinctions between races was false (White, 1795).

A disciple of Morton and fellow polygenesist, Dr. Josiah Clark Nott, a physician in Mobile, Alabama, showed that mulattoes were less fit in terms of longevity. In a chapter in **Types of Mankind** (1854) entitled *Hybridity of Animals, Viewed in Connection with the Natural History of Mankind,* Nott maintained that whites and blacks are distinct species. He argued that 1) mulattoes have shorter lives than any other human race; 2) mulattoes are intermediate in intelligence between whites and blacks; and 3) mulattoes are less prolific than other races. Thus, Nott concluded that mulattoes were a hybrid, the product of two distinct species, similar to the mule produced from the horse and donkey. He also explained that some species crossings were more successful than others because of diversity of type among Caucasians. For instance, mulattoes living on the Atlantic coast were different from those in the Gulf States because Teutonic and Celtic populate those from the former whereas in the Gulf States there are a lot of emigrants from Southern Europe. If blacks mixed with southern Europeans their offspring were more prolific than those produced from matings between Teutons and blacks.

Although polygenesis was not as popular as monogenesis, its supporters (Morton, Broca, White, Knox, Nott, Gliddon) were very influential (Gould, 1981; Stanton, 1960; Banton and Harwood, 1975). It was used to explain the economic gap between whites and Africans and to justify European and white American imperial domination (Stocking, 1982). Polygenesis was entrenched in European and white American social values and racial worldviews (Stocking, 1968).

The distinction between species and varieties, in terms of contemporary variation is still problematic for people. For example, a chair of a psychiatry department asked me if blacks had the same number of chromosomes as whites. So even today people question the unity of humans and wonder if there are fundamental innate differences behind outward visible characteristics.

As you can see, knowledge is legitimated and the *status quo* is maintained through a circular process. That is, knowledge can be used to justify the social order and in doing so affect the worldview of scientists and lay people. Simultaneously, the worldview of scientists influences how they interpret data. This circularity not only maintains the existing social structure but also prevents other ways of thinking from being seriously considered.

THE TOOLS OF RACE BIOLOGY: QUANTIFICATION AND COMPARISON

Milic (1984) also stated that the social function of knowledge and ideas is practico-technical. There is a practico-technical knowledge that each professional group learns for their professional practice. Quantification and comparison are the practico-technical tools used by scientists, in the past and present, to examine human variation. According to Buffon "all our knowledge is ultimately derived from comparison" (Buffon, 1791a: 355). The standard for comparison was always people of European ancestry. For instance, White contended that

> ...taking the European man as a standard of comparison, on the one hand, and the tribe of simiae on the other; and, comparing the classes of mankind with the standards, and with each other, they may be so arranged as to form a pretty regular gradation, with respect to the differences in the bodily structure and economy, the European standing at the head, as being farthest removed from the brute creation (1795:83).

Today, people of European ancestry continue to be used as a standard for comparison. To many scientists, deviation from people of European ancestry in terms of behavior, cultural elements, genetics, health, et cetera still suggests inferiority, weakness, retardation, or unacceptable behavior.

In the post-emancipation era comparison and quantification were the practico-technical skills used in race science. The premier polygenesist provides an example of the use of comparison and quantification to validate folk beliefs. In *Crania Americana* (1839) George Samuel Morton concluded that the larger the size of the cranium, the greater the average intelligence and in *Crania Aegyptica* (1844) he showed that heads of Caucasians were larger than those of mulattoes and pure Negroes. While it could be argued that climate could affect skin color, like White, Morton argued that climate could not change skeletal traits. The environment was not involved in producing racial distinction, rather, it was God's doing. God adapted each race to its particular region (Morton, 1839).

Gould (1978, 1981) published a comprehensive study of Morton's methods and showed how he manipulated his data to produce desired results. Gould stated that:

> ...Morton's summaries are a patchwork of fudging and finagling in the clear interest of controlling *a priori* convictions. Yet—and this is the most intriguing aspect of the case—I find no evidence of conscious fraud; indeed, had Morton been a

conscious fudger, he would not have published his data so
openly (Gould, 1981:54) .... The prevalence of *unconscious* fi-
nagling, on the other hand, suggests a general conclusion about
the social context of science. For if scientists can be honestly
self-deluded to Morton's extent, then prior prejudice may be
found anywhere, even in the basics of measuring bones and tot-
ing sums (Gould, 1981:55-56).

Unfortunately, this data was reprinted repeatedly in the nineteenth century as
"hard" data on the mental ability of human races (Gould, 1981).

The master craniometer and polygenesist was Paul Broca (1824-1880), professor of clinical surgery in the faculty of medicine and founder of the Anthropological society of Paris in 1859. He collected over 2,000 skulls but noted that
the head was too irregular to allow accurate statistical comparisons. He concluded that individual differences are greater within a given race, than between
races and that measurements could change between individuals and on the same
individual (Gossett, 1965). Broca chose to measure and weigh brains directly although such measurements also presented irregularities. He could never "accu-
rately" weigh brains and partition human diversity into races but he continued to
believe that measurements of the brain provided insights into individual and racial moral and intellectual worth (Stocking, 1982).

Scientists thought that if they took enough measurements they could fit overlapping variation into discrete categories and rank them. They believed human
variation could be divided into discrete categories because in the distant past
there were pure races with a narrow range of variation. As such, a few individuals could represent a population, the "type" for that group. Morton and others
believed certain skulls represented pure types. How closely contemporary skulls
conformed to these types determined if they belonged to that "classic" race. For
them, races were real but classification was problematic because of intermixture. For instance, based on differences in bone structure, Africans were the
product of three types: Bush, Boskop, and Negro. According to Dart (1940), the
Bantu is made from Bush and Negro types, ... " but before they fused, the Bush
race had already been infiltrated with Brown (Mediterranean) racial elements
and the Negro with Nordic elements" (1940:22).

When the data did not show a hierarchical relationship between races anthropologists did not give up. Gossett (1965:83) stated that:

There was a fundamental fallacy behind this whole vast nineteenth-century
search for methods to measure race differences. Many a racist awaited breath-
lessly some scheme of race classification that would withstand the testing methods of science and was prepared—once such a method was found—to pile
mountains of ad hoc theory concerning the character and temperament of the
races onto any discoveries concerning their measurable physical differences.
How little the search really mattered may be seen in the tendency of racists,

when a physical basis of measurable race differences eluded them, to assume immense innate psychological differences in any case. They did not really need proof for what they knew was there.

RACE AND CULTURE

The idea that blacks never contributed to civilization has already been examined. However, it should be noted that this belief continued into the 1800s. For example, in 1817 George Cuvier argued that Egyptian civilization was not created by blacks but by Europeans who had large brains (Stocking, 1982). In *Crania Aegyptica*, Samuel George Morton argued that only Caucasians developed a great civilization and that the social position of blacks ... "in ancient times was the same that it now is, that of servants and slaves" (Morton, 1844:66). By showing that blacks had been slaves since ancient times, Morton implied that their subjugation was inevitable and natural.

The idea that black Africans never contributed to civilization persists today. There continues to be a debate about the physical makeup of Egyptians and especially Cleopatra. People seem to think that Cleopatra looked like Elizabeth Taylor because she starred in the epic motion picture where she portrayed the Egyptian Queen. Did Cleopatra really look like a Greek, a Nubian, or a mixed race person? Because of hypodescent in the United States, if Cleopatra was a mixed race person she would be considered black. However, that is not how her physical appearance is usually interpreted.

While visiting the National Library of Medicine I was reminded of another reason that race matters. The library had an exhibit of an 855-year-old medical book, *Treatises on Medicine* (the book is untitled but was given this name for the traveling exhibition). It contains the *Aphorism of Hippocrates*, the treatise that gave rise to the theoretical and practical branches of the 'art of medicine.' The book includes writings by a number of authors including a passage by Constantine the African (d. 1087). If his racial classification had not been stated I would not have know that an African contributed to such an important work. Given world history and negative stereotypes about people of African descent, it is important that all people recognize the contributions of people of African ancestry to world civilization. Constantine the African is one example.

In the 1800s and currently, the importance of this question and concern about the physical appearance of Egyptians, who created the pyramids and other cultural wonders, are related to the idea that physical makeup is connected to culture and civilization, or lack of it. Scientists in the 1800s tried to prove that the inferior biological makeup of black Africans 'caused' them to be incapable of attaining a 'high' civilization. Today, African Americans try to prove that Cleopatra was a black African to show that blacks are capable of attaining a 'high' civilization. In both cases, there is still a commitment to the connection between biological makeup and culture.

Unilinear Evolution

Unilinear evolution was the preeminent theory that explained cultural development in the late nineteenth and early twentieth century. Lewis Henry Morgan, an American anthropologist, author of *Ancient Society* (1878), and unilinear evolutionist concluded that races had to pass through three cultural stages from savagery to barbarism to civilization. According to Morgan and John Wesley Powell (1888, 1899), the most influential American anthropologist after Morgan's death, savagery was characterized by nomadic life that was based upon kinship such as clans with totems, belief in ghosts and animal worship, and hunting/gathering mode of life, while barbarism was described as tribal, sedentary, also based upon kinship with a patriarchy, priests, city-states, and domestication of plants and animals. Civilization was the highest cultural stage and was portrayed as the use of machinery, iron tools, accumulation of wealth, walled cities, nations and most importantly, inductive reasoning.

In 1899 Powell partitioned civilization into monarchy, and republicanism in which the former was distinguished by slaves, serfs, taxation, private ownership of land, aristocracy determined by hereditary descent, guilds, and castes, while the latter included invention of machinery and development of scientific processes of production as well as representative government and democracy. W.J. McGee (1899), Powell's protégé at the Bureau of American Ethnology, followed the civilized stage of cultural evolution with a fourth cultural stage, enlightenment, characterized by inventions.

Unilinear evolution actually presents a circular argument for culture change. For instance, according to Powell (1888), activities are products of the mind where "knowledge is always born of one and diffuses to the many" (1899:729). This knowledge prompts a change in the culture and the cultural change stimulates more mental changes that bring about more cultural changes. It was believed that as societies passed through cultural stages there was a qualitative and quantitative change in the brain with the 'civilized' having larger and more complex brains (McGee, 1899). In this regard, the acquisition of inductive reasoning (due to changes in the brain) made research and civilization possible. According to Herbert Spencer (1891) inductive reasoning was impossible for savages because they lack the ... "ability to select facts from conclusions"... (Spencer, 1891:79) and therefore cannot distinguish natural from unnatural causes. In other words, inductive reasoning was a new type of mental activity that made civilization possible (Powell, 1888).

Not only are cultures ranked in unilinear evolution, but the "organization of living bodies is hierarchic" (McGee, 1899:424). McGee (1899), Brinton (1890), and Spencer (1891) proposed major racial differences between cultural stages. Africans, as indicated by their dark skin color, were at the stage of savagery. The 'yellow' races were barbarians with better minds than savages while the 'civilized' white race had the best minds and, of course, the highest level of civilization (McGee, 1899). In other words, darker-skinned people were less evolved and therefore their consciousness was more dependent upon sensation and impulsiveness rather than reasoning (Spencer, 1891).

The body represented the culture stage but the culture stage was due to the quality of the brain that was housed in the body. Brinton and Spencer listed traits of inferior physical form such as wide nasal aperture, early union of cranial sutures, and prominence of the jaws and teeth, and stature. Spencer implied ... "some connexion between barbarism and inferiority of size" (1891:40) and that 'inferior' races have early puberty compared to "superior" races. "This early cessation of development [among savages] implied both low intellectual nature and a great impediment to intellectual advance, since it makes the larger part of life unmodifiable by further experiences" (Spencer, 1891:88).

The physical environment was thought to be the reason for differences in mental development (Powell, 1888; McGee, 1899; Spencer, 1891; Ripley, 1899). According to McGee, "incongruities in mode of thinking displayed by diverse peoples... are traceable to environment; for other things equal, the mental operations of peoples vary with their surroundings" (1899:430). The environment of Europeans was considered more hospitable, therefore, it was assumed that this made possible superior minds that resulted in civilization. Even in the 1700s, Buffon contended that

> The most temperate climate lies between the 40th and 50th degree of latitude, and it produces the most handsome and beautiful men. It is from this climate that the ideas of the genuine colour of mankind, and of the various degrees of beauty, ought to be derived (Buffon, 1791b: 205).

In addition, White stated that "inhabitants of warmer climates have a 'dull torpid brain" compared to Europeans (White, 1795:65). The poor environment of the 'savages' retarded their mental development and therefore their cultural advancement (McGee, 1899). And, Spencer concluded that:

> ...development of the higher intellectual faculties has gone on *pari passu* with social advance, alike as cause and consequence; that the primitive man could not evolve these higher intellectual faculties in the absence of a fit environment; and that in this, as in other respects, his progress was retarded by the absence of capacities which only progress could bring (1891:90-91).

According to this reasoning, the environment stimulated mental development that brought about cultural change. A change in culture then stimulated further mental development and so on.

Ontogeny Recapitulates Phylogeny

Another way to explain the relationship between physical form and culture was the advocacy of 'ontogeny recapitulates phylogeny' (Spencer, 1891). Spencer hypothesized that during growth and development the "civilized" passed through physical and physiological stages representing phases passed through by the other races. Civilized whites, however, continued to develop while other races stopped at earlier stages of development. This partially explained the early puberty of darker-skinned people. They stopped growing and developing at an earlier stage compared to whites that continued to evolve. Children of the civilized, for instance, have the minds of savages but as they develop their minds become civilized. Another way to look at it is that savages are children who have not developed into civilized whites.

This discussion provides a background to explain the strong dislike by blacks to being called boy or girl by whites. One cannot say that these ideas are in the past when some adult whites still call blacks by these terms or when adult blacks are still insulted by these terms. Something similar happened while I was in a take-out restaurant. A none black woman called an elderly black woman "mama." Use of this term toward the elderly woman irritated every black person in the room. There are still depictions of blacks as "Aunt Jemimas" and children. Just as there are contemporary legacies of slavery, there are contemporary legacies of race science from this period.

SOCIAL DARWINISM, EUGENICS, AND IMMIGRATION

Unilinear evolution and 'ontogeny recapitulates ontogeny' are early examples of scientific paradigms in which human physical and cultural variation was considered solely the product of biology. Biology produced particular cultures and social or physical forces could not modify this association. In the early 1900s this connection was a major concern among "Old Americans", those of western European ancestry, because of concerns about mass immigration from southern and eastern Europe.

Old Americans were especially fearful of racial intermixture. They feared that the inferior new immigrants would contaminate or mongrelize the "American stock". For them, intermixture with new immigrants would bring about a decline in the biological makeup of "Americans." Two publications during this time, Madison Grant's *The Passing of the Great Race* (1916) and Theodore

Lothrop Stoddard's *The Rising Tide of Color* (1920) are examined because they epitomize these beliefs and attitudes toward the new immigrants.

The Immigration Scare

Madison Grant (1865-1937) was a major alarmist about mass immigration. In the initial pages of *The Passing* it is clear that he is a polygenesist. While this view was contrary to the bible, people of color, especially dark-skinned people, seemed so different from Europeans that it was believed they were not created in God's image. Such differences and a polygenesist perspective may be the basis for his conviction that any intermixture between European and another race resulted in ... "a race reverting to the more ancient, generalized and lower type" (1916:18). According to Grant:

> The cross between a white man and an Indian is an Indian; the cross between a white man and a Negro is a Negro; the cross between a white man and a Hindu is a Hindu; and the cross between any of the three European races and a Jew is a Jew (1916:18).

Like many scientists in this era he assumed that complex traits such as hair and skin color followed simple Mendelian inheritance. According to Grant, "the blond is consequently recessive to the brunet because it recedes from view in the first generation" (1916:14). A student of mine made similar statements in a paper about Australian aborigines. He assumed that Australian aborigines were inferior to Europeans because of recessive genes. According to him, the mutation for dominant intelligent genes appeared among Europeans and since they were a large population, it spread. The gene for intelligence did not spread to Australia because they were isolated and a smaller population. Since they did not receive the dominant gene for intelligence, they only had the recessive gene resulting in inferiority. Even today, with all of our technical and biological advances, people do not understand inheritance, especially when it involves complex traits. More seriously though, it suggests that individuals cannot reject myth even if there is an abundance of evidence to the contrary. The idea of simple inheritance for traits such as intelligence is so ingrained in the belief system of some individuals that exposure to knowledge is not enough to overcome preconceived notions.

Based upon beliefs about inheritance, Grant and other Americans were concerned about losing the Nordic racial character. Throughout the volume, he argued that civilizations rose and fell because of racial attributes. The same thing could happen in the United States if Old Americans interbred with new immigrants.

During the period of mass immigration, southern and eastern Europeans were considered a different race from Western Europeans and therefore "not-quite white". Melbourne Tapper (1999) shows how sickling (a genetic mutation that affects the hemoglobin) was used in the debate about the new immigrants. According to Tapper, after sickling was discovered in a black student from the Caribbean in 1910, it was linked to people of African ancestry and was used as an indicator of racial purity or the degree of blackness. During the 1920s, however, sickling was observed in other groups such as whites and Arabs. Because of preconceptions about sickling, these individuals were thought to have African ancestry. Tapper states that

> As increasing numbers of cases of sickling in "whites" were reported, physicians were faced with the dilemma of either rejecting these cases on the grounds that the diagnosed individuals were not truly "white" or that the cells found in their blood were not authentic sickle-shaped cells, or creating a space within which sickling in whites would cease to be problematic. They chose the latter solution and refined existing strategies to determine who was and who was not "racially pure white," without accepting the position that sickling could be found in "whites" (1999:20).

Sickling in whites, e.g. Italians and Greeks, was viewed as the result of mixture with blacks. Because of their exposure to blacks, southern Europeans were "not-quite-white" and therefore distinct from other whites (western Europeans). Sickling was used as a racial marker to determine who was white, "not-quite white", and black (Tapper, 1999).

These ideas form the background for immigration restriction efforts. Grant and other Americans believed that politics, such as immigration restriction, laws against miscegenation, and sterilization of the unfit were simply the application of biological laws. While nature would weed out the inferior through the process of natural selection, these laws would do artificially and faster what nature was doing naturally and slowly, maintaining the "higher" races. In essence, artificial selection or eugenics made possible the political application of biological laws (Stein, 1988).

Many scientists during this period believed that eugenics could speed up the process of social Darwinism, the application of natural selection to society. Grant discussed social Darwinism when he stated that

> Where two races occupy a country side by side, it is not correct to speak of one type as changing into the other. Even if present in equal numbers one of the two contrasted types will have some small advantage or capacity which the other lacks toward a perfect adjustment to surroundings. Those possessing these

> favorable variations will flourish at the expense of their rivals
> and their offspring will not only be more numerous, but will
> also tend to inherit such variations. In this way one type gradu-
> ally breeds the other out. In this sense, and in this sense only,
> do races change (1916:46).

Grant believed nature would weed out nonwhites. This belief had a precedent in unilinear evolution, which placed people of color low on the biological and cultural scale. People of color were considered physically deficient which produced cultural inferiority. Over time, the superior would dominate while the inferior would become extinct. This is noted among premier unilinear evolutionists such as McGee (1899) who argued that the 'lower races' would become extinct because they lacked the 'strong present among the 'higher races'. In addition, Brinton (1891) contended that mixed race people would become extinct because of their short lives, feeble constitution, or sterility. Social Darwinism was the ultimate solution to the white man's burden. It was a scientific paradigm that predicted the eventual extinction of nonwhites through natural competition. Simultaneously, individualism and competition were given scientific justification for black subordination as well as their projected extinction (Franklin, 1991).

Another advocate of immigration restriction was Theodore Lothrop Stoddard (1883-1950) who formulated the term *underman* (similar to the current term underclass) to describe individuals from eastern and southern Europe (Cravens, 1996). Stoddard aroused the nation about race in a popular series of illustrated travelogues that he published as Stoddard's Lectures and numerous articles for popular magazines such as the Saturday Evening Post (Gossett, 1965). In these publications and *The Rising Tide of Color* (1920) Stoddard, like Grant, was concerned about the larger reproductive rate among the "colored races" relative to the "white race". In addition, Stoddard argued that the white race is removing checks on population size such as tribal warfare, famine, and disease, among people of color. He argued that people of color dislike white domination and are expanding into "white areas".

> Where, then, should the congested colored world tend to pour
> its accumulating human surplus, inexorably condemned to
> emigrate or starve? The answer is: into those emptier regions of
> the earth under white political control. But many of these rela-
> tively empty lands have been definitely set aside by the white
> man as his own special heritage (Stoddard, 1920:9).

According to Stoddard the "colored world" is … "restive under white political domination" and will try to erode white supremacy (1920:9). In response to the "colored threat", Stoddard stressed the need for white solidarity against the encroaching colored masses. His words were realized in the revitalization of the Ku Klux Klan (see last section).

Both books were used on the floor of the U.S. senate to support discriminatory quotas against immigrants from Eastern and Southern Europe (Metress, 1993). Therefore, both publications provided fuel for nativist movement's anxieties about the new immigrants (Cravens, 1996).

THE SOCIOLOGY OF RACE SCIENCE

Scientific societies and institutions such as universities created a collective political correctness for race science. Using the methods of 'normal science,' measurement and comparison, physiognomy, phrenology, craniometry, unilinear evolution, and social Darwinism were validated. In the process, folk beliefs were also validated. In addition, "normal science" validated colonialism, slavery, imperialism, classism, sexism and racism.

Entrenchment in normal science (e.g. gradations, polygenesis, unilinear evolution) obscured research findings. Premier anthropologists and natural historians of their day twisted the most important theory in biological history, natural selection, to fit folk 'science.' It was not only exposure to particular theories in the literature and the educational process that prevented scientists from concluding that races are nonexistent or cannot be ranked. Races and concepts associated with races were needed to scientifically justify the exclusion of non-Europeans from American socioeconomic and political life.

Commitment to folk beliefs based upon exposure to tacit knowledge was apparent to me in a study on unintended pregnancies. During data collection and analysis, researchers attempted to find support for every negative stereotype imaginable about African Americans. For instance, researchers wanted to discuss drug use in their research findings although participants refused to talk about drugs. Participants would only say that some people used drugs. However, researchers stated that they could discuss the "normative use" of drugs because the literature provided numerous examples of drug use among African Americans. The point of data collection is to determine what people are actually doing. The approach of the researchers, however, was to inject the literature into the research findings as if it was part of the data collection process. In that way, it would appear that drug use among African Americans was supported by data collected in the current project. Researchers' commitment to the belief in rampant drug use among African Americans was not altered by lack of data. Rather, there was an attempt to generate data, through the literature, to confirm what they already believed.

Milic (1984) stated that in order to understand the sociology of knowledge, we need to examine the position of scientists within the class system of the society. Participants in the production of scientific knowledge were the elite, upper class of the society. Scientists, as members of the upper class, are granted epistemic warrant, "a covert form of distributing power" where a 'cult of experts' determine what is appropriate for people outside their group (Fuller, 1987). Since access to and control of knowledge is determined by the upper class, value biases exist in knowledge. Because knowledge is controlled by a 'cult of experts,' usually members of the upper class, we must always ask who benefits from the knowledge claim.

Examination of scientific publication processes and academic training also are necessary to understand why one paradigm is more popular than others (Milic, 1984). In academia mentors and professors determine the direction of scientific endeavors. For instance, Nott and Gliddon were disciples of Morton and all were members of the upper class. Stocking (1982) suggested that Knox had considerable influence on racial thinking in British science in the 1850s and 1860s. Knox influenced physicians, and his disciple, James Hunt who formed the Anthropological Society of London in 1863 (Banton and Harwood, 1975).

Among scientists, intellectual evolutionary trees can be constructed to demonstrate the social inheritance of ideas about human diversity. Figure 4.1 provides an example of such a tree. In the transmission of knowledge, ways of thinking about science and biological diversity are passed from professor to student over a number of generations. In this way, knowledge diffuses but the paradigm may remain the same. This is so because historic and contemporary scientists work within social, political, economic and cultural ideologies of "scientific communities" which were/are the mechanisms for the transfer of knowledge.

Another factor in paradigm transmission is the 'Matthew effect' in which eminent scientists are more rapidly and easily published (Milic, 1984). The fact that some individuals at large institutions collaborate and are able to publish more means they have a greater impact on the scientific community. Over time, collective activity can have the appearance of objectivity (Fuller, 1987). That is, paradigms can appear objective because of the preponderance of publications by popular scientists. For example, George Combe, founder of the Edinburgh Phrenological Society in 1820 (actually a debating society for the upper class) and the first editor of the Phrenological Journal in 1823 (Fulton, 1927; Davies, 1955), popularized phrenology not only by lecturing, but also by publishing a wide variety of articles, books and pamphlets (Parssinen, 1974). Between 1803 and 1857 there were over fifty-five major books published on the subject in Europe alone. Although phrenology was based on weak documentation, because of wide publications it was a branch of psychology for over 140 years (McCoy, 1985).

The overview of the formation of the race concept given here highlights the influence of certain leading scientists during this period. While there were opposing viewpoints, those advocating racial scaling were the leaders in this area.

Their popularity rested in the production of science that supported the existing social order.

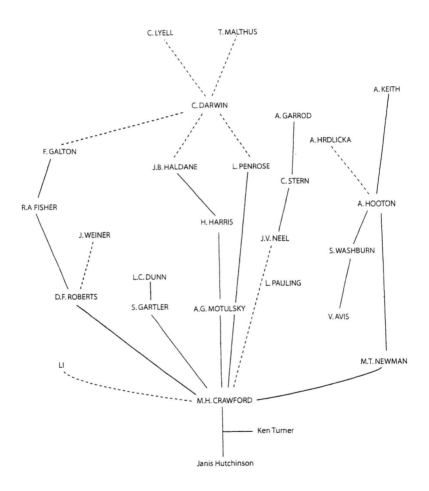

Figure 4.1. Intellectual Genealogy (Adapted from the Genealogy of Michael Crawford, u.m.).

Today, science continues to rationalize and legitimize enculturated prejudice about people who are biologically different from those of European ancestry. Quiet advocates of scientific racism generate hypotheses and frame data collection and analysis in such a way that the outcome is congruent with racist ideology. Scientific racism, as a function of collective racism, is a part of the process of generating knowledge about people of color in western science (Hutchinson, 1997). In other words, race science in the nineteenth century provided the basis for modern beliefs about human variation that are still the foundation for racism and discrimination as we move into the twenty-first century.

UPDATE: THE KU KLUX KLAN

Books by scientists such as Grant and Stoddard reflected the mood of the country. With these pseudoscientific beliefs entrenched in American society, U.S. culture was a fertile ground for organizations such as the Ku Klux Klan (KKK). The KKK originated less than a year after the Civil War, December 1865 in Pulaski, Tennessee near the border of Alabama. Six college men and former Confederate officers who were bored organized the KKK as a social club. They had a secret initiation that was the focal point of their roughhouse. The terms Ku Klux were adapted from a Greek term, *kykos* meaning circle, and their small circle of friends. The word Klan comes from the old Scottish clans in writings by Sir Walter Scott, a popular author in the South (Chalmers, 1987; Tucker, 1991).

While the Klan began for fun, later groups had purposes that were more insidious. They drove out northern schoolteachers, storekeepers, and politicians, and threatened and attacked free blacks that had land, prospered or talked about equal rights. They attacked officials who registered blacks, or who did not give whites privilege and priority. To accomplish these tasks the Klan committed atrocities such as floggings, tar and feather parties, kidnappings, killings, mutilations, and acid branding of KKK on the forehead (Chalmers, 1987; Tucker, 1991).

White supremacist groups had various names such as Order of the White Rose, Knights of the White Kamilia, and White Brotherhood. However, the Klan with its symbols and regalia became the leader among white supremacist groups. In 1867 their program was formulated when General Nathan Bedford Forrest, a former Confederate officer, became the first Grand Wizard (Chalmers, 1987; Tucker, 1991).

Over time common criminals began to use the Klan regalia to commit robbery, rape, or arson causing many in the upper class in the south to turn against them. Then in 1915 William J. Simmons revived the KKK. Many believe he was influenced by D.W. Griffith's the *Birth of a Nation* which was based on Thomas Dixon, Jr.'s novel *The Clansman*. Dixon was a classmate and friend of

President Woodrow Wilson. His novel was subtitled: *An Historical Romance of the Ku Klux Klan*. In it he portrayed blacks as illiterate rapists who took over southern legislatures and property. Simmons placed an advertisement for his secret lodge adjacent to the one for *The Birth of a Nation* in Atlanta (Chalmers, 1987; Tucker 1991) and Klan membership increased.

In the beginning, the Klan was a Protestant lodge that was not openly anti-Catholic or anti-Semitic although there were racial and religious restrictions on membership. During mass immigration in the early 1900s, Catholic immigration from Europe polarized the Klan against immigrants and Catholics. They thought that the Vatican in Italy and the Pope would take over the country and sought to revitalize small-town xenophobia where Roman Catholics, Jews, and blacks were the aliens. Today, the Klan is a protestant organization although it has recruited Catholics and a minority of Jews (Tucker, 1991).

The early Klan stressed patriotism and white exclusivity. It also sought to protect white womanhood (Tucker, 1991). White women were at the core of property, chivalry and culture. Not being accessible to blacks she was the ultimate distinction between the two groups (Chalmers, 1987). In addition, the Klan has always wanted one language and sought one school system, public schools, and separation of church and state. This was meant to separate the Roman Catholic Church from the state because Klansmen did not see a conflict with state-mandated prayer and bible reading in public schools (Chalmers, 1987; Tucker, 1991). Among southerners the Klan was a law and order movement because it was to restore the proper social order (Chalmers, 1987).

The impact of the Klan on civility in the United States is exemplified by the tragedy in Tulsa, Oklahoma on June 1, 1921. On that day an affluent all-black community in Tulsa was bombed from the air and burned by an angry white mob. In less than twelve hours over 3,000 African Americans were dead. More than 600 successful black-owned businesses and over 1,500 homes were destroyed along with a hospital, six private black owned airplanes, a post office, libraries, schools, law offices and a bus system. The driving force behind this massacre was the Ku Klux Klan along with ranking city officials and other sympathizers. The response of poor white males returning from WW I to prosperous "Black Wall Street" in Tulsa was mass murder and pillage. It was the largest massacre of non-military U.S. citizens in the history of America. While the Klan claims to be the defenders of the American way of life, they committed the greatest atrocities against Americans in the history of this country (Wilson and Wallace, 1992) until September 11, 2001.

In the 1950s and 1960s the Klan bombed churches, shot civil rights workers and assaulted integration-minded bus riders. Nevertheless, they did not stop the civil rights movement. In the 1970s there was sporadic Klan violence and its revival was related to economic uncertainty, new leadership and black-white confrontation (Chalmers, 1987).

On the website of the Knights of the Ku Klux Klan it is clear that they, like Stoddard and Grant, are concerned about the "dwindling numbers of whites" compared to others such as Mexicans, blacks, and Asians. In particular, they focus on changing demographics in California where in a few years whites may be the minority. They believe that white American freedoms and uniqueness are threatened by high birth rates among people of color and non-white immigrants. According to them, they will be voted not only out of power, but also out of existence (Knights of the Ku Klux Klan website, 2001).

The Klan claims to be a revitalization movement by trying to rid society of "foreigners," (Chalmers, 1987). Evidence of this is evident in their concern about afrocentricity in public schools. According to the Knights of the Ku Klux Klan (2001, website) only those of European ancestry should be included in U.S. history books because they are the only group instrumental in building America.

They also claim to be a political party of whites who want to preserve Western Civilization and those of Western European ancestry. To accomplish this goal they are against integration because they believe it reduces academic standards. According to them the white majority is discriminated against in terms of employment, promotions, college entrance and scholarships. They call for an end to immigration and use of the welfare system to control birth rates. In other words, in order to receive federal aid, individuals would have to reduce the number of children they have (Knights of the KKK website, 2001).

Examination of the Knights of the KKK reveals a continuation of the ideology espoused by Grant and Stoddard in the early 1900s. Review of the website also shows that they continue to think of themselves as the preservers of American culture and tradition. As stated by Chalmers (1987: 21) "most of the time the Klan rode to prevent future rather than to stop present and punish past actions." This was true for the Klan in the past and seems to be their current situation.

CHAPTER FIVE

RACE, RACISM, AND SCIENCE II

> Physical form and characteristics mattered in the discourse of
> scientific racism for two reasons: they made it possible for sci-
> entists to identify particular races with relative ease, and physi-
> cal form and traits had a presumed relationship to cultural abil-
> ity. Cultural ability, or, more precisely, mental heredity for in-
> dividuals and groups, was central to this discourse (Cravens,
> 1996:479).

Former slaves never received forty acres and a mule from the government.
Consequently, according to the 1930 Census Tract data, out of a total of over a
million black agricultural workers only 13% were landowners (Myrdal, 1975)
compared with 42% among a white agricultural workforce of almost three million (Wilson, 1996). While blacks did not own land, they continued to be tied to
it. Initially, this connection was through the gang labor system discussed in the
previous section. However, through work slowdowns, refusal to sign labor contracts, and threats to leave the job during the season, former slaveholders were
forced to abandon this system (Royce, 1985). Land, however, continued to be
centralized in the hands of the dominant class who began to exploit labor in a
different way. They used tenant farmers and sharecroppers to accumulate wealth
and, simultaneously, to continue the post-emancipation slavery of blacks. For
example, while most sharecroppers were white, a greater percentage of the
black population (28.2%) compared to the white population (13.0%) were
sharecroppers (1930 U.S. Department of Commerce Census data). In the black

belt of the South over half of the sharecroppers were black (Mandle, 1992; Wilson, 1996).

Sharecropping was a system in which croppers received a share of the crop at the end of the season in exchange for their labor (Royce, 1985). The credit system allowed planters to either advance loans or provide supplies on credit using the crop as collateral. Interest rates could be as much as 71% of the loan. The crop share system allowed sharecroppers to pay rent as a percentage of the crop yield, usually 50%. The planter determined how much the cropper owed him and how much to subtract from the cropper's share. It was not necessary to cheat the cropper because under the fairest conditions the planter was enriched (Mandle, 1992).

Sharecropping was a continued attempt by the ex-planter class, now industrial leaders, to maintain a cheap labor force. A hierarchy was created with black sharecroppers at the bottom, white landowners at the top, and other whites in the middle. This ranking meant that there continued to be a need to justify this hierarchy and science continued to be the source of that justification.

BLOOD GROUPS AND RACE

While the preceding chapter focused on connecting outward physical characteristics with culture to define/describe races, the current section uses inward biological traits, i.e. blood groups and genes, to accomplish the same end. In other words, genetics was used to accomplish the goal, making race real, that cranial measurement was unable to do. Moreover, like the heyday of craniometry, blood group systems were/are used to explain inter-group differences in terms of health, behavior, and intelligence. Biological determinism moved from measurement and observation of the outside of the body to blood groups and genes inside the body.

For example, when the ABO and other blood group systems were discovered in the early 1900s they became the quantifiers for "classic races". Like bones, blood groups were considered stable and not subject to the pressures of natural selection. Blood groups were thought to be selectively neutral. Rather, mutations created blood group systems and their distributions were related to migration, drift, and isolation (Wiener, 1946; Boyd, 1949, 1950). For these classifiers, blood groups provided an objective analysis of human variation because they follow simple Mendelian laws of inheritance (Wiener, 1946; Boyd, 1950). Since the mode of inheritance is known ... "we can distinguish a different serological race for each of the major geographical areas" (Boyd, 1949:105). Since the mode of inheritance was known, these blood factors were considered objective measures of "classic" race. While these researchers considered their work to be unbiased, Blakey (1987), acknowledged that interpretation of natural phenomena is not objective but clouded by our worldview.

Ottenberg (1925) provides an early example of attempts to classify populations based upon blood groups, the ABO system. Using this single system, he
classified humans into six races (see Table 5.1).

1)	Europeans — Swedes, Norwegians, English French, Italian, Danish, German, Austrian, Bulgarians, Servians, and Greeks
2)	Intermediate— Arabs, Turks, Russians, and Jews (Spanish)
3)	Hunan— Japanese, South Chinese (Hunan Province), Hungarians, Roumanian Jews
4)	Indomanchurian— Koreans, Manchus, North Chinese (Peking), Gypsies (Hungary), Hindus (Indians)
5)	African South Asiatic (Negroes (Senegal), Americanized Negroes, Madagascans, Sumatrans, Sumatra Chinese, Javans, Annamese
6)	Pacific American Indians— North American Indians, Australian aborigines, Icelanders, Filipinos

Table 5.1. Racial Classification using the ABO System (Adapted from
Ottenberg, 1925)

Being a cultural anthropologist, Ottenberg stated that he did not intend to

> draw conclusions concerning an anthropologic question [racial
> classification] on which I am wholly incompetent to pass. I
> wish merely to arrange the available blood group data in as
> natural a manner as possible ... (1925:1395).

His classification scheme was not taken seriously since it did not conform to
preconceived "classic" racial classification (Boyd, 1950).

It did, however, indicate the commitment by anthropologists and biologists to
racial classification. For them, such taxonomy was possible whenever they identified the best available method of measurement, in this case the ABO system.
In doing so, they conformed to the "scientific method", measurement, using
whatever variables were available.

Continued efforts to find the best method to classify human diversity is seen
in the work by Lahovary (1946 in Boyd, 1950). He added the MN and some
other blood group systems with the ABO to distinguish seven races. His classification was: European, Mediterranean, Mongolian, African, Indonesian,
American Indian, Oceanic, and Australian. When the ABO system did not separate racial groups, he sometimes used the MN and other blood factors. In this
way, his classification conformed to older ideas about racial taxonomy and was
therefore more acceptable to scientists. Mostly, however, Lahovary found sero-

logical clines in Europe but he found various ways to subdivide populations so they conformed to classic racial thinking.

Use of blood groups to identify racial groups was taken more seriously in the work by Wiener (1946) and Boyd (1949, 1950). Based on the ABO and Rh factors, Wiener partitioned humans into Caucasoid, Negroid, and Mongoloid. He argued that ... "it is possible to demonstrate certain *qualitative* differences in the *distribution* [my italics] of the blood properties in different peoples" (1946:484-486). Puerto Ricans, for instance, were intermediate between Caucasoids and Negroids because of their intermediate distribution of the Rh blood factor. In other words, quantitative differences indicated degree of relatedness for both Wiener and Boyd. A quantitative analysis indicated how different races were even if they did not know what proportion of, for instance, Mongoloid genes "co-operate" to produce a Mongoloid phenotype (Boyd, 1950).

Using the ABO, MN, Rh, PTC, and secretor systems, Boyd (1949, 1950) suggested a classification that corresponded to geography. He identified 1) Early Europeans, a hypothetical group that differed from modern Caucasoids, 2) Europeans (Caucasians), 3) Africans, 4) Asiatics, 5) American Indians and 6) Australoids. Since blood groups conformed to traditional racial classification schemes: "Far from discouraging us, this should be a sign that our new methods are not doing so badly" (Boyd, 1950:273). These researchers never found blood factors that were distinctive of one group and completely absent in another. Yet, they continued to try to make races real. To do this, "classic race" was reified with blood group frequencies. Commitment to race prevented scientists from acknowledging the arbitrariness of their selection criteria and cutoff points. Any manipulation of the "data" that supported traditional folk taxonomies was considered scientific and proved that races were real.

THE ADAPTATION PARADIGM

In the 1960s, there was a paradigm shift with human diversity being viewed as the product of the interactive effect of environmental factors and mechanisms of evolution such as natural selection. This shift was initiated by a number of factors such as the work by Allison (1954a, b, c), Raper (1955, 1956), and Livingstone (1958) who showed that blood types are subject to natural selection. For instance, Allison (1954a,b) and Raper (1955) showed that the red-blood cells of sicklers (AS genotype) are less likely to be parasitized by *plasmodium falciparum*, the malaria parasite, than nonsicklers (AA genotype). Therefore, sicklers are less likely to exhibit clinical symptoms of malaria such as blackwater fever and cerebral malaria. Consequently, sicklers have lower mortality from complications associated with falciparum malaria that result in death (Raper, 1956). Sickling, then, provides immunity to malaria.

Then, Livingston (1958) showed that the prevalence of sickling and malaria followed yam cultivation. With the clearing of the forest a suitable habitat for *Anopheles gambiae*, the mosquito carrying the malaria parasite, was created. The only large animals in this domesticated environment available for infection were humans. Those with the sickling gene, however, had increased survivorship in such an environment. A cline in the frequency of sickling was found to coincide with the spread of yam cultivation from East to West Africa. During this period Livingstone made his classic statement: "There are no races, there are only clines" (Livingstone, 1964: 47). Now, population geneticists tried to explain genetic polymorphisms in terms of their impact on physiological function and disease.

A number of other factors also facilitated the paradigm shift. For example, during WWII the deployment of armies in diverse environments prompted governments to provide funds to understand what happens to servicemen in different climates. The U.S. army wanted to know, for instance, why white soldiers were fatigued in the deserts and why some soldiers could not consume milk. The government funded research that examined human physical responses to climatic stresses (Baker, 1958, 1966, 1975). For example, in high altitude studies, highlanders were compared to lowlanders in terms of ventilatory efficiency or work capacity. While assessment of adaptation at high altitude differs depending upon the level of analysis (infra-individual, individual, and population levels), the main stressor is hypoxia. Increased production of red blood cells and larger lung capacity among native highlanders were considered adaptive in a hypoxic environment (Monge, 1948; Hurtado, 1932). Also, in hot climates individuals with a linear body build are at an advantage because it facilitates sweating while in colder climates a short stocky body conserves heat (Schreider, 1950, 1963; Roberts, 1953, 1973; Newman, 1952, 1955a, 1955b, 1960; Baker, 1958, 1959; Newman and Munro, 1955; Briggs, 1960). These studies showed the short-term and long-term plasticity of the human species.

In addition, as a result of international aid programs there were attempts to improve nutrition world wide, understand variation in nutritional needs, and the impact of nutritional status on behavior and potential (Baker, 1975). In 1942 the U.S. government began cooperative health programs with a number of Latin American countries. Also, with the founding of the World Health Organization and extension of U.S. technical aid programs to Asia and Africa after the war, numerous public health programs were initiated. From this, it was apparent that health and disease were as much cultural and social related, as they were biological phenomena (Foster and Anderson, 1978).

The mood of the country also changed. With the Vietnam War, the hippie, women's, and civil rights movements, people wanted new or different answers to old questions. In particular, the civil rights movement illuminated social disparities resulting from racism and discrimination. Racial hatred was constantly on the news. The media showed a side of America that killed, maimed, and oppressed blacks, including their children. When the Sixteenth Street Baptist Church was bombed, it seemed like the entire black community in Birmingham was wounded. Now we knew we were not safe at home or in church. The mother of one of the children who died was my library teacher, Mrs. Robertson. I remember one day she sat at her desk and cried in class. We all sat there in sadness and cried too. Everyone felt for her because she had just lost her child. There was no need to say anything. Everyone knew why she was crying. There was nothing we could do for her. We couldn't protect her. We couldn't help her. No one could bring back her child. No one could bring back our community. It was group mourning. A grieving that took place. This was the atmosphere in which an environmental approach to human diversity flourished, although briefly.

THE UNDERCLASS

Numerous genetic and physiological studies led scientists to view human diversity as the product of the complex interaction between genes, culture, and the environment. I am not suggesting that biological reductionism was nonexistent during the 1960s. For instance, in *The Origins of Races* (1962) Carlton S. Coon continued the old paradigm of biological determinism. He argued that Africans, Asians, and Europeans evolved separately and that Europeans evolved the most. This was a popular view among physical anthropologists while I was an undergraduate. Although I was not aware of opposition to this theory within the academic community, it did exist, especially in cultural anthropology.

Social and climatic factors were common explanations for population differences in the late 1950s and 1960s, but this perspective was short lived. By the 1970s, there was a shift back to biological determinism to explain human social diversity. In this section, I suggest a possible reason for the reemergence of the genetic model. In particular, I argue that this shift was in response to the "underclass."

Gunnar Myrdal first used the term underclass in 1962 to describe all victims, irrespective of color or gender, of structural changes in the economy. In the 1980s the term emphasized cultural and behavioral traits and singled out African Americans. It is believed that members of the underclass do not share traditional values of home, money, work, and life. They resist any effort to solve their problems, receive more than their fair share of welfare and other benefits; and cause political and social turmoil disproportionate to their membership in society. They are trapped in cycles of alcohol, crime, illiteracy, disease, and welfare dependency (Patterson, 1995).

In the 1970s and 1980s blacks accounted for almost 30% of the poor but were only 12% of the U.S. population. In 1990, nearly 10 million of 30 million blacks (30%) were officially defined as residing in poor households. This does not mean that poverty is a black issue. Two-thirds of the poor since the 1960s have been white; this has not changed over time (Patterson, 1995). However, blacks were singled out as the cause of their own poverty and for urban decline.

Brett Williams illuminated stereotypes about the underclass: "They are poor while the rest of us are affluent; "dependent" while we are "stable" (Williams, 1994: 348). Because the underclass does not fully participate in patriarchal, heterosexual households, they are portrayed as a sex-segregated population composed of gun holding men and unwed mothers (B. Williams, 1994). Evidence for this came from statistics that showed that the proportion of black families headed by females increased from 17% in 1950 to 42% in 1986 (for whites the proportions were 5% and 13% respectively). The percentage of black births to unmarried women increased from 17% to 61% compared to 2% to 15% for white women in 1950 and 1986 respectively. For obvious reasons female-headed household are likely to be poor (Patterson, 1995).

While some would argue that there is not a connection between slavery and the underclass, others would disagree. For instance, Moynihan (1965) argued that the destruction of black culture by slavery encouraged pathology and disintegration among blacks. However, slavery and poverty after the civil war did not destroy the two-parent black family. Just the opposite, emancipation allowed blacks to reunite families divided by slavery. In 1950, 83% of black families with children lived in two-parent nuclear families (Gutman, 1975; Patterson, 1995).

Another hypothesis focused on black cultural development in the South in the years after emancipation. The argument is that blacks caught in the sharecropping system could not develop an economic base so they became dependent on paternalistic white employers. When blacks moved north in large numbers after the 1940s they carried their dependent ways with them and by the 1970s government welfare replaced southern paternalism, but dependency remained a dominant cultural trait (Patterson, 1995).

Murray (1984) blames expansion of the public assistance program, Aid to Families of Dependent Children (AFDC), for promoting separation, divorce, and illegitimacy among women and sexual irresponsibility among men. However, there is no correlation between amount of AFDC benefits, which vary by state, and illegitimacy or divorce (Patterson, 1995).

In *The Truly Disadvantaged* (1987) Wilson attributed the growth of black poverty to: the decline of older industries, use of the split-labor market by working class and poor whites to disenfranchise blacks, and the low educational achievement of central city blacks. In particular, Wilson argued that race cannot explain increases in the black urban underclass because of: 1) the passage, in the 1960s, of civil rights legislation; 2) institutional affirmative action policies in the 1970s; and 3) the dramatic growth of the black middle class. But, Wilson underestimated the power of "those in power" who want to and can maintain their power/privilege. He also overestimated the effect of the civil rights movement and affirmative action policies. These policies may have ended blatant racism but have been much less effective with institutional, collective and cultural racism.

The underclass did not suddenly appear but were culturally and institutionally constructed. Emancipation and desegregation did not mean the end of institutional racism or the role of the state in maintaining and legitimizing popular racism. In the post-WWII years, for instance, there was strong support for suburbanization. By 1965, 98% of more than $120 billion worth of housing was owned and occupied by whites. This was due to official government policies through the lending decisions made at the Veterans Administration and the Federal Housing Agency. These racialized economic transactions resulted in loss of jobs, tax revenues, and affordable housing in the inner cities where blacks were displaced from southern sharecropping and then went north in search of work. Decisions of the state produced racialized ghettos with under-resourced education and health systems, poor housing and high levels of unemployment and underemployment (Kushnick, 1996).

The underclass was a new social problem. Whenever problems appear to be insurmountable, biological reductionism gains popularity. This was the case with the underclass. With black poverty differentiated from white poverty through the category underclass, biological determinism became an acceptable way to explain the new category. The following sections are examples of popular biological explanations for behavior.

INTELLIGENCE

The difficulty in understanding how the underclass exists in the most prosperous country in the world and the failure of programs to rectify the problem led many Americans to believe that the problems of the underclass are unsolvable. It is assumed that the reason for the underclass is genetics. Behavioral traits associated with the underclass are believed to be related to their biology. They are the source of their problems.

In the 1960s, there continued to exist, along with the environmentalist interpretation of human variation, a deterministic view of culture and social life. Some scholars, such as Arthur Jensen switched from an environmental to a biological reductionist paradigm. In the early 1960s, for instance, Jensen argued that decades of "socio-economic and cultural disadvantages" explained lower IQ scores among blacks and Mexicans (Jensen, 1967 in Chase, 1980:465). However, by the late 1960s Jensen converted to a hereditarian perspective and argued that genetic heritability for intelligence was high (85%). Like Galton in *Hereditary Genius*, who argued that occupational ability was biologically transmitted, Jensen contended that genetic differences explained lower IQ scores among blacks compared to whites. Consequently, the difference was not due to discrimination or inequality in education, but to genetic differences (Jensen, 1969). This being the case, education and other pedagogics could not rectify this situation. So programs like Head Start (just beginning) were doomed to failure and should be eliminated (Jensen, 1969, 1972).

Jensen (1972) and later Herrenstein and Murray in *The Bell Curve* (1995) attempted to show that social and class differences have an hereditary basis. For instance, in *The Bell Curve* Herrenstein and Murray incorporated data with no merit and presented it as scientific evidence of inherent intellectual differences between classes and races. Studies cited in the book were debunked in the sixties, seventies, and eighties but it appealed to the masses because it validated modern folk beliefs (which are the same as the folk beliefs in the sixteenth through the twentieth centuries) concerning racial differences. The political implications of such scientific endeavors were apparent then and now.

For instance, political action is explicit in the actions by the Pioneer Fund, a conservative group that gave Jensen and Rushton large sums of money between 1986 and 1990. The Pioneer Fund also supported the Federation of American Immigration Reform that in 1994 waged a successful effort to pass proposition 187 in California that denied public services to undocumented immigrants (Baker, 1998b). "Popular 'science' is emerging from privately funded think tanks that are dedicated to formulating policy and shaping public opinion in order to reinforce particular agendas" (Baker 1998b: 216).

Proponents of the belief that there are intellectual differences between racial groups do not consider inherent problems in this proposition. For instance, the Intelligence Quotient is not equivalent to intelligence. I.Q. is an achieved and not an inherent score. The I.Q. score tells us how well an individual performs relative to a standard population, usually a European American group, and indicates achieved learning (I.Q.) and not the potential for learning, intelligence. IQ tests are actually indices of enculturation for white, middle-class values. Such tests measure ability as modified by sociocultural and emotional factors and have little cross-cultural validity. These factors were ignored or considered unimportant in Jensen's model and in *The Bell Curve*.

SOCIOBIOLOGY AND EVOLUTIONARY PSYCHOLOGY

Sociobiology

Two paradigms represent the switch to biological determinism in contemporary times: evolutionary psychology and sociobiology. In *Sociobiology: The New Synthesis* E.O. Wilson defined sociobiology as "the systematic study of the biological basis of all social behavior, including the evolution of social behaviors and their relationship to genetic change" (Wilson, 1975:4). Henry Harpending and colleagues (1987:127) redefined sociobiology as "the study of human behavior based on a Darwinian paradigm." While the former definition focused on the genetic basis of behavior, the latter is concerned with the effect of natural selection on behavior; and researchers may or may not be concerned with genes.

The core of the theory is the idea of maximization of inclusive fitness. This refers to *behaviors* that increase the likelihood that an individual's alleles will be transmitted to the next generation. For example, physical examinations increase the likelihood of finding health problems early and receiving beneficial treatment thereby increasing your survivorship or fitness. Parental investment, a related concept, refers to parental behaviors such as feeding, clothing and other care for offspring that increase the likelihood that children will survive. Another concept, altruism, is a behavior that natural selection should eliminate over time because it can put the individual at risk and reduce rather than maximize inclusive fitness. Sociobiologists, however, believe that kin selection (Hamilton, 1964, 1972) alters the benefit of altruism. According to them, altruistic behaviors are selected for when it involves biological relatives. For instance, if your mother dies to save you, half of her genes will survive in you and can be transmitted to the next generation. With kin selection sociobiology enters human families and the arena of sociocultural organization (Freese, 1994).

Altruism can also be adaptive with non-relatives through the concept of reciprocal altruism (Trivers, 1971). By helping others to survive it is more likely that you will receive help in the future (Wilson, 1975). For instance, in helping victims of hurricanes, earthquakes, and other disasters you may receive aid when you are the victim of such catastrophes. With sociobiology individuals only want to maximize the chances of their genes surviving. Therefore, other members of their species are their natural competitors and are only important if they help the individual to pass on his genes.

The concepts of sociobiology remind me of possessive individualism (MacPherson, 1962) of sixteenth century England. In possessive individualism you own your body and your labor, which you can sell. This was a justification for slavery because if you could sell your own labor then you could sell or use the labor of someone else, especially if they were considered inferior by nature. With sociobiology there is possessive individualism for genes. You own your genes and they are yours to pass on to the next generation. The goal of individual behavior is to increase the likelihood that these genes will be transmitted to the next generation and others are considered competitors in this transmission. Because you own your genes, you carry out behaviors that will ensure transmission of your genes to the next generation. The basic belief behind sociobiology is that we are walking genes and these genes simply operate to perpetuate themselves. Barkow (1978:8) wrote: "sociobiology is a theory of selective pressures generated by intra-specific competition among organisms each of which is seen as striving to maximize its genetic representation in the next generation."

Using this type of logic, genes determine the degree to which an individual will behave altruistically toward relatives. They will be more altruistic toward individuals that they are closely related to them such as siblings as opposed to cousins. Pheromones are hypothesized as the mechanism for determining degree of relatedness (Barkow, 1978). If an individual is altruistic toward nonrelatives then reciprocal altruism is invoked. Sociobiology is the ultimate model for biological reductionism. It can explain everything and there is always another concept to account for a genetic basis for behavior.

For instance, racial prejudice and discrimination are related to kin selection. Van den Berghe (1978) argued that racial bias has a genetic based component and that racism, ethnocentrism and nationalism derive from the same source, kin altruism. Similarly, Dawkins (1976) suggested that racial prejudice is the product of an irrational generalization of a kin selected tendency to identify those physically similar to oneself and to be insulting to those who are different in appearance. Therefore, sociobiology provides a biological explanation for racism. Racism is genetic and out of human control although genes for racism, and other social behaviors, have not been found. Since a link between genetics and social relations is lacking ..."sociobiology may be useful and illuminating, or reductionist, racially biased, and absurd" (Washburn, 1978:36). *Without a link between social behavior and genetics, natural selection cannot be invoked to explain such phenomenon* (Caplan, 1984).

In terms of behavior, sociobiologists assume that if there is a good fit between the structure of the organism and the environment, that it is the product of natural selection. Over evolutionary time, this process is expected to produce optimal traits. However, there are no optimal traits among humans. For example, among females, adaptation for locomotion and the birth canal are in conflict (Oliwenstein, 1998). For bipedal locomotion, the ligaments for the knees should be stronger. "Even in behaviors that are largely genetically determined, there is no reason to suppose that the behaviors are necessary, ideal, or more than the compromise that survived in evolutionary competition" (Washburn, 1978:39). Rather, organs and systems are the result not of millions of years of perfection, but evolutionary compromises that represent reproductive benefit at a low cost (Oliwenstein, 1998).

Sociobiologists do not attempt to explain any type of human behavior. They postulate genes to account for human social relations such as parental care, bonding, aggression, and altruism. However, specific types of social behaviors do not aggregate within families and do not follow predictable patterns of degree of genetic relatedness. Within families, members may or may not be aggressive, criminal or loving. Sociobiology attempts to explain complex social interactions in a modern industrialized world without considering culture history, enculturation, and socialization processes (Washburn, 1978).

Sociobiology selects certain aspects of human social behavior for reification such as a man jumping on a grenade to save his friends, a mother risking her life to protect her child, or doctors risking infection while working in leprosy colonies. These actions are grouped under a common feature, self-sacrificing and categorized as altruistic behavior (Rose, 1979). Once the concept of altruistic behavior is developed, the source of the behavior is sought within the individual, genes.

This type of reification is similar to that of phrenologists who atomized behavior into discrete categories and then sought the source within the individual. Phrenologists, for instance, believed one only had to observe a particular skull shape to know the mental faculty of the individual. Once a label exists for the behavior, one can look for the source of that behavior within the individual. For phrenologists this was a bump at a particular location on the skull. If these traits are seen as a part of the individual, then one can search for the region of the brain that produced these behaviors and the genes behind the brain. In modern times, some consider a brain dysfunction to be the cause of disrespect toward teachers by inner city children. Since the source of the deviant behavior is biological, it can be corrected with ritalin, an amphetamine-like substance (Rose, 1979).

Similarly, Mark and Ervin (1970), psychosurgeons, tried to determine the cause of riots in the United States in the 1960s. They argued that there was something wrong with the centers of aggression in the brains of some black leaders. Mark and Ervin believed that rioting in the ghettoes of America and urban violence could be eliminated if a certain area of the brain, the amygdala, was removed from about 5 to 10% of urban ghetto blacks. Unrest in urban areas was reified as violence and the source was located in a specific region of the brain (Rose, 1979). If you eliminate the source of the 'deviant' behavior, the behavior is altered. Such explanations are given without an understanding of the dynamic environmental circumstances that created these behaviors.

Evolutionary Psychology

In the 1990s sociobiology was refashioned into evolutionary psychology, the study of the evolutionary basis of psychological mechanisms that underlie behavior (Cosmides and Tooby, 1987). In *Human Universals* (1991) Brown noted that natural selection does not select for behaviors but for the psychological processes that control or produce behaviors. Evolutionary psychologists emphasize the importance of the interaction between an individual's cognitive mechanisms and environmental inputs for the production of behavior (Tooby and Cosmides, 1990; Wiederman and Allgeier, 1992). They examine diverse areas of human experiences such as rape (Thornhill and Thornhill, 1990), homicide (Daly and Wilson, 1988) and human sexuality (Symons, 1987; Buss, 1989, 1995; Buss et al., 1990).

In *The Adapted Mind* (1992) Barkow, Cosmides and Tooby put forth the central premise of evolutionary psychology: there is a universal human nature at the level of evolved psychological mechanism not at the level of expressed behavior. Evolutionary psychologists assume that the existence of human universals is evidence that a universal human genetic nature exists like the "psychic unity of man." In other words, these universals or "psychic unity" are due to the human genome. Like European thinking in the eighteenth and nineteenth centuries, evolutionary psychologists believe the genetic makeup of the population produced variation in cultural, political, economic, social, and religious systems. Similar to unilinear evolution, in evolutionary psychology culture is not arbitrary but determined by innate predisposition.

The human brain, and therefore culture, is the product of mechanisms that evolved in response to specific adaptive problems encountered by early hominids during the Pleistocene (Tooby and Cosmides, 1990; Buss et al., 1990). They assume that psychological mechanisms developed for adaptation to a hunter/gatherer lifestyle and that natural selection altered these mechanisms to produce variation in cultural behavior. Successful behavior continued to appear in biological evolution because these behaviors made survival and the transmission of certain genes possible.

But, these behaviors appeared in a unique ecological niche that included social interactions where the biological capacity for learning also evolved. For instance, when considering the throwing of objects, both apes and humans can throw things. Evolutionary psychologists and sociobiologists would argue that this behavior is the product of selection favoring defensive mechanisms during prehistoric times. However, people throw objects not only to be aggressive, but also in play. Throwing involves not only biological potentialities, but learning and social encouragement as well (Washburn and McCown, 1972).

Evolutionary psychology is actually an elaboration of sexual selection. In the latter, according to Trivers (1971) the sex that invests more in offspring will evolve to be more discriminating about mating than the sex that invests less. Buss (1989) contended that during the Pleistocene, females evolved mechanisms that led to greater discrimination than men because of greater investment, minimally nine-month gestation period. Since access to resources was the main problem faced by females during the Pleistocene, females preferred mates with high levels of such access. Men, whose minimal parental investment is contributing sperm, evolved to be more competitive with members of their own sex in order to gain sexual access to the opposite sex (Buss, 1989, 1995).

This scenario was used to explain attractiveness. For instance, since male reproductive success was more dependent on the number of partners, males were/are more likely than females to value physical attractiveness in a potential mate (Symons 1979). Male adult brains evolved through natural selection to produce maximal sexual attraction to certain physical traits correlated with female fertility such as youth, smooth skin, full lips and good muscle tone (Buss et al., 1990). So men can increase their chances of transmitting their genes if they find and mate with young fertile females as indicated by attractiveness. Sexual selection and evolutionary psychology purport to explain differences in mate selection patterns between males and females based upon the genetic makeup of males and females as opposed to social environmental factors.

This type of biological reductionism has also been used to explain sexual harassment. The theory predicts that men will initiate most sexual harassment that single young women will usually be the victims and that women will experience more negative reaction than men in the workplace. According to evolutionary psychology, male sexual psychology was designed by natural selection to motivate males to actively seek out and exploit all potential sexual opportunities. The prediction in evolutionary psychology is supported since sexual harassment of women by men is much more frequent than sexual harassment of men by women (Studd and Gattiker, 1991). However, can we conclude that sexual harassment is the product of natural selection and is therefore adaptive? If so, for whom is it adaptive? Also, if sexual harassment is genetically based, should it be subject to legal consequences?

With the appearance of modern sapiens only about two hundred thousand years ago, there would not have been enough time for natural selection to bring about genetic adaptations to social behaviors that are found in contemporary societies. If conditions examined by sociobiologists and evolutionary psychologists such as territoriality, bonding, aggression, and human sexuality are related to adaptations in past environments, then these conditions cannot be used to explain contemporary social relations. Conditions that persisted through most of the evolution of hominids no longer exist. Altruistic behavior may no longer be advantageous. Today people increasingly decide to reduce their family size and most interactions are with nonrelatives. Evolutionary theory   ..."cannot be indiscriminately applied to human evolution as if the contemporary situation were similar to that of millions of years ago" (Washburn, 1978:36). Over a short period of time, it is more likely that these behaviors are the product of nonbiologically based cultural and behavioral adaptations.

THE SOCIOLOGY OF BIOLOGICAL DETERMINISM

During the 1960s and early 1970s social explanations were routinely used to explain social facts. Since the publication of E.O. Wilson's (1975) *Sociobiology: The New Synthesis*, biological explanations for human behavior have been more popular. This section examines possible reasons for the current popularity of sociobiology, evolutionary psychology and other biological deterministic explanations of social phenomenon among researchers and the average citizen.

Using the family to investigate the origin of morality and deviance, Gray and Wolfe (1982) considered factors that popularized sociobiology. They claim that our belief system, which places the American family at the center of our culture, presumes that deviation from this family type is related to moral deviance. For example, promiscuous females or lazy males cause matrifocal family units. In other words, ... "deviant families do not produce human beings, but animals who are not capable of controlling themselves since the rationality provided by nature was not transmitted by the approved family form" (Gray and Wolfe, 1982:583). Major shortcomings of deviant families are used to show that the *ideal* family type is the *natural* family unit and..." to stigmatize class or ethnic groups with different family forms" (Gray and Wolfe, 1982: 583).

Female-headed households are considered deviant and according to the paradigms discussed in this chapter there is a genetic basis for the deviancy. If there are only a few deviations from the ideal family type, they may be overlooked or rationalized. However, if a large number of deviations occur, it is assumed that social rules are not enough to control the deviance. Deviation, the underclass, must be outside of the *cultural* domain, it must be *nature* (Gray and Wolfe, 1982).

When large numbers of individuals lose faith in social explanations for problems, movements are generated to determine the cause of the deviance outside of their former belief system. Evolutionary psychology and sociobiology performed this task by showing that social inequality is not needed to explain immorality and deviance. Then, they connected this discourse with the secular worldview, science (Gray and Wolfe, 1982).

> People must be convinced that the discourse is 'only natural' in that it is the logical outcome of applying common sense to the observation of reality, while at the same time being 'scientific' in that it will lead to the solutions of the problems facing society. The appropriation of science ...is vital because science is still seen by most Americans as a successful strategy for coping with nature. We doubt that any discourse that does not manage to appropriate the prestige of science to its cause can gain the adherence of the majority of Americans (Gray and Wolfe, 1982:587).

Therefore sociobiologists claim that human behavior is being studied scientifically (Gray and Wolfe, 1982). So science fills in the gap left by culture to explain human behavior (Leach, 1981). These movements then become 'culturally fashionable.' Gray and Wolfe (1982) argued that sociobiology has attained the status of cultural fashion because people have lost faith in traditional belief systems regarding morality and deviance. They resorted to a new movement, sociobiology, to explain what rationality cannot explain. The same is true for evolutionary psychology.

From the perspective of the citizenry, which scientists are a part, Gray and Wolfe (1982) provided an explanation, cultural fashion, for the popularity of sociobiology (and evolutionary psychology). However, from the perspective of scientists, who are supposed to examine the facts and draw logical conclusions based solely on the facts, additional reasons must be considered. Solutions may be found among social, economic and political ideologies of the research community.

In the scientific community, what to study and test are determined by philosophical, ideological and social prejudices. In other words, the sciences are grounded in philosophical and ideological premises (Bitsakis, 1987-88). That individual, institutional and scientific racism are factors in deciding what to study and how to interpret data are usually not discussed within the scientific community. They are never part of the discussion in terms of research questions, methods or interpretation of findings. Gould (1981) wrote:

> Science, since people must do it, is a socially embedded activity. It progresses by hunch, vision, and intuition. Much of its change through time does not record a closer approach to absolute truth, but the alteration of cultural contexts that influence it so strongly. Facts are not pure and unsullied bits of information; culture also influences what we see and how we see it. Theories, moreover, are not inexorable inductions from facts. The most creative theories are often imaginative visions imposed upon facts; the source of imagination is also strongly cultural (Gould, 1981:21-22).

In particular, science and the average citizen often do not consider the significance of inequality in contributing to social problems or the importance of inequality in reducing the likelihood that social programs will be successful. For instance, researchers such as Okongwu (1993), Vincent (1993), Gilliam (1992) and B. Williams (1994) critiqued the "reproductive underclass" by examining the 1980 proposal to jail "dead beat" dads and force women to work. These acts were considered justified because it was/is believed that African Americans inflict poverty on themselves. Okongwu (1993) criticized the media for reinforcing stereotypes about poor mothers that do not address the ways gender, race, and class shape female-headed households and structure the allocation of resources.

More recently, the media has focused on inequality in the legal system. Research indicate that a higher percentage of whites use and sell drugs than blacks but blacks and other minorities are more likely to be arrested and jailed

(Gilliam, 1992; Buck, 1992). Gilliam (1992) noted that the term "cocaine mother" is almost synonymous with "pregnant black women" although black and white women have the same test rates for the drug. Nevertheless, black women are ten times more likely to be arrested (Gilliam, 1992). Buck (1992) related increased incarceration of minorities to media coverage that rationalized the privatization of prisons and exploitation of the labor of people of color. Also, preoccupation with drug consumption and trafficking does not deal with the more widespread suburban consumers and top-tier traffickers of the international drug industry (Gilliam, 1992).

Child support, workfare, and welfare have continually differentiated between fit and unfit women with white women considered worthy of support while women of color are considered unworthy. The latter have been forced to work to *improve* their character and have "only conditional rights to raise their children" (Brodkin, 2001:368). It may be that the term underclass was socially constructed not only to identify a group in a cycle of poverty but, also to provide social and psychological explanations for their status that are considered outside the realm of solutions by the structures that created the situation.

Given that biological determinism has been dismissed each time it has arisen, why has it reappeared in the form termed sociobiology and evolutionary psychology? No new information has been found to replace previous findings that refuted biological determinism. There are no unambiguous facts to support the reappearance of biological determinism. Support appears to be related to social and political influences. Biological determinism has reemerged because of: ... "pedestrian pursuits of high royalties for best sellers to pernicious attempts to reintroduce racism as respectable science. Their common denominator must lie in our current malaise" (Gould, 1977:239).

Biological determinism has always been used to support and defend the existing social structure. It has been disproved throughout the centuries but remains popular because it maintains the *status quo* (Gould, 1977; Rose, 1979). Maintaining the *status quo* means transmitting to students and to the general population a genetic explanatory model for group differences. In that way, the social order or *status quo* is 'natural' and is not due to unequal access to resources.

UPDATE: RACIAL PROFILING[1]

Definitions of the underclass include a laundry list of social and behavioral traits. For instance, it is believed that they do not have traditional values concerning home, money, and work, and that the underclass participates in a cycle of alcoholism, criminality and welfare dependency. According to Dinesh D'Souza (1995) values of the underclass shape the cultural norms of African Americans. For him, characteristics of the underclass are also "black group traits", illegitimacy, criminality, and dependency on welfare. The underclass is equated with minority status and poverty where it is assumed that certain minorities and poor people are criminals, alcoholics, and depend on welfare.

This profile of the underclass represents a stereotype about blacks and poor people. It discounts the working poor and others living in poverty that are not alcoholics or criminals or the environment/history factors that produced the situation. As a result, there is prejudice and discrimination by the majority population toward the poor and groups associated with poverty.

This profile of the underclass has been extended to minority groups as a racial profile. In racial profiling the profile is linked to the individual's "classic" racial classification. While Gotanda (2000) contends that the profile is conceptually and linguistically different from a racial classification because it does not suggest biological inferiority, I would argue that it is not different. Racial profiles represent negative stereotypes that are the product of the same sociohistorical factors that produced "classic" race and racism in America. The racial profile of, for instance, African Americans includes stereotypes such as criminality that can be traced to slavery and the post-emancipation era. Therefore, racial profiles represent collective and institutional racism in the same sense that "classic" races are the product of racism.

Racial classification schemes are associated with racial profiles that represent racial understandings by the profiler. For the profiler, racism is not overt. To circumvent racism, the profiler moves the examination of race from racial classification with associated beliefs about inferiority to the production of "culturally situated racial profiles" (Gotanda, 2000:1691). Gotanda (2000) suggests that in this racial understanding the profiler develops 1) a racial category, 2) a profile of subordination, 3) the social context, and 4) a political conclusion. For instance, among African Americans police officers' profiles may flow from: a) black, b) the underclass, c) legacies of slavery such as the belief that people of African descent are immoral and criminals, and d) a presumption that all African Americans are criminals. Profilers argue that racism is not involved in the development of a racial profile. Rather, the profile is based upon their cultural understanding of racial groups. Racial profiles and "classic" racial classifications are similar in terms of generalized stereotypes that are used by those in power, profilers, to construct racial identities (see chapter 8), racial profiles of minority groups.

Well-know examples of racial profiling include Wen Ho Lee, a nuclear physicist accused of espionage although after years of investigation the government produced no evidence (Gotanda, 2000). Another example is the case of Sergeant First Class Rossano V. Gerald who with his 12-year old son in 1998 drove across the Oklahoma border, was stopped twice by police officers and searched once. Gerald and his son sat in a hot police car while officers ransacked their car for two hours (no contraband was found). They maintained that they were stopped and searched because they are black. However, it was determined that failure to signal a lane change was reasonable suspicion that justified the search (Trende, 2000).

The world is well aware of the racial profiling of Arab men in airports after September 11, 2001. For instance, Mohamed El-Sayed, a U.S. citizen of Egyptian descent, was denied boarding on a United Airlines flight to Washington on September 21 because the pilot refused to fly with him on board. While refusing to service passengers because of their race on airlines is illegal according to Title 42, Section 1981 of the U.S. Code, it has been continually violated since September 11. Airlines admit that pilots are wrong and some individuals of Arab descent have successfully sued. But, currently there is an ingrained fear of flying with men who appear to be Arab (Polakow-Suransky, 2001).

Racial profiles and "driving while black" are more commonly discussed today because of media attention, the drug courier profile and the introduction of the Traffic Stops Statistics Act of 1997 (Beck and Daly, 1999; Trende, 2000). The "drug courier profile" was developed by the Drug enforcement Agency (DEA) to help prevent drug smuggling. The profile consists of a list of sometimes-contradictory factors considered useful in arresting suspects. For example, factors used by agents include being the last off the plane, being the first off the plane, traveling alone, traveling with a companion, or being too calm or nervous. It is not an exact science (Trende, 2000).

Representative John Conyers of Michigan introduced the Traffic Stops Statistics Act of 1997 to Congress. The Act would have required the Justice Department to study the rates at which black American motorists are stopped by police officers. While it passed the House the same did not occur in the Senate, mainly due to strong opposition by police officers. Passage in the House, however, brought media attention to the issue of racial profiling and the American Civil Liberties Union (ACLU) launched a nationwide campaign to end racial profiling among police officers (Trende, 2000).

Racial profiling is not illegal because it is a component of pretext. In pretext, not only is race considered, but other factors such as vehicle violation and "suspicious" behavior (Beck and Daly, 1999). In other words, race/ethnicity is one factor, along with others that can be used in any investigative stop. For example in United States v. Coleman, a black male was detained by a DEA agent in an airport because 1) he was coming from Los Angeles, 2) had no luggage, and 3) he was black. The court held that the stop was founded upon unreasonable suspicion and suppressed the evidence (controlled substance) but stated that race was an appropriate factor, along with others, to justify the stop (Trende, 2000).

Stopping a vehicle based on pretext does not violate the Fourth Amendment (Beck and Daly, 1999) that states that:

> The right of the people to be secure in their persons, houses, papers, and effects, against unreasonable searches and seizures,

shall not be violated, and no Warrants shall issue, but upon
probable cause, supported by Oath or affirmation, and particularly describing the place to be searched, and the persons or
things to be seized (The Constitution of the United States).

The Supreme Court in Whren v. United States pointed out that while racial
profiling is unconstitutional, motor vehicle stops based upon pretext are not
prohibited by the Fourth Amendment (Beck and Daly, 1999; Trende, 2000).

In the Whren case, in 1993 Michael Whren was the passenger in a vehicle in
Washington, D.C. Plainclothes vice-squad officers were suspicious of Whren
and the driver because of

the pair's youthful appearance, the truck's temporary license
plate, and the fact that the vehicle remained at a stop sign in a
"high drug area" for "an unusually long time" while the driver
looked into the lap of his passenger. When the officers made a
U-turn in the direction of the truck, they observed the vehicle
turn suddenly to its right, without signaling, and sped off at an
'unreasonable' speed. At a traffic light, they approached the
vehicle, with the asserted intention of giving the driver a warn-
ing about the traffic violation he had just committed. Once at
the driver's side window, the officers saw that Whren was
holding two large bags of crack cocaine. Whren was arrested
and ultimately charged with several violations of federal drug
laws (Beck and Daly, 1999: 603-604).

Whren argued that the police officers were suspicious of them solely because
of their race and that the minor traffic violation was just an excuse to investigate
them. Whren urged that without their unsubstantiated suspicions they would not
have stopped them for the traffic violations. If so, suppression of the seized
drugs was proper because it violated the Fourth Amendment. However, the Supreme Court rejected an analysis of the officer's underlying motivations and
noted that the only relevant inquiry is the traffic infraction. In Whren v. United
States the Court affirmed that police officers who observe a traffic violation can
stop a vehicle even "if their actual reason for stopping the car was not the violation they observed" (Beck and Daly, 1999: 605). In essence, the Court contended that race as the sole reason for a vehicle stop is improper but the inclusion of race as part of the probable cause for the stop is appropriate (Beck and
Daly, 1999).

To challenge racial profiling, the Court indicated that the practice must be attacked using the Equal Protection Clause (Beck and Daly, 1999; Trende, 2000).
This Clause "prohibits the discriminatory application of laws and precludes law
enforcement agencies, exercising discretion, to go forward with a case based on
an unjustifiable standard such as race, religion or other arbitrary classification"

(Beck and Daly, 1999: 612). While it is easy to allege that there was police interference because of race, it is difficult to prove. For instance, you must prove that racial profiling is more likely to happen to minorities and that it is intentional discrimination. In other words, it must be proved that similarly situated whites are not prosecuted. "The court concluded [citing United States v Armstrong] that without a showing of different treatment of similarly situated persons, either through statistical or other evidence, plaintiffs' Equal Protection claim is dismissed" (Trende, 2000:354). However, in Washington v. Vogel defendants introduced testimony interpreting videotaped stops that showed that 60% of the stops on videotapes were blacks. This was not enough. The court argued that the jury could not draw any reasonable conclusion from it (Trende, 2000).

Other studies show similar statistics. Numerous statistical studies show that being black significantly increases the chances of a person being stopped and searched by police officers. This is true although blacks that are stopped are no more likely than whites to possess drugs. For instance, David Cole and John Lamberth in the *New York Times* showed that in Maryland 73% of those stopped and searched on a particular section of Interstate 95 were black but police reported that equal proportions of blacks and whites who were searched statewide had contraband or drugs. In New Jersey, blacks were less likely than whites to be carrying drugs. Cole and Lamberth reported that contraband was found on 25% of whites, 13% of blacks and only 5% of Latinos (Forman, 2001).

Such statistics are not enough to prove racial profiling because they are aggregate statistics and courts deal with individual officers. For instance, in Whren the Court contended that officers should not be second-guessed (Trende, 2000) indicating that group statistics cannot reveal individual intentions. Not only must a defense attorney prove that a reasonable officer would not have made the stop, but that this particular officer's training, habits, as well as those of his colleagues and supervisors support racial profiling (Beck and Daly, 1999; Trende, 2000).

Also, the accuser must prove that race was used as a guide in violation of the Equal Protection Clause. In order to prove this they must have proof of violation as, for example, in the case of the two New Jersey State troopers who falsified their official paperwork. Also, in New Jersey the Office of the Attorney General released a report where they admitted the existence of racial profiling in the state's law enforcement associations. Usually, however, the accused will request documents from the prosecution such as the officer's personnel file, prior arrest records, documents from the law enforcement agency such as departmentwide arrest and investigation statistics, policies and procedures and training manuals. If they receive these documents they must prove that "the police agency has an officially sanctioned or 'de facto' policy of selective enforcement against minorities" (Beck and Daly, 1999:613). The data needed for this type of analysis are usually not gathered on a regular basis. Even if they had the data it may not sway the courts (consider data on the death penalty which shows that minorities are more likely to be subjected to it than whites but it remains a constitutional form of punishment).

In addition, to prove racial profiling the defendant must suffer a concrete injury that must be "actual or imminent, not 'conjectural' or 'hypothetical'" and the injury must be traceable to the action of the accused. Gerald, for instance, could not prove a real injury or threat of injury. Being forced to sit in a hot squad car for two hours is not a "real injury." Also, while Gerald alleged that he would continue to use the Oklahoma highway there is no 'confidence' that the event will occur again. This would be conjecture rather than concrete intention (Trende, 2000).

Finally, if it can be proved that the Equal Protection Clause was violated, there must be a remedy that the individual is entitled. Violation of the Fourth Amendment has sanctions that suppress evidence seized as a result of the violation. Such relief may not be possible for the individual who is forced to stand in the rain with his family while his car is searched. A remedy could be dropping the charge for, for instance, drug possession but in a pretext case, with other violations, it does not fit neatly within the prosecution model. The Court has declined to determine what type of remedy a criminal defendant is entitled to in the case of racial profiling. Therefore, use of the Equal Protection Clause to fight racial profiling is only theoretical (Beck and Daly, 1999).

Rather than using racial profiling to reduce crimes, data show that police forces that reduce crime are the ones that win the respect of high-crime communities. For example, in the 1990s the San Diego police force engaged the community in dialogue to solve problems and recruited over 1,200 citizen volunteers to aid police officers. This is contrary to Guiliani's approach in New York where he pursued a zero tolerance policy that resulted in the city's notorious Street Crimes Unit becoming hyperaggressive and adopting a "We Own the Night" motto. While the situation in New York has not improved, San Diego has greatly reduced crime with a smaller police force. As the Heritage Foundation has shown, ...

> cities that have instituted genuinely community-oriented approaches to policing have reduced crime while simultaneously developing strong relationships with citizens. The most successful forces do not rely on ironfisted special units like New York's but rather invest in neighborhood patrols (Forman, 2001:27).

Racial profiling and its legitimization by the courts and police agencies represent institutional racism. Blacks, Hispanics, Asians, and Arabs are profiled, but there was no profile of whites after the militiaman Timothy McVeigh bombed the Alfred P. Murrah federal building in Oklahoma. No one discussed detaining white civilians wearing military clothing. It is assumed that minorities such as blacks are criminals and drug users although blacks do not disproportionately use drugs. That is, blacks use drugs in proportion to their share of the population (14%). But they are more likely to be arrested 35%, convicted, 55%, and sentenced for drug use, 74%, compared to whites (Cole, 1999). We must ask does profiling cause the sentencing disparity or does disparity (e.g. oppression, poverty) cause the profiling? I would contend that collective and institutional racism are integral components to racial profiling that are antithetical to democracy and the constitution but are a part of social life in America.

CHAPTER SIX

RACE, RACISM, AND HEALTH IN AMERICA

Research that viewed racial differences in health as primarily biological in origin diverted attention from the social origins of disease, reinforced societal norms of racial inferiority, and provided a so-called scientific rationale for the exploitation of blacks (D. Williams et al., 1994: 27).

INTRODUCTION

Since at least the colonial period, racial variation in health has been dominated by a model that views race as a function of biological homogeneity and black-white differences in health as mainly biologically determined (D. Williams et al., 1994). This model is still used today where it is based on the following three assumptions: 1) Race is a valid biological category; 2) genes that determine race are linked to those that determine health; and 3) the health of a population is mainly determined by the biological constitution of the population (Krieger and Bassett, 1986). Although there is no scientific evidence to support these assumptions, in the medical community and in public health a genetic etiology for disease is equated with racial-genetic susceptibility to that disease (Goodman and Armelagos, 1996).

The aim of this chapter is to examine the impact of the genetic model and its assumptions on the health of minorities in the United States. I argue in this section that since colonization of the New World, commitment to the genetic model and its assumptions formed the basis for the health care of nonwhite minorities in the United States. Belief in the innate inferiority of, for example, Africans and their descendants included a conviction that by nature they were a diseased population. Because disease was thought to be a part of their biological constitution, mainstream medicine was considered ineffective in this population. Considering their diseased nature, expenditure of funds for health care, education, or quality housing was a waste of money. It is argued that individual, collective, institutional and scientific racism are factors in the continued commitment to the genetic model in the health care of minorities. It is further contended that adherence to this model significantly contributes to the poor health status of minorities in the United States.

RACIAL DIFFERENCES IN DISEASE PREVALENCE

In the United States, like all multiracial societies, there are racial differences in disease pattern (Cooper and David, 1986). For example, life expectancy at birth for black men in 1992 was 65.5 years compared to 73.2 years for white males. For black and white women the figures were 73.9 years and 79.7 years respectively (Herman, 1996).

A 1990 study by the Centers for Disease Control revealed the striking gap between black and white populations in terms of excess mortality. Excess mortality is the difference between the actual number of deaths in a minority population and the number of deaths that would have occurred if the mortality experience of that group were the same as among the white population. It was reported that the all-cause mortality rate for blacks exceeded that for whites by 149% for 35-44 year olds and by 97% for those 45-54 years (Otten et al., 1990). The minority death rate is higher than those of the white population in almost every category of mortality listed (see table 2). For example, a greater proportion of minorities die of heart disease, stroke, lung cancer, female breast cancer, and HIV/AIDS compared to the white population.

As shown in table 6.1, the minority death rate is higher than that of the white population in almost every category of mortality listed. This includes infant deaths, neonatal deaths, and postnatal deaths, which are, for instance, twice as high among blacks compared to whites (Sullivan, 1989; Krieger et al., 1993). Differences in infant mortality rates may be related to levels of residential segregation. For instance, in the United States in 1990 the black infant mortality rate was 17/1,000 in large US metropolitan statistical areas, but was a low 13/1,000 live births in some least-segregated areas (Polednak, 1996). Segregation and the social conditions that correspond to it such as discrimination and inequality contribute to high black infant mortality in the United States.

Minority populations in the United States suffer poorer health, more illnesses and incidence of disease and die in larger numbers than the nation as a whole (Mullings, 1989; Payne and Ugarte, 1989). They experience shorter life expectancy, higher rates of debilitating and chronic diseases and lower protection against infectious diseases (Rice and Winn, 1990). While both blacks and whites are living longer, blacks still bear a higher burden of disability, death, and disease and experience poorer health status compared to white populations. This situation is not new. The following section provides an historical context for contemporary health disparities between minorities and whites in the United States.

Cause of Death	Black	Hispanic	American Indian Or Alaska Native	Asian or Pacific Isl.	White
*Heart Disease	188.0	84.2	97.1	67.4	123.6
*Stroke	42.5	19.0	19.6	22.7	23.3
*Lung Cancer	46.0	13.6	25.1	17.2	37.0
*Female Breast Cancer	26.1	12.1	10.3	9.8	18.8
**Pneumonia	17.8	9.7	14.0	9.9	12.2
**Diabetes	28.8	18.8	27.8	8.8	12.0
**HIV/AIDS	41.4	16.3	4.2	2.2	7.2
*Suicide	6.1	6.0	13.4	5.9	11.8
*Homicide	26.1	9.9	9.9	3.7	3.2

Table 6.1. Age-adjusted death rates based on population estimates for certain causes of death by race in the United States, 1998 (Keppel et al., 2002)* and age-adjusted death rates per 100,000 U.S. resident population 1950-1996 (Adapted from the National Center for Health Statistics, 1998)**

RACE AND HEALTH: AN HISTORICAL PERSPECTIVE

Slavery and its legacies resulted in race relations in the United States being dominated by black-white comparisons. This comparison is illuminated in the one-drop rule. The one-drop rule holds that a person with any African ancestry is black regardless of physical appearance or socioeconomic status. While every nation in the Western Hemisphere has persons with African ancestry, the one-drop rule only applies to the United States. In other nations, miscegenation involves the creation of an elaborate racial hierarchy. This did not occur in the United States. Here, the only important factor is yes or no to the question of African ancestry. In addition, the one-drop rule only applied to blacks (R. Jones, 1997). As noted in this rule, blacks are considered to be so physically and socially different from other minorities that they are thought to be distinct and unassimilatable. Belief in the biological uniqueness of people with African ancestry, then, formed the basis for the health care of slaves, free blacks, and African Americans.

Since the 1800s mainstream American society and the medical community believed disease was linked causally with black African descent (McBride, 1991). Biology was considered the reason that in 1900 the life expectancy at birth for whites in the United States was 47.6 years compared to only 33 years for nonwhites (mainly blacks) (Herman, 1996). Blacks were viewed as the source of their own disease as well as contagion for whites. Followers of this paradigm tried to establish a fundamental connection between phenotypical race traits among minorities and mental illness, criminality, low intelligence, biological inferiority and susceptibility to infectious disease. The backdrop for this perspective was social Darwinism, eugenics, and Euronationalism (McBride, 1991).

However, from slavery to emancipation, reconstruction, and in contemporary times the health of blacks has been related to living conditions. This means that their health was determined by allocation of resources from the white majority. In addition, institutional, collective, and individual racism insured a low standard of living among blacks, continued poverty, and the health ills that go along with disenfranchisement.

Early evidence for this is demonstrated in the health-related treatment of slaves. Two major types of seasonal diseases that afflicted slaves reflected living conditions within most slave communities. For instance, respiratory illnesses were prominent during the cold months when slaves were forced to spend more time indoors in intimate contact with family and friends. Contagious diseases such as tuberculosis, diphtheria, colds, upper respiratory infections, influenza, pneumonia, and streptococcal infections were important during the cold months. Pneumonia was the most serious acute respiratory malady affecting not only individuals and families, but also entire neighborhoods (Savitt, 1978) (this is still true today; see table 2). During slavery pneumonia had twice the fatality among blacks compared to whites (Kiple and King, 1981).

With warmer weather intestinal diseases caused by poor outdoor sanitation were major health problems. Infectious diseases were not only related to overcrowding of individual slave houses, but pathogens were transmitted during the course of everyday life, aided by general uncleanliness, and ignorance of the cause of disease (Savitt, 1978).

Nutritional deficiencies aggravated their exposure to the environment (Kiple and King, 1981). Many vitamins, as well as calcium, and iron were inadequate. For example, since their diet was based on corn it lacked niacin contributing to pellagra that caused physical and mental symptoms in late stages. In addition, black slaves had diets high in starch and fat and low in protein unless they supplemented their rations on their own (which some did) (Waring, 1971).

Laboring in rice swamps had unfavorable effects on the health of slaves. Slaveholders discussed the sickness of their slaves such as ague, shakes, chills and fever. Often the fevers were some form of malaria. Blacks were not immune to malaria and in the swamps it was a major affliction along with yellow fever although slaves had greater resistance to both compared to whites. Blacks usually, for instance, contracted yellow fever in a milder form and suffered fewer fatalities (Stampp, 1961).

The Asiatic cholera, on the other hand, hit the United States in 1832 and was more deadly among blacks than whites (Stampp, 1961). Cholera epidemics in Charleston in 1834, 1836, and 1852 were particularly devastating to African Americans relative to whites. For example, in the 1836 epidemic there were 339 deaths among blacks but only 69 among whites (Waring, 1964). While environmental exposures probably accounted for the differences in infection rate, cholera was labeled a black disease (Kiple and King, 1981).

Infant mortality is an index of the health of a population. In Charleston between 1822-1848 adult death rates were similar for blacks and whites but it was twice as high among black children relative to their white counterparts (Waring, 1964). Tetanus or "jawfall" was a major cause of death, especially among infants (Kiple and King, 1981). For those under nine years old deaths due to teething, tetanus, and convulsions were three times higher among blacks than whites (Waring, 1964).

Disease	Black	White
Consumption	532.52	269.42
Pneumonia	356.67	180.31
Diarrhea diseases	193.19	151.41
Diphtheria and croup	44.58	82.06
Diseases of the urinary system	133.75	60.81
Heart disease and dropsy	257.59	157.16
Cancer and tumor	37.15	56.63
Disease of the liver	12.38	27.82
Malaria	7.43	5.66
Typhoid	91.64	72.82
Stillbirths	203.10	135.61
Suicides	3.20	12.99
Accidents and injuries	99.07	78.78

Table 6.2. Death Rate Per 100,000 From Specific Diseases, Philadelphia, 1890 (Adapted from DuBois, 1899)

Diseases of arteries and heart and malignant tumors accounted for few slave deaths. They died from other afflictions before these scourges became a major menace (Stampp, 1961).

Using the 1884-1890 U.S. Census, DuBois (1899) provided a descriptive epidemiology of the health status of blacks and whites. Table 6.2 indicates higher death rates among blacks related to consumption, pneumonia, heart disease, stillbirths, dropsy and urinary system and infections such as malaria and typhoid. DuBois noted that the health of blacks is largely related to situations such as poor housing and unsanitary living conditions. Similarly, Savitt (1978) argued that diseases among slaves were related to lack of proper shelter, clothing, food, occupational hazards and unsanitary conditions on the plantations and in slave quarters. Clearly, diseases among slaves were associated with living conditions. It is argued that diseases among minorities today continue to be related to living conditions. Why then, is disease still linked to race in medicine and public health?

POPULATION BIOLOGY, RACE, AND DISEASE

Studies include race in the demographic triad of age, sex, and race where race is considered a biological trait and a predictor of health in the same way that age and sex are. Studies define and operationalize every variable in the analysis except race (Herman, 1996) and it is assumed that any association with the race category in the analysis is due to genes. But in many epidemiologic studies race is a label of convenience (Cooper, 1984). Using the classic anthropological concept of race with discrete categories, researchers in medicine and public health never define race and the criteria for assignment to a racial category is not stated (Cooper and David, 1986).

Physical criteria for racial classification such as skin color, facial features and hair texture are inconsistent. In addition, racial traits are discordant and there are no qualitative differences between racial groups. Those who have the same skin color are assumed to belong to the same race group and group identity is assumed to be associated with differing degrees of health risk. It is assumed that there is no variance in nationality, ethnicity and biology within races. For instance Cubans, Nicaraguans and Mexican-Americans are grouped under Hispanic while Nigerians, Jamaicans and African Americans are grouped under the heading black (LaVeist, 1996). In other words, health risks of blacks, based upon physical features, are compared to health risks of whites (based on their physical appearance) and differences are presumed to be due to the risk of belonging to the defined group.

Because race is a social and not a biological construct, an individual's race may change during the course of their life. For example, there are problems in the classification of race in vital records. For instance, of infants classified as white at birth, 1.2% had a different race at death. For black infants 4.3% had a different race at death and 4.2% of infants in other races were classified differently at death. Inconsistencies in coding race are low for whites, greater for blacks and greatest for races other than black or white. Similar results have been reported for classification of race at death for adults (Hahn et al., 1992; Hahn and Stroup, 1994).

Such variation occurs because determination of race is subjective. A funeral director or clerk may determine race/ethnicity at death based upon their observation of physical appearance that differs from self-perceived identity. For instance, Hahn and associates (1996) found that 96% of individuals who classified themselves as American Indian in interviews were classified as white on their death certificate and 4.1% were classified as black. In addition, individuals may change their racial classification over time. For example, in the same study, using NHANES I data, it was reported that 42% specified different ancestries at different interviews.

Because of this problem, some researchers have moved away from measuring race as a categorical variable. Instead, they measure it as a continuous one such as skin color. Osborne and Feit (1992) argued that measuring skin color and using 'a priori' hypotheses to test the association between skin color and disease allows the reader to determine the validity of the measures and the hypotheses. But the researchers are assuming that genes associated with skin color are linked to or also cause disease. There is no empirical evidence to support this.

Public health, like other biological disciplines, proceeds on the assumption that a significant proportion of racial differences in health are due to population genetics (Cooper and David, 1986). However, biological differences between racial groups account for a small difference in disease between racial groups. Richard Cooper, for example, demonstrated that of the thousands of excess black deaths in 1977, only 0.3% was attributed to diseases such as sickle cell. In addition, there is no evidence that susceptibility to disease falls along racial lines (Cooper and David, 1986). However, such diseases are used to support genetic explanations of racial variation in twentieth century diseases such as cancer, stroke and heart disease. But, no evidence exists to justify such extrapolation (Krieger and Bassett, 1986). Genes ... "are almost always a minor, unstable, and insufficient cause" of disease (Goodman, 2000:1700).

Genes linked to skin color have not been shown to be critical determinants of disease. Rather, skin color (race) is a centrally determining characteristic of obligations, social identity and a determinant of access to desirable resources (D. Williams et al., 1994). Rather than race being used as a risk factor, it should be viewed as a risk marker. In terms of health outcomes, race is a measure of exposure to health risks. Examples include occupational health hazards, environmental toxins, and poor quality of medical care (LaVeist, 1996). For example, racial differences in exposure to toxins and carcinogens in residential and occupational contexts could lead to systematic differences in biological profiles. In addition, hemodynamic profiles for hypertension may differ between blacks and whites because blacks consume less potassium. These differences could be due to socioeconomically determined dietary differences between the two racial groups (D. Williams et al., 1994). Race does not determine disease but serves as a risk marker for unequal access to resources, racism, and poor health care that result in poor health status.

The Institute of Medicine (IOM) (Haynes and Smedley, 1999), Cooper (1994) and Fullilove (1998) suggest using ethnicity rather than race in surveillance and public health research. For instance, the IOM recommends a shift away from race as a biological construct to examination of cultural and behavioral factors that affect health risk. However, Thomas (2001) suggests that in using ethnic group researchers would focus on individual behavior rather than examining social inequality and power relations in society. Such a shift would minimize the impact of racism on health and the importance of inequality and unequal access to resources as major factors that contribute to health disparities. Race is needed as a variable in research as a proxy for racism and inequality, not as a possible risk factor for disease.

RACE AND CLASS

Definitions of social class or socioeconomic status may include race as a component of class (Boudon and Bourricaud, 1989). Race is sometimes used as an index of social rank reflected in criteria such as linguistic, residential location, or education. Race is most often used as a proxy measure for socioeconomic status (SES), discrimination, and cultural factors. It is assumed to be a measure of class that is imposed from the outside (Herman, 1996). That is, what are considered racial traits, such as skin color, are used by out-groups to identify social class among "others". It also implies that class has a biological component.

Social and economic factors are considered confounders of the association between race and disease (Herman, 1996). In other words, there is a link between race and disease that is "fuzzied" in the analysis by class or socioeconomic status. However, it is more likely that race predicts socioeconomic status because race precedes it (Cooper and David, 1986).

In addition, socioeconomic measures are not usually equivalent between races. For example, social and economic measures such as education, occupation, and income are not equivalent proxies of economic measures for blacks and whites (Herman, 1996) because, for instance, returns on education are higher for whites than blacks (Jaynes and Williams, 1989). Also, the same income level may provide less purchasing power for blacks than whites (low SES blacks pay more for rent and food than their white counterparts) (Cooper, 1984; Alexis et al., 1980). In addition, the poorest white applicants are more likely to obtain loans for mortgages than blacks in the highest income group. When blacks do receive loans they pay higher interest rates (Harrison, 1998).

Also, socioeconomic status is not completely assessed. The income and class status of black and white populations is different because the upper end of the income distribution is absent for blacks (Cooper et al., 1981). In addition, similar employment may not represent similar work experiences. For example, employed blacks are more likely to be exposed to occupational hazards and environmental toxins and carcinogens than whites even after controlling for education and job experience (Robinson, 1984; D. Williams et al., 1994; LaVeist, 1996). Therefore, black-white comparisons are being made between two populations that are not comparable (Cooper et al., 1981).

Another reason SES measures are not equivalent between races is that they do not capture lifetime exposure to marginal conditions. Among minorities, for example, a substantial proportion of the black population may experience long-term health consequences linked to problems of infancy (King and Williams, 1995). Geronimus (1992, 1996) proposed a "weathering hypothesis" to account for such patterns that lead to higher morbidity among blacks. She argued that the health status of women may deteriorate in detectable ways in young adulthood in response to persistent social and environmental insult or prolonged coping with stressful situations. Minorities experience stress related to environmental factors (i.e. racism, poor health care, unequal access to resources) that have a cumulative affect over the course of their life (Geronimous, 1992). SES does not capture this lifetime of health problems. SES status may change but individuals and populations are still burdened with a lifetime of exposure to environmental insult. So race plays a role in ill health independent of class. That is, the greater oppression of blacks, in terms of racism, has a separate and independent effect on health (Cooper et al., 1981; Krieger and Bassett, 1986).

Often, racial differences in infant mortality and low-infant birth weight are used to show the importance of genes in producing health disparity. For example, black infant mortality exceeds that for whites in each category of socioeconomic indices. There is an excess of black infant mortality beyond that proportion attributed to socioeconomic status. For instance, the highest SES blacks have more infant mortality than whites in the lowest SES.

In other studies it has also been shown that cumulatively and interactively, U.S. born black women experience higher infant mortality than white women and foreign-born black women. For instance, Singh and Yu (1996) and David and Collins (1997) found that foreign-born women had lower risk of low-birth weight infants and infant mortality compared to U.S. born women. The incidence of low-birth weight was 13.2% among infants of U.S. born black women and 7.1% among infants of African-born black women, as compared with 4.3% among infants of U.S. born white women (David and Collins, 1997). This suggests that it is not race but living conditions and life experiences that are important.

Similarly, it has been argued that a higher prevalence of congestive heart failure among blacks compared to whites is due to a pathophysiology that results in lower nitric oxide in the blood of blacks compared to whites. It has been reported that blacks are two times more likely to die from heart failure compared to whites (this statistic is controversial or should be) because they have a genetic tendency for this pathophysiology. As evidence for this, researchers point to a retrospective multivariate analysis of the SOLVD data (Studies of

Left Ventricular Dysfunction) trials that examined racial differences in the natural history of left ventricular dysfunction (Kahn, 2004). Because they controlled for educational level and "history of financial distress" and found higher mortality among blacks, researchers concluded that this observation suggests that certain genetic polymorphisms may explain the observed differences (Yancy, 2002). Based upon this type of research we have the first ethnic drug, BiDil. This is not to say that there are not populational differences in the metabolism of certain drugs or that consideration of differences in metabolism should not be used in medical treatment, only that standardization for some socio-economic factors does not mean that any differences found must be genetic in origin. By 2005 or 2006 Bidil will be approved as an ethnic drug to treat only African Americans for heart failure (Kahn, 2004).

Standardization for SES does not mean that any differences found are due to genetics. Rather, a lifetime of insult and poor health care are more likely explanations for higher rates of heart failure among blacks. In essence, standardization for SES does not mean that the variable is captured or measured because the meaning of the variable varies across groups. "Weathering" associated with racism and unequal access to resources in the United States may account for racial, including SES, differences in the prevalence of low-birth weight infants, infant mortality and congestive heart failure among blacks.

RACISM AND HEALTH

In surveillance, medicine, and public health, race as a variable suggests a genetic base for the differences in prevalence, severity, or outcome of health conditions (Herman, 1996). A review of the health literature revealed a tendency to make black/white comparisons for diseases associated with promiscuity, underachievement, and antisocial behavior (Osborne and Feit, 1992). This leads readers to assume that specific races have a certain predisposition, risk or susceptibility to the illness or behavior under study. Since such assumptions are not substantiated, this type of comparison may represent a subtle form of racism because "racial differences in mortality are in all likelihood not due to fundamental biological differences, but are in large part due to racism and discrimination" (Herman, 1996:13).

Access to health care

A number of epidemiologic studies reported differences in access to health care and differential treatment based on race. Giachello (1996) examined the sociodemographic disadvantages of Latinos in the U.S., especially women. Latina access to health care is restricted by 1) lack of health insurance, 2) white male orientation of health services, 3) institutionalized sexism and racism, and

4) the inability of the medical system to recognize and adapt to the needs of the poor and those of diverse cultures and languages.

Recommendations for specific medical treatments differ between black and white patients (Council on Ethical and Judicial Affairs, 1990). For instance, numerous studies report differences in the use of cardiovascular procedures by race and sex of patient (Wenneker and Epstein, 1989; Carlisle et al., 1997). After adjustment for clinical status and health insurance, whites were more likely than blacks to receive coronary angiography, bypass surgery, angioplasty, chemodialysis, kidney transplants, and intensive care for pneumonia (Anderson et al., 1986). Studies have shown that blacks and women were less likely than whites and males to receive cardiac catheterization or coronary-artery bypass graft surgery when they were admitted to the hospital for myocardial infarction or chest pain (Wenneker and Epstein, 1989; Ayanian and Epstein, 1991).

With similar severity of illness, in a national survey, black men were only half as likely to have angiography and one third as likely to have bypass surgery as white males (Ford et al., 1989). In another study, while blacks and whites had similar hospitalization rates for circulatory disease or chest pain, whites were one third more likely to undergo coronary angiography and were twice as likely to receive bypass surgery or angioplasty. This disparity persisted after controlling for income and severity of disease (Wenneker and Epstein, 1989).

In a study of physicians, Schulman et al. (1999) found that women and blacks were less likely to be referred for cardiac catheterization than men and whites, respectively. Examination of race-sex interactions indicated that African-American women were significantly less likely to be referred for catheterization than white men. The authors suggested that the race and sex of a patient independently influenced the decision-making process for physicians' management of chest pain. In other words, after adjustment for symptoms, the physicians' estimates of the probability of coronary disease, physician's perceptions of the personalities of the patient, and clinical characteristics, race and sex still affected the physicians' decisions about whether to refer patients with chest pain for cardiac catheterization. This suggests a bias on the part of the physician. This bias may be overt prejudice or the result of subconscious perceptions (subtle racism) rather than deliberate actions.

Louis W. Sullivan, Secretary of Health and Human Services stated that "... there is clear, demonstrable, undeniable evidence of discrimination and racism in our health care system" (Sullivan, 1991:2674). For instance, racism is found in patterns of organ donation. The Task Force found that blacks wait for a first kidney transplant twice as long as whites (Sullivan, 1991). In a review of patients who received long-term dialysis in the United States, nonwhite dialysis recipients were two thirds less likely as white patients to receive a kidney transplant (Kjellstrand, 1988). Also, whites were disproportionately on waiting lists for transplants (Held et al., 1988). According to Sullivan (1991), there is a two-tiered health care system.

Prior to 1992 it was common practice to exclude racial and ethnic minorities from clinical research. It was presumed that racial and ethnic minorities could affect the scientific validity of the study because of uncontrolled heterogeneity between racial groups. But, Italians, Danes or the Irish are placed in a homogeneous group, white, for clinical research although there is substantial ethnic diversity among white Americans (LaVeist, 1996). Clinical marginalization meant that the impact and utility of, for example, certain oral contraceptives and drugs to combat various diseases might not be as effective for blacks.

There also is a long history in the United States of minorities being devalued and having their illnesses labeled deviant. Stigmatized minorities are socially ostracized and marginalized by AIDS when it is seen as another reason to dissociate from them (Cancela, 1989). A prime example is the experience of the Haitian community. Because they were at one time considered a risk group for HIV, Haitians lost their jobs simply because they were Haitian (Landesman, 1983). They experienced racial discrimination because of the racism within American society and because of their minority status within the larger black population (Forstein, 1984).

In addition, minorities are less likely to have health insurance because of historical and contemporary inequality in America. For instance, in 1997 thirty-three percent of Hispanics, 19% of blacks and 12% of whites were uninsured. At the same time, 45% of poor Hispanics and 43% of near poor Hispanics under 65 years old were uninsured (NCHS, 2002).

Lastly, the poor are usually sicker before they seek health care and require more services for longer periods. Therefore, they are usually excluded from programs because they are high-risk patients. Often the health care needs of poor minorities are served by emergency rooms where the treatment is expensive, slow, impersonal, even hostile and usually delivered by relatively inexperienced personnel (Jones, 1986). Poor minorities end up going from one physician to another without receiving long-term health care from one or a few physicians (Blendon et al., 1989).

Experimentation

Historically, since blacks were viewed as a separate species that were biologically, mentally, and morally inferior, they were considered appropriate subjects for experimentation. While the Tuskegee Syphilis Experiment illuminated the enormity of problems in the recruitment of disenfranchised people in medical research, this type of racism has a long history. For example, Dr. James Marion Sims (1813-1883), the father of gynecology and president of the American Medical Association (1875-76), experimented on slave women between 1845 and 1849. He was a plantation doctor who tried to deliver the baby of a 17-year-old slave woman, Anarcha. Using forceps he pulled the baby's head out. We do not know if the child lived. But Anarcha suffered a fistula or tear in her vagina wall making her not as valuable to her owner. So the doctor tried to improve the owner's property by developing a surgical procedure to cure vaginal fistula. He operated on Anarcha over 40 times and used other slave women to test his theories on vaginal repair. Finally, using silver wire sutures rather than the usual silk ones he cured Anarcha's vaginal tear. She became the first woman to be cured of vaginal fistula (McGregor, 1998).

Anarcha and the other women were also turned into dope addicts because part of the treatment regimen was to give them large doses of opium after the surgeries to calm their nerves (Richardson, 1994). Experimentation on these women was considered acceptable because of their "inhuman" status. When Dr. Sims operated 30 times on Mary Smith, a poor Irish woman, however, his colleagues censured him. While Mary was poor she was still white (McGregor, 1998).

Experiments on disenfranchised people continued into contemporary times. For instance, Jones (1993) and Brandt (1978) examined the Tuskegee Syphilis Experiment (1929-1972) and its sponsorship for forty years by the United States Public Health Service (USPHS). From the beginning it was assumed that blacks in Macon County, Alabama constituted a "natural" syphilitic population. This was the rationale for the experiment. The USPHS believed the study might show that treatment for syphilis was unnecessary for blacks and that existing knowledge concerning treatment for latent syphilis did not apply to them. To the USPHS, syphilis was a different disease in blacks as opposed to whites (Jones, 1993).

In the 1960s the experiment was still ongoing. At this time the Centers for Disease Control had a meeting in which they concluded that the men were getting better health care than they would under any circumstances and that the study should continue because they would never have another study like this. By the mid-1970s the Department of Health, Education and Welfare (HEW) report suggested that failure to provide penicillin was the major ethical problem with the study but Brandt suggests that lying to the men about treatment was the major problem. The HEW investigation of the experiment did not discuss the fact that the men participated in the study under the guise of treatment (Brandt, 1978). The fact that a comparative sample of whites was not included in the research design shows the racist orientation of the USPHS. Nothing scientifically useful resulted from this experiment.

The persistence of the genetic model in the medical community is evident when dealing with black Americans, as well as the racist underpinnings of this experiment. This is shown by the fact that the study was widely reported for almost forty years without evoking widespread protest within the medical community and at the USPHS (Brandt, 1978). For this study to be published in major journals for almost forty years without vocal condemnation highlights the various levels that racism operates on in the world society.

CONCLUSIONS

Blacks today suffer from excess morbidity and mortality related to the same factors that affected their slave ancestors, living conditions. These living conditions include daily individual racism, collective and institutional racism. As a result, blacks are marginalized and ghettoized and ill health is a known consequence of such environmental conditions.

Ghettoization can affect the health of poor minorities in a number of ways that include poor housing, lack of sanitary environment and overcrowding. Economics is not the reason that blacks have been circumscribed to ghettoes. Ghettoization is the outcome of social forces that represent institutional racism as shown by U.S. government policies, restrictive covenants, real estate systems, zoning laws, and violence against blacks (Reed, 1981).

Ghettoization began with the New Deal with segregation in urban cities in the 1930s. This program extended social rights but reinforced racial separation. Congress, mainly southern members, used the Social Security Act of 1935 to create a two-tiered racially segregated benefit system for senior citizens and the unemployed. In essence, the New Deal legitimized racial discrimination in employment and housing (Quadagno, 1994). For instance, since the 1930s the Federal Housing Administrations had an official policy of segregating and redlining residential areas. Another form of racial exclusion is zoning ordinances to keep public housing out of white areas since many blacks live in public housing (Reed, 1981).

By the 1960s this was an obstacle for an effective government so Lyndon Johnson reoriented the Nation's social policy with the War on Poverty by funding education and housing in disenfranchised communities. Resources were transferred from the federal government and the local "machines" to those in need of equality. This orientation changed with Nixon who attempted to reach an alienated white working class. In order to gain their support he attempted to replace Aid to Families with Dependent Children with a Family Assistance Plan (FAP) that would guarantee an annual income to poor people. But FAP threatened southern employers who feared that the program would undermine the wage structure (low-wage for workers) in the south. Ghettos and low wages benefited the employer class (mainly white) in America. As a result, "the long-term legacy of coupling social policy to racial issues has diminished America's ability to stem the decline of the inner cities" ... (Quadagno, 1994:14).

Millions of dollars are funded each year to change individual health behavior with little result. With so little change, considering the money spent, one might wonder why the paradigm does not shift. That is, that there is more of a focus on changing behavior within society as opposed to changing the behavior of people who are disenfranchised and not part of the power structure that makes decisions about their health. The genetic model is part of the culture of public health. Genes are important but racism is not. As a result, the health of minorities has not significantly improved since slavery because U.S. health researchers continue to focus on genetic causes when there are known environmental factors that can be addressed.

UPDATE: ENVIRONMENTAL RACISM

Environmental racism is a type of collective racism that results in racial discrimination. It involves institutions and mechanisms that affect the living conditions and quality of life of disenfranchised people. For instance, lack of access to freeways from communities, unsafe public transportation, proliferation of billboards that promote harmful products such as tobacco and alcohol, poor housing and paucity of police patrols are examples of environmental racism. In addition, structural factors needed for survival are controlled by the majority population and are differentially distributed in such a way as to negatively impact the quality of life of minorities.

An example in the United States is the distribution of hazardous waste sites. Race is a significant predictor of proximity to hazardous waste facilities even after controlling for socioeconomic factors (Commission for Racial Justice, 1987). Bullard (1983) found that solid waste sites were not randomly distributed in Houston but were more likely to be found in black neighborhoods and near black schools. Before 1970 blacks and Hispanics did not hold a city council seat in Houston. An all-white and all-male city council made key decisions on where to dispose of the city's waste with the assistance of planning and solid waste departments. The Texas Department of Health permitted twenty-one solid waste sites in Houston between 1970 and 1978. Fifty-four percent were located in predominantly black neighborhoods (Blacks were 26% of the Houston population in 1970 and 27.6% in 1980). Five of the six Houston landfills were located in predominantly black neighborhoods. Black children were more likely to attend schools near a solid waste site. These factors contributed to black neighborhoods becoming the dumping ground for Houston's solid waste (Bullard, 1983).This is the reason that after controlling for education and job experience, African Americans are more likely than whites to be exposed to carcinogens and occupational hazards (Robinson, 1984).

Environmental racism results in a reduction of public services, inferior services, over utilization of black communities for disposal of toxins, or targeting minorities for products that put them at risk for various illnesses. For example, using the 1973-87 General Social Survey, Williams et al (1995) examined factors related to access to pistols among urban low-income males. It was shown that low-income African-American males have easier access to guns than their white counterparts.

Hackbarth et al. (1995) studied billboard advertising of tobacco and alcohol products in Chicago. They found that minority neighborhoods had three times as many tobacco billboards and five times as many alcohol-billboards as white neighborhoods. These findings are congruent with other studies that show that tobacco and alcohol advertisers target poor and minority neighborhoods.

Eighty percent of the 60,000 annual excess black deaths are related to cardiovascular disease, cancers, homicide/suicide/intentional injury, diabetes, infant mortality, and cirrhosis of the liver. Cigarette smoking and alcohol abuses are risk factors for five of these six causes of death (U.S. Department of Health and Human Services, 1985). Today, blacks are more likely to smoke and abuse alcohol than whites but prior to the 1950s whites had higher rates of both smoking and alcohol abuse (Williams, 1992). The tobacco and alcohol industries command financial resources that have led to a symbiotic relationship with the state (King and Williams, 1995). In this relationship these companies are equipped to co-opt the state to prevent mobilization against their actions. The result is poor health among minorities.

CHAPTER SEVEN

SCIENTIFIC STATEMENTS ON RACE

> The battle against racism is crucial in the deconstruction of the race idea because racism lies at the heart of the race concept and lends the concept its vitality (Lieberman and Reynolds, 1996:147).

This chapter examines scientific statements on the concept of race by the United Nations Education, Scientific, and Cultural Organization (UNESCO), the American Anthropological Association (AAA) and the American Association of Physical Anthropologists (AAPA). These statements provide insight into the state of "scientific" knowledge and "belief systems" of natural and social scientists on the subject of biological and social aspects of race. In particular, I analyze the approach used to deal with myths and stereotypes about race and their treatment of social and biological aspects of race within professional organizations from the 1930s to contemporary times.

THE PREWAR YEARS AND RACIAL THINKING

Racial thinking in pre-WWII Europe and the United States was linked to nineteenth century racial theorists who thought of races as fixed types which spread across the map without changing their character. There was no adaptation to the environment (Barkan, 1996), only intermixture. Races were unchangeable and primarily determined by biology. Besides morphology, culture and personality were also considered biologically based. Nations and cultures were ranked using the Great Chain of Being with some cultures, European and white American, considered superior to other nations and cultures of the world. This was the intellectual and social climate of Germany in the early nineteen hundreds. Germans continued to believe in the Aryan myth and considered themselves superior to all other nations in the world. It was manifest destiny for them to rule the world. As such, certain populations such as Jews were considered inferior. Although Jews were Germans, they were not 'Aryans' and therefore not members of the superior race.

The Nazis argued that only Aryans were Germans. But Franz Boas argued that Jews were Germans because nationality and language were cultural and not biological designations. He contended that a nation was defined by language and custom and not descent. As such, their persecution of Jews was misguided and not based upon science. In 1938 at the urging of Boas, the AAA passed a resolution denouncing Nazi racism (Visweswaran, 1998). The 1938 AAA Resolution had three statements:

> 1) Race involves the inheritance of similar physical varia-
> tions by large groups of mankind, but its psychological
> and cultural connotations, if they exist, have not been as-
> certained by science. 2) The terms 'Aryan' and 'Semitic'
> have no racial significance whatsoever. They simply de-
> note linguistic families. 3) Anthropology provides no sci-
> entific basis for discrimination against any people on the
> ground of racial inferiority, religious affiliation or lin-
> guistic heritage (AAA 1939:30).

In placing Jews in the same group with other Germans, Boas made the distinction between culture and biology. He put race in biology and everything that was not biology was culture. Boas made the distinctions between race, language and culture that are the basis for the current subdivisions within American anthropology. In doing so, most anthropologists, i.e. cultural anthropologists, did not consider race to be within their area of study (Visweswaran, 1998). Race was in the realm of biology and biological anthropology and therefore outside the cultural domain. Ironically, this is what physical anthropologists had always argued (although they also assigned cultural and personality traits to race). In an attempt to eliminate racism against Jews, Boas unknowingly supported the position that physical anthropology should be the sole proprietor of the race concept within anthropology.

THE EARLY POSTWAR YEARS AND RACIAL THINKING

The international scientific community after WWII was different from the previous one (Barkan, 1996). That is, anti-racist scientific positions were more acceptable because of the atrocities committed by the Nazis. Race was now associated with racism. This is the environment in which UNESCO was founded in 1945. In its constitution UNESCO declared

> ... that ignorance of each other's ways and lives has been a common cause, throughout the history of mankind, of that suspicion and mistrust between the people of the word through which their differences have all too often broken into war... (UNESCO, 1945:3).

With this as their base there was a receptive international environment for an anti-racist universal declaration by UNESCO (Barkan, 1996).

The United Nations General Assembly adopted the Universal Declaration of Human Rights (UDHR) on December 10, 1948. The Declaration put forth civil, political, economic, social and cultural rights as one integral set of rights necessary for human dignity and world peace (UNESCO, 1950). As a philosophical concept, human rights refer to the reasonable demands for personal security and well being that all humans should have by virtue of being members of the species *Homo sapiens* (Messer, 1993). It was proposed because it was believed that governments that systematically disregarded the rights of their own people would not respect the rights of other nations and were likely to seek their objectives by coercion and force in the world (Martenson, 1992). It also was a refutation of the fascist and nazi theories that devalued the human person (Bureau of Public Affairs, 1988). But, the meaning of these rights and who was protected under them varied historically, socially, and politically (Messer, 1993).

Race was at the heart of the atrocities in WWII. As such, in 1950 UNESCO published the first formal statement on race by the international scientific community. The committee consisted of scholars from around the world. Ashley Montagu of the United States was the chief architect and rapporteur for the committee. His scholarship and reputation in the scientific community as well as his advocacy against racism and his book *Man's Most Dangerous Myth*, made him an obvious choice to lead the committee. Other committee members included members from the fields of genetics, psychology, sociology, and social and physical anthropology. But the statement was still strongly associated with Montagu (Montagu, 1972; Shipman, 1994).

The 1950 statement discussed three aspects of race: what it is, what it is not and equality. First, the statement attempted to educate the international public about the origin and maintenance of human variation. The statement began with

... " all men belong to the same species, *Homo sapiens*" (UNESCO, 1979a:23).
Two definitions of race were given:

> ... as one of the group of populations constituting the species
> *Homo sapiens*; and ... a group or population characterized by
> some concentrations, relative as to frequency and distribution,
> of hereditary particles (genes) or physical characters, which ap-
> pear, fluctuate, and often disappear in the course of time by
> reason of geographic and/or cultural isolation (1979a:23-24).

Differences were attributed to evolutionary forces such as isolation, drift, mutation and natural selection but it was stated that similarities among humans are
much greater than differences. Then the committee conformed to racial thinking
by classifying present-day populations into Mongoloid, Negroid and Caucasoid
and stated that there is no general agreement on the number of races although
they already named three.

It was also noted that race is not a biological construct but a 'social myth.'
But their prior classification of the world's populations into pre-established
races nullified this statement. By naming three races that scientists and lay people already recognized they validated race and biological racial classification
and thereby reduced the usefulness of the statement.

There is no discussion of the selection of characteristics to be used or the
reason for classifying people. Why is skin color more important than stature?
What is the purpose and use of racial classification? They missed the opportunity to highlight the social construction of race that may have been implied by
the attempt to substitute ethnicity for race (an obvious inclusion by Montagu).

"Whatever classification the anthropologist makes of man, he never includes
mental characteristics as part of those classifications" (UNESCO, 1979a:25).
Examination of the history of scientific racism and the history of physical anthropology do not support this statement. Physical anthropologists (e.g. Edward
Tylor, George Samuel Morton, W.J. McGee, Daniel Garrison Brinton and John
Wesley Powell) were leaders in the dissemination of correlates of race with
mental ability.

The statement goes on to pronounce that intelligence tests do not allow us to
distinguish between what is due to innate ability and environmental influences.
Tests, where there are allowances for differences in environment, show basi-
cally similarity in mental ability among all human groups. They stated that the
average achievement of each ethnic group is the same once allowances are made
for cultural opportunity and that based upon the scientific data available, inherited genetic differences are not the cause for differences between races in cultural achievements. Rather, the cultural history of populations is the reason for
such differences (UNESCO, 1979a).

Miscegenation was a hot topic. Race mixture has been taking place since earliest times and is one of the chief mechanisms for race formation, absorption and extinction. It was stated that evidence does not indicate that race mixture produces undesirable traits, either physically or mentally and that there is no biological reason to prohibit miscegenation (UNESCO, 1979a). Montagu and the committee wanted to acknowledge that hybridization or race crossing is important in producing human diversity and also in the unification of humankind (Montagu, 1972).

Lastly, it was recognized that the race myth causes enormous suffering, prevents the normal development of humans and deprives civilization of productive minds. While the committee concluded that "It must be asserted with the utmost emphasis that equality as an ethical principle in no way depends upon the assertion that human beings are in fact equal in endowment" (UNESCO, 1979a:27). Individuals in all ethnic groups vary among themselves in endowment but differences between human groups are exaggerated and used to question the validity of equality (UNESCO, 1979a).

With comments from the advisory members, UNESCO officials such as Metraux sought to modify the positivist claims in the statement and to play down the 'universal brotherhood' part of the statement that said ... "cooperative spirit is not only natural to men, but more deeply rooted than any self-seeking tendencies" (UNESCO, 1979a:26). "Biological studies lend support to the ethic of universal brotherhood; for man is born with drives towards cooperation, and unless these drives are satisfied, men and nations alike fall ill" (UNESCO, 1979a:28). This statement was severely criticized by the commentators. Montagu rejected these attempts and since he was the final arbiter the statement was included in the publication. Although it was severely criticized, Montagu's views briefly became the official international scientific truth about race (Barkan, 1996).

The fact that a panel of international experts convened to advocate an egalitarian racial perspective and repudiate the idea of racial ranking exemplified the revolutionary transformation in thinking about race in the postwar years. The UNESCO statement provided continuity with anti-racism of the pre-war years but presented a break with pre-war theories of race. In one generation the race concept shifted from a biological category that explained all social traits as genetic to a sociological category with skepticism regarding biological causes (Barkan, 1996).

Criticism of the statement rested on those who believed that race had a significant biological component and those who objected to the assertion that humanitarianism was biologically based. The most outspoken were those who opposed the repudiation of a biological base for race or objected to the environmental nature of the declaration (Barkan, 1996). For instance, Dover (1950) considered race to be a taxonomic issue and believed that taxonomists should

write any statement on race and not social scientists. He questioned that all
"men" belong to the same species and are derived from the same stock and
seemed to question the statement that likenesses between races is greater than
differences. He does not appear to understand the difference between groups
formed as a culture and groups formed because of genes but considered all
variation to be related to biology; and argued that a few genes could produce
major differences between races.

Likewise, Hill (1951) stated "That race is more than a social myth is endorsed by the plain facts of physical anthropology and ethnography" (Hill,
1951:17). Like Dover, Hill concluded that the Statement was the ... "misguided
opinions of a particular school of anthropologists whose assertions appear to be
motivated by wishful thinking" (1951:16). Little (1951) also stated that the
UNESCO panel suggested ... "philosophical or ideological doctrine rather than
a 'modern scientific' one" (Little (1951:17).

The claim that was the source of much criticism was the statement that "biological studies lend support to the ethic of universal brotherhood, for man is
born with drives towards co-operation" (Stepan, 1982; Barkan, 1996). Dover
(1950), Little (1951) and Fleure (1951) stated that there is no proof that humans
have a biological drive towards universal brotherhood and cooperation. "We
cannot presume the existence of the tendency to universal co-operation in mankind at large; we have to try to build up this universalism bit by bit" (Flueure,
1951:16). A universal drive to cooperation could also imply genetic drives for
racial discrimination.

In response to the UNESCO statement Hill (1951) argued that intermating
may or may not be a good thing. Gunnar Myrdal (1948) in *An American Dilemma* may have identified the motivation behind Hill's statement. Myrdal
found that the item that aroused the highest intensity of emotion in those who
discriminate was intermarriage and sexual relation involving white women. According to Hill intermarriage was maladaptive because:

> Nature, in evolving different racial types, was endeavoring to
> produce the best fitted each to its own environment. On the
> whole a good job seems to have been made of it; why interfere?
> A categorical denial that ill may result seems premature in
> the present state of knowledge (1951:17).

In general, the public had strong negative feelings about miscegenation. This
is illustrated in *Man's Most Dangerous Myth* where Montagu provided data on
thirty states in which interracial marriage was prohibited. For example, in Alabama you were prohibited from marrying a white person if you were a "Negro
or descendent of a Negro to the third generation inclusive, though one ancestor
of each generation was a white person" (1942:263). In Arizona it was illegal for
whites to marry "Negroes, Mongolians, Indians, Hindus, or members of the Ma-

lay race" (1942:266). In some states participants would also be guilty of a felony. Such discrimination was 'strong' in the United States.

Another area of contention was the belief that races did not differ in mental abilities. Some scientists argued that this statement was without scientific evidence (Shipman, 1994). This was noted in Hill's commentary:

> The range of mental capabilities is 'much the same' in all races is scarcely a scientifically accurate statement. It is at most a vague generalization. It is, however, scarcely true, for temperamental and other mental differences are well known to be correlated with physical differences. I need but mention the well-known musical attributes of the Negroids and the mathematical ability of some Indian races. ... Even if it were true that there is 'no proof that the groups of mankind differ in intelligence, temperament or other innate mental characteristics,' it is certainly the case that there is no proof of the contrary (Hill, 1951:17).

Some scientists contended that because mainly sociologist framed the 1950 statement it did not carry authority with scientists in biology such as geneticists and physical anthropologists (Montagu, 1972). In response, UNESCO published a second Statement on *The Nature of Race and Race Differences* in June 1951. Montagu (physical anthropologist) was the only member to remain on the second panel (a number of its members were commentators on the first statement). The Rapporteur for the second committee was L.C. Dunn, a geneticist. The 1951 panelists were anti-racist because of their fight against fascism but were not "precise" egalitarians. That is, there was conformance to folk beliefs by wavering on correlates of race and not emphasizing that hybridization did not result in biological degeneracy. The second statement was an additional explanation of race, not a revision of the first one (Barkan, 1996).

The 1951 statement also classified the world's populations into three groups but stated that the classification was not based on a single trait such as skin color because by itself this trait did not differentiate one major group from another. It discussed overlapping or intergrading of racial groups and indicated that individual differences in a race were greater than the differences between the averages of two or more races.

In terms of mental ability, they stated that innate ability and environmental factors influence intelligence tests and personality although the relative contribution of each is uncertain. Mental diseases are genetically transmitted while the heredity of normal mental ability is less clear. The possibility that races differed in their innate intellectual abilities was left open.

They failed to reach consensus about the inborn nature of humans with respect to behavior toward their fellow human beings. The section on the ethic of

universal brotherhood was removed. It was reiterated that equality does not necessarily mean equal in endowment.

Overall, the committee believed that hybridization was biologically advantageous but reported that they had insufficient evidence to support this claim
(UNESCO, 1979a). The writers retreated from the 1950 statement that emphasized a lack of maladaptation related to hybridization.

UNESCO AND RACE IN THE 1960s

There was a changed social and intellectual environment in the United States
and in the world in the 1960s. The Vietnam War caused people to reevaluate in-
terventions by the superpowers. Simultaneously, the mass media brought the
war into our homes. Nightly views of Americans dying and women and children
killed may have softened people's perspective of the 'other.' In addition, the
civil rights movement pushed for a change in race relations with its nonviolent
approach being used as a model for freedom and equality efforts around the
globe. It was an effective emotional war against racism and discrimination.
Lastly, the women's movement incorporated members of the dominant population, white females, in the fight for equality at home. All of these events, along
with numerous studies on race, race relations, biology and genetics moved the
world toward a more egalitarian perspective on race although the implementation of this perspective was a slow process. Statements on race in the 1960s reflected this changed atmosphere.

Proposals on the Biological Aspects of Race, Moscow, August 1964

The 1964 statement on race by UNESCO reiterated much of the 1950 statement. Three major racial groups were recognized but not named. Many anthropologists, while stressing the importance of human variation, believe that the
scientific interest of these classifications is limited, and even that they carry the
risk of inviting abusive generalizations (UNESCO, 1979a:36). This is the first
time the lack of scientific purpose in racial classifications was discussed. Unfortunately, there was not a discussion on whether or not such classifications are
useful and under what circumstances they might have utility. Given a lack of
utility, there could have been a discussion of why such classifications are conducted in the absence of a scientific purpose. If such a discussion had occurred,
it would have to include a discussion of racism.

Similar to previous statements, this one examined the discordance of traits in
terms of the difficulty of categorizing humans into discrete groups.

> Human races in general present a far less clear-cut characteriza-
> tion than many animal races and they cannot be compared at all

to races of domestic animals, these being the result of height-
ened selection for special purposes (1979a:37).

Some 'intermediate populations' are difficult to classify. Again the race concept is validated. The use of the phrase 'intermediate populations' suggests that
some populations are intergradations between groups (splitter or classifier) and
it presupposes that populations can be categorized.

Because of the mobility of humans and social factors, matings between different populations have played an important role in human history. Obstacles to
intermixture are geographical, social and cultural. There is nt evidence that intermixture has biological disadvantages for our species. To the contrary, it
maintains the unity of the species (UNESCO, 1979a). In the 1960s they reem-
phasized the lack of biological maladaptation related to intermixture.

In the statement, panelists contended that race is a biological concept. But, it
has a cultural component because people who speak the same language and
share the same culture are more likely to intermarry and therefore there is a certain degree of overlap between physical characteristics and linguistic and cultural traits. However, it is not valid to attribute cultural traits to the influence of
genetics. There is no causal relation. People today possess equal biological potentialities for reaching 'civilizational level' and differences in achievement are
attributed only to cultural history (UNESCO, 1979a). Again it is emphasized
that culture is not biologically based.

While heredity may play a role in variability between individuals within a
population, in terms of psychological tests, they stated that a plethora of data
supports the influence of physical, cultural and social environment in response
to tests. Some psychological traits are attributed to particular people but there is
no basis for ascribing such traits to hereditary factors. In terms of hereditary potentialities for intelligence, there is no justification for the concept of inferior
and superior races. The Statement now makes a stronger case against genetic
differences in intelligence.

> Racist theories can in no way pretend to have any scientific
> foundation and the anthropologists should endeavor to prevent
> the results of their research from being used in such a biased
> way that they would serve non-scientific ends (UNESCO,
> 1979a:39).

This is the first scientific statement on race that addresses the use of scientific research for racist ends.

Statement on Race and Racial Prejudice, Paris, September 1967

The 1967 statement on race and racial prejudice focused on racism and re-affirmed the 1964 statement in Moscow. It emphasized the historical, social and political causes of racism and makes specific recommendations for political and social action to effectively combat racism. UNESCO defined racism as antiso-cial beliefs and actions that are based on the false belief that discrimination against groups is justified on biological grounds.

The hidden agenda of racial classification is provided. It is argued that pro-moters of racist doctrines claim to have a scientific base for ranking groups in terms of psychological and cultural traits that are innate. However, they are really seeking to insure that existing differences appear unchangeable so that current race relations are permanent (UNESCO, 1979a).

The statement also outlined the historical roots of racism. It noted that racism arose out of conditions of conquest, justification of black slavery, its aftermath of racial discrimination in the West and out of the colonial experience. They be-lieved that it was possible to eliminate racism because former colonies and their people, who were classified as inferior, now have "full political rights" (UNESCO, 1979a:43). [In the 1960s a number of African countries gained in-dependence, at least on paper.] It was believed that participation of these na-tions in international organizations undermined racism. But in some instances, the groups that had been the victims of racist doctrines applied policies with racist implications in their freedom struggle (UNESCO, 1979a).

Since its inception, members of UNESCO argued that in order to end racism one must do more than expose its fallacies. Scientists must demonstrate its causes. UNESCO stressed examination of the social structure and provided ex-amples such as settler societies with disparity of power and property and urban ghettos with unequal access to housing, education and employment opportuni-ties. The writers stated that the foundations of prejudice could be found in the social and economic system of a society (UNESCO, 1979a). Then the perpetra-tors of racism were discussed.

> Individuals with certain personality troubles may be particu-larly inclined to adopt and manifest racial prejudices. Small groups, associations, and social movements of a certain kind sometimes preserve and transmit racial prejudices (UNESCO, 1979a:44).

The main way to cope with racism entails changing certain social situations that gave rise to prejudice, preventing those who are prejudice from expressing their prejudice and combating the false beliefs. Education and other mechanisms for social and economic 'progress' can be effective for broadening understand-ing. However, schools can also be used to perpetuate inequality and discrimination. It was proposed that resources for education should be used to reduce prejudice. For example special attention should be given to the training of teachers because they can reflect current prejudices in society. Also, because of historical factors there are disparities in education and income. Therefore, societies should take corrective measures such as limiting the transfer of poor environments (such as poor housing, health care and education) to children (UNESCO, 1979a).

Preventing people from expressing their prejudices often requires political action. Law is one of the most effect means to ensure equality between individuals and to fight racism. The Universal Declaration of Human Rights and related international agreements could contribute on the national and international level to the fight against racism and national legislation could be used to outlaw racist propaganda and discrimination. Like Martin Luther King, UNESCO argued that legislation cannot immediately eliminate prejudice, but it can protect victims from acts based upon prejudice and in the long run it can change attitudes (UNESCO, 1979a).

For the first time there is an advocacy for cultural self-determination. It was noted that sometimes the dominant group tolerates ethnic groups that are the object of discrimination if they abandon completely their cultural identity. Efforts of these groups to maintain their cultural values should be encouraged so that they can contribute to the culture of humanity (UNESCO, 1979a).

UNESCO stressed that researchers should prevent the misuse of their work by those who wish to promote racial prejudice and discrimination (UNESCO, 1979a).

The International Covenants on Human Rights

The International Covenants on Human Rights consists of 1) the International Covenant on Economic, Social and Cultural Rights; 2) the International Covenant on Civil and Political Rights; and 3) the Optional Protocol to the International Covenant on Civil and Political Rights (UNESCO, 1967). Along with the Universal Declaration of Human Rights, these Covenants are the International Bill of Human Rights. These covenants were proposed to promote "...universal respect for, and observance of, human rights and fundamental freedoms for all without distinction as to race, sex, language or religion..." (UNESCO, 1967:1). For instance, the following elements are included in the International Covenant on Economic, Social and Cultural Rights: the right to self-determination; implementation of the Covenant without discrimination based on race, sex, language, religion, political or other opinion, national or social origin, property, birth or other status (however, developing nations could determine the degree to which they will adhere to the economic rights to non-nationals); equal rights for men and women; right to employment; right to a standard of living that ensures well-being and health; right to form trade unions; right to education; and free compulsory primary education.

The International Covenant on Civil and Political Rights includes the following elements: self-determination; right to life however the death penalty is allowed "for the most serious crimes in accordance with the law in force at the time of the commission of the crime" (UNESCO, 1967:15). This was an attempt to outlaw genocide. It ...

> is understood that nothing in this article shall authorize any State Party to the present Covenant to derogate in any way from any obligation assumed under the provisions of the Convention on the Prevention and Punishment of the Crime of Genocide (United Nations, 1967:15-16).

The Covenants also include the abolition of torture and slavery; right to liberty and security (those deprived of liberty, jail or prison, should be treated with humanity); freedom of movement; equality before the courts; right to protection of the law, freedom of thought, conscience and religion; prohibition of war propaganda; freedom of association; and pledge an effective recourse whenever these rights are violated (UNESCO, 1967).

The Covenants do not provide for adjudication or arbitration if there is disagreement concerning their interpretation. Terms are general rather than precise and there is no provision for complaints by States that a party failed to fulfill its obligations from individuals claiming that rights outlined in the Covenant were violated. Unrestricted reservations, the absence of provisions for judicial determination of disputes or questions relating to their interpretation, limited measures of implementation, and the need for ratification to bring them into force limits the potential effectiveness of the Covenants (Jenks, 1968).

International Convention on the Elimination of All Forms of Racial Discrimination

UNESCO initially adopted The International Convention on the Elimination of All Forms of Racial Discrimination (ICERD) in 1965. The purpose of the Convention was to prohibit ethnic and racial discrimination in public life (Banton, 1996). Racial discrimination was defined as:

> any distinction, exclusion, restriction or preference based on race, colour, descent, or national or ethnic origin which has the purpose or effect of nullifying or impairing the recognition, enjoyment or exercise, on an equal footing, of human rights and fundamental freedoms in the political, economic, social, cultural or any other field of public life (1965 in UESCO, 1994: 4-5).

UNESCO met at a time when many states were trying to move the UN to complete the decolonization process. Therefore, the responsibilities of former colonial powers for racism and racial discrimination were accentuated. In particular, disgust for apartheid was probably the main motivation for the adoption of ICERD (Banton, 1996). But, while states considered situations like South Africa or Nazi Germany to represent racial discrimination, most of the signatories associated racial discrimination with other countries rather than their own. Also, there was confusion about the meaning of racial discrimination (which CERD continued to clarify) and resistance to applying it to the plight of indigenous peoples. Examination of compliance reveals that usually articles of the Convention have not been met. The United States is among the noncompliant states (Banton, 1996).

ANTHROPOLOGICAL PERSPECTIVES ON RACE: 1960s-1970s

While the nation and world were developing a more egalitarian and anti-racist worldview, these orientations had mixed receptions among anthropologists. Cultural anthropologists argued against biological reductionism and espoused the view that humans were more than biology, that biology did not determine culture, and that social, economic and historical factors were the source of cultural differences and inequities. The Boasian school led this approach by demanding proof of racial differences in mental abilities (Lieberman and Reynolds, 1978).

Although Boas trained his students to renounce scientific concepts of race, to ignore folk concepts of race, and to work toward an egalitarian society, upon his death in 1942 sociocultural anthropology was indifferent to skin-color differences that were/are the basis of racial, folk, classifications. Instead, they were concerned with salvaging ethnography and expanding the field of ethnology among small-scale societies. Race did not matter and therefore racism was irrelevant to the study of anthropology (Shanklin, 1998). Sociocultural anthropologists, with some notable exceptions, did not return to the study of race and racism until the 1990s.

The AAA's response to the civil rights movement and racist hostilities during the fifties and sixties was reactionary in nature. For example, at the annual meeting in 1956 the AAA passed a resolution in support of Section H (Anthropology) of the American Association for the Advancement of Science (AAAS) to forgo its annual meeting rather than hold it in Atlanta, Georgia under conditions of segregation (AAA, 1956). However, there was no organized activist effort within the AAA to aid in the demise of segregation and racial discrimination.

Then in 1961 the Executive Board of the AAA passed a resolution on race at its annual meeting in Philadelphia. The resolution stated that:

> The American Anthropological Association repudiates state-
> ments now appearing in the United States that Negroes are bio-
> logically and in innate mental ability inferior to whites, and re-
> affirms the fact that there is no scientifically established evi-
> dence to justify the exclusion of any race from the rights guar-
> anteed by the Constitution of the United States. The basic prin-
> ciples of equality of opportunity and equality before the law are
> compatible with all that is known about human biology. All
> races possess the abilities needed to participate fully in the de-
> mocratic way of life and in modern technological civilization
> (AAA 1962:616).

This too was reactionary and lacked actions since there was no institutionalized effort by the AAA to end racial discrimination against the people who were
the primary subject of anthropology. That is, anthropology was built on study-
ing people of color, however in the early days of the civil rights movement the
AAA did not, as a unit, actively advocate or 'fight' for their rights.

The AAA added a section in response to Arthur Jensen's 1969 article in the
Harvard Educational Review. They stated that his work is not consistent with
the facts of psychology, biology or anthropology. The AAA ... "repudiated any
suggestion that the failure of an educational program could be attributed to genetic differences between large populations" (AR 1969:40). At the same meeting a resolution on *Racial Inferiority and Public Understanding* was passed.
The AAA asked all of its members ... "to use available outlets in the national
and local media to inform the general public concerning the correct facts about
the nature of human variability" (AR 1969a:40). Unfortunately members were
not provided with any guide in terms of how to accomplish this task.

Another resolution at the 1969 New Orleans meeting dealt with Minorities in
Anthropology. They noted that

> ...participation in research and teaching of persons of diverse
> backgrounds is essential to objectivity and relevance in anthro-
> pology ... knowledge of significant aspects of communities and
> groups is often accessible only to persons with roots in those
> communities and groups ...persons with roots in other than the
> white middle class sector of American society can make invalu-
> able contributions to knowledge of all sectors of contemporary
> life, ... few persons from other than the white middle class sec-
> tor now enter anthropology in the United States and achieve
> professional recognition...   Be it resolved that the American
> Anthropological Association urges vigorous recruitment of stu-
> dents of Black, Chicano, American Indian, Asian and other
> such backgrounds into anthropology in universities and col-
> leges, and vigorous efforts to hire and facilitate the careers of
> such persons in the profession (AR 1969b:37).

Unfortunately, there was disagreement about how to contribute to these efforts. In the 1990s, discussions of a minority fellowship funded by the AAA drew considerable controversy. Some individuals, even in the nineties, objected to such a fellowship and considered it to be a "ghettoized" scholarship. The AAA requested that each section contribute 10% of its fund balance to support a minority fellowship that would provide a full-year dissertation fellowship of $10,000 to a minority doctoral candidate in anthropology. Some sections of the AAA did not believe they should be asked to give part of their fund balance to a minority fellowship. Others believed they were already providing opportunities for minorities. Although some sections contributed 10%, others gave less, and some sections did not contribute. Without full financial support from all sections of the AAA, the Executive Board of the AAA funded the first minority fellowship in 1999.

The following resolution on *Theories of Racial, Sexual and Class Inferiority* was ratified by mail ballot in May, 1972. "That the American Anthropological Association condemns as dangerous and unscientific the racist, sexist or anti-working class theories of genetic inferiority propagated by R. Herrnstein, W. Shockley and A. Jensen." They stated that there is no scientific warrant for ascribing to genetic factors the oppressed condition of classes and ethnic groups and condemned as irresponsible the support of these unfounded conclusions through publication and wide dissemination by *The Atlantic Monthly, Harvard Educational Review* and the *New York Times Magazine*. The AAA stated that theories of genetic inferiority of races, sexes, or classes facilitate and shift the burden of the present economic situation onto the oppressed (AR 1971).

Then, at its annual meeting in Toronto, the AAA passed a motion to condemn the killing of two black students by the police at Southern University in Baton Rouge, Louisiana on November 16, 1972. The students were shot while participating in a demonstration against oppressive conditions and racial discrimination at the university. The AAA urged "...the immediate settlement of all the students' legitimate grievances, opposes the threatened closing of southern University through a merger with Louisiana State University, and demands the prosecution of those responsible for the killings" (AR 1972a:58). There was no follow up to these 'demands.'

Also in 1972 the AAA passed a motion "*Against Racist Distortion in Scientific Discourse*" and endorsed a statement entitled "*A reply to "hereditary reasoning" and racist distortion*." In these statements they encouraged people to challenge the theory and practice of racism and condemned the attempt to present virulent racism under the guise of scholarly "scientific" research (AR 1972b,c).

While cultural anthropologists passed such resolutions during the 60s and 70s such beliefs were not unanimous. For example, Nash, a cultural anthropologist, espoused numerous negative stereotypes of blacks as biological truths in the

1962 *Current Anthropology*. He stated that "the social, moral and political as well as the physical history of the Negro race bears strong testimony against them; it furnishes the most undeniable proof of their mental inferiority" (Nash, 1962: 286). He says a lot more than that in his article. At the same time, physical anthropologists were having their own discussion about human variation.

The nature of the differences among physical anthropologists can be divided into the classifiers (splitters) (Hooton and his students, Coon, Garn and Birdsell; Dobzhansky, Mayr, Glass) and clinalists (lumpers) (Livingstone, Montagu (Boas' student), Brace, Lieberman). Following the recommendation by Brace (1982) and Brace et al. (1993) I will use the term clinalists and classifiers rather than lumpers and splitters because the latter two concepts assume the existence of categories and imply inclusiveness in those categories. Keep in mind that the race concept implies categorization of the worlds' populations into discrete biological groups, subspecies. Classifiers or the believers in the race concept hold that this is possible. According to them such populations were produced through thousands of years of isolation making races incipient species that differ in the frequencies of only a few genes (Garn, 1964) and that interracial clines exist within and between populations (Coon, 1964). The classifiers replied, like the craniometrists of the eighteen hundreds, that new methods and data were needed and then they would be able to provide discrete races (Lieberman, 1968).

Clinalists, no-race group, claimed that biological variability does not conform to discrete categories that can be labeled races. Rather variability exhibits overlapping gradients with discordance in racial characteristics (Montagu, 1942; Livingstone, 1962, 1964; Brace, 1964, 1982; Brace et al., 1993; Lieberman and Reynolds, 1978). The no-race physical anthropologists argued that human variation is the product of natural selection operating in varied ecosystems that do not coincide with national boundaries. Races do not exist because gene flow has always occurred and populations have not existed in isolation (Lieberman, 1968). Therefore, boundaries between races are subjective and arbitrary (Brace, 1964).

Although Montagu was an early supporter of the no race concept and an advocate of the idea of ethnic groups, his position was challenged or ignored until the 1960s. It did, however, lay the foundation for the rejection of race by Livingstone and Brace and they in turn stimulated this thinking among other anthropologists (Lieberman and Reynolds, 1996).

Both groups examined the same variation but interpreted it in completely different ways (as they do today). The 1962-1964 volumes of *Current Anthropology* and *Science and the Concept of Race* edited by Mead, Dobzhansky, Tobach and Light (1968) contain numerous articles on this topic. In the latter volume some scholars such as Marshall (1968) rejected the race concept. She argued that race is a biopolitical concept because racial ideologies and typologies, in various historical periods, reflected the existing sociopolitical consensus. Others, such as Dobzhanzky defended the race concept by stating that "if man has no races, where are races to be found? And if they are nowhere found, why then are the inhabitants of different countries often recognizably different" (Dobzhansky, 1968:78). This discussion was taking place, not because of anthropology, but due to changes in U.S. society such as Brown versus Board of Education, i.e. civil rights movement, the Vietnam War and the women's rights movement.

The edited volume was a response to "scientific research" that attempted to change the 1954 decision in Brown vs Board of Education by proving the biological inferiority of blacks. For instance, certain statements published during this period by scientists in the academic community asserted that scientific evidence proved that blacks were inherently less competent than individuals of other races. The authors of these statements also claimed that the alleged scientific data justify inequities in "Negro" civil rights and ought to invalidate the U.S. Supreme Court decision of 1954 on school segregation. These scientists also claimed that research findings were being stifled to support a more egalitarian environment (AAAS, 1963).

The AAAS responded to such criticism within the scientific community by commissioning a report that was published in *Science* in 1963. The report was a response to writings by W.C. George and Carleton Putnam (author of *Race and Reason*, 1961). George wrote a report for the Governor of Alabama on *The Biology of the Race Problem* (1962). George and Putnam made two assertions: 1) the 1954 decision failed to realize that scientific evidence definitely showed that Negroes are inherently less capable of benefiting from education than whites and Negroes are mentally inferior to whites with respect to intelligence. 2) Some scientists have misled government officials and the public about this evidence for political reasons (AAAS, 1963).

In response the AAAS reexamined the 1954 decision and noted the Supreme Court decision was based on *whether or not segregation resulted in unequal education*. The AAAS stated that research by George and Putnam did not address the issue of the *effects of segregation* on blacks and ... "available scientific data about human heredity and racial differences are not applicable to the ethical judgments that determine the civil rights of racial groups (AAAS, 1963: 560). In other words, the Supreme Court decision concerned whether there was a difference (unequal) education for blacks, not whether blacks were incapable of learning. The AAAS did not present opposition to George's and Putnam's claim that blacks were biologically inferior, rather they stated that this was not the issue in the Supreme Court decision.

AAAS did not attack George's and Putnam's assertion that blacks are genetically inferior to whites by presenting the voluminous data available at that time on, for example, black-white I.Q. For instance, classic Studies by Otto Klineberg (1935, 1944) could have been cited where he examined I.Q. scores for blacks and whites in the south and north and found that northern blacks scored higher on I.Q. tests than southern whites. Klineberg concluded that differences in I.Q. scores were related to environmental factors. Instead, the AAAS allowed racist allegations to be unchallenged by a premier scientific association. In doing so, members of the scientific community could legitimately continue a racist orientation in their research and academic positions.

The AAPA was also involved in this discussion, especially concerning Putnam. At the 1962 annual meeting in Philadelphia the AAPA condemned racism and the writings by Putnam such as *Race and Reason* (1961). Based on southern ideology, this book dealt with negative stereotypes of blacks such as, 'blacks have never contributed to civilization.' The resolution sympathized with colleagues who were forced by administrators to teach race concepts and affirmed that ... "there is nothing in science that justifies the denial of opportunities or rights to any group by virtue of race" (1962:445). Again, a respected scientific organization that focuses on human variation did not take the opportunity to vigorously attack myths related to human diversity.

Diamond (1963) noted that this statement could have been more positive. He stated that they could have argued that there is no scientific basis for the belief in differential capacity for culture between the races, that races have been interfertile throughout history and that racial equality is supported by science. According to Diamond, the AAPA showed "restraint" on this matter.

UNESCO AND RACE: 1970s-2000

UNESCO's Declaration on Race and Racial Prejudice, Paris, November, 1978

UNESCO's *Declaration on Race and Racial Prejudice* in 1978 supported other international agreements and covenants on race and racial discrimination. UNESCO also reaffirmed its role in implementing the program of the *Decade for Action to Combat Racism and Racial Discrimination*. This program dealt with the right of self -determination. For instance, identity of origin does not "preclude the existence of differences based on cultural, environmental and historical diversity nor the right to maintain cultural identity" (UNESCO, 1979b:12). It also noted equality in terms of mental ability and stated that differences in achievements were due to geographical, historical, economic, social, political and cultural factors.

> Any theory which involves the claim that racial or ethnic groups are inherently superior or inferior, thus implying that some would be entitled to dominate or eliminate others, presumed to be inferior, or which bases value judgements on racial differentiation, has no scientific foundation and is contrary to

the moral and ethical principles of humanity (UNESCO, 1979b:12).

In this statement UNESCO provided an inclusive description of racism. Racism included prejudiced attitudes, discriminatory behavior, racist ideologies, structural arrangements and institutionalized practices that result in racial inequality and erroneous beliefs that discrimination between groups is morally and scientifically justifiable. Racism is also exhibited by discriminatory measures in legislation and discriminatory practices, and antisocial beliefs and acts. Racism prevents the development of its victims, perverts those who practice racism, divides nations internally, impedes international cooperation and contributes to political tensions between groups. It is contrary to the fundamental principles of international law and therefore impedes international peace and security (UNESCO, 1979b). Again the origin of racism is considered.

> Racial prejudice, historically linked with inequalities in power, reinforced by economic and social differences between individuals and groups... (UNESCO, 1979b:13).

Laws in themselves are not sufficient to eliminate racism, therefore States should supplement them with administrative mechanisms for the systematic investigation of racial discrimination. They should develop a comprehensive framework of legal remedies against acts of racial discrimination and broadly based education and research programs to combat racism. To combat racial prejudice researchers in the natural and social sciences, as well as scientific organizations and associations should undertake 'objective' research on race and race relations on an interdisciplinary basis. And again, it is stated that researchers should insure that their research findings are not misused (UNESCO, 1979b).

Decade of Action to Combat Racism and Racial Discrimination

There have been three *"The Decade of Action to Combat Racism and Racial Discrimination."* The first one (1973-1983) and a special program for the period 1980-1983 were aimed at the complete elimination of all forms of racism and racial discrimination (UNESCO, 1980). Given the history of race relations, this was a naive stance. There was controversy at the 1975 meeting to implement the proposal and convene the first conference. The issue revolved around the definition of racism and racial discrimination. In addition, States were asked to include bilateral assistance to people that are victims of racial discrimination; outlaw racial discrimination or to counter policies or regulations that create or perpetuate racial hatred; establish recourse for rights violations; insure the elimination of discrimination in education and school systems; and to include the subject of human rights in school curricula. Racist regimes were to be denied support or assistance that would enable them to perpetuate racist policies or practices. They stated that Apartheid "is a crime against humanity and an affront to the dignity of mankind and is a threat to peace and security in the world" (UNESCO, 1980:4). The General Assembly revoked the resolution by a vote of 111 to 25 (Banton, 1996).

For the first time UNESCO discussed the rights of foreign origin people such as migrant workers. Those of foreign origin, such as migrant workers and their families, who contribute to the economic well being of the host country should also benefit from measures designed to provide security and respect for their cultural values and to aid in their adaptation to the host environment and their professional advancement (UNESCO, 1979b).

UNESCO called for global restructuring of economic and political systems to end racial discrimination and racial inequality. Now Third World Nations, especially in Africa pressed for a more equitable socioeconomic order and a sustainable environment (Messer, 1993).

Although the principal objectives of the first Decade had not been attained, the General Assembly of the United Nations mandated the *Programme of Action of the Second Decade to Combat Racism and Racial Discrimination (1983-1993)* (Banton, 1996). With the Second Decade member states and international organizations attempted to reexamine the origins of racism (such as religion, historical such as colonialism and slavery, and economic interests that led to racism) (UNESCO, 1988). Besides the origins, UNESCO examined contemporary forms of racism such as apartheid, xenophobia and heterophobia when States organize around one culture or one religion. Activity against apartheid and other racist policies were a major focus of the Second Decade (UNESCO, 1988; Banton, 1996). Self-determination among indigenous peoples was emphasized and that migrant workers and refugees were particularly vulnerable to racism (UNESCO, 1988). Indigenous people are currently adding another generation of indigenous rights to protect their control over socioeconomic development and rights to political self-determination (Messer, 1993).

International organizations have been slow to respond to human rights abuses against indigenous people and to recognize their needs and aspirations. Within the General Assembly of the UN the Third Committee considers humanitarian and social issues and the Fourth committee deals with decolonization. But due to inadequate international legislation and political constraints, little effort has been put forth by these committees regarding indigenous issues (A Report for the Independent Commission on International Humanitarian Issues, 1987).

In 1982 the Economic and Social Council of the United Nations established the Working Group on Indigenous Populations with a mandate to

> review developments pertaining to the promotion and protection of human rights and fundamental freedoms of indigenous

populations' and to give special attention to the evolution of standards concerning the rights of indigenous peoples' (Burger, 1988:108).

This council is informed of human rights violations of indigenous peoples worldwide but cannot act on complaints (A Report for the Independent Commission on International Humanitarian Issues, 1987; Burger, 1988).

The UN implemented the *Third Decade to Combat Racism and Racial Discrimination (1993-2003)* although the objectives of previous ones have not been met. There is little support for the Third Decade as shown by insufficient funds and lack of success in fundraising and generating interest and commitment to the program (Harrison, 2000; www.hri.ca/fortherecord1999/vol1/racism.htm). The mandate of the third decade is to continue to focus on contemporary forms of racism, racial discrimination, any form of discrimination against Blacks, Arabs and Muslims, xenophobia, Negrophobia, anti-Semitism, and related intolerance. The assembly accords special attention to the situation of migrant workers and called upon states to ratify the International Convention on the Protection of the Rights of All Migrant Workers and Members of Their Families. The Third Decade also paid particular attention to the situation of indigenous peoples (www.hri.ca/fortherecord1999/vol1/racism.htm).

The Third Decade emphasized measures to ensure a peaceful transition from apartheid to a non-racial and democratic government in South African and attempted to establish measures to remedy the legacy of apartheid. The UN also sought successful national models to eliminate racism and racial prejudices in, for example, education of children, racism against migrant workers, ethnic minorities and indigenous peoples (Banton, 1996).

Today racism is relatively neglected in comparison to other UN human rights concerns such as gender and "women's rights as human rights." This is so although there has been an increase in human rights offenses that implicate racial discrimination and violence. This includes situations in which race is the background for ethnic and religious conflict and where it is the primary source of inter-group tensions (Harrison, 2000).

Racism and Racial Discrimination

There has been a continual debate over the definition of racism and racial discrimination at the United Nations. The term discrimination was not used in the UN Charter or in the Universal Declaration of Human Rights. In the 1940s the Sub-Commission on the Prevention of Discrimination and Protection of Minorities defined discrimination as:

> A detrimental distinction based on grounds which may not be attributed to the individual and which have no justified conse-

quences in social, political, or legal relations (colour, race, sex, etc.), or on grounds of membership in social categories (cultural, language, religious, political or other opinion, national circle, social origin, social class, property, birth, or status) (Banton, 1996:51).

The Sub-Commission on *The Elimination of All Forms of Racial Discrimination* (1963) had differing approaches to eliminate racial discrimination. For instance some members of the committee wanted the elimination of racial discrimination to be linked to colonialism while others argued that its manifestations had not always been tied to the existence of colonial territories. Former colonizers, the Western states, considered human rights to be individual rights while those from the Soviet group and the Afro-Asian delegations maintained that rights in the West were in reality enjoyed by only a minority and in the colonies by just a small elite group. For them, individual desires were not a good starting point to eliminate racism because individuals had been conditioned by societies in which they were raised. Both the East European and African groups criticized the continued influence of the former colonial powers and the policies of southern African governments. Differences in worldviews conditioned the ways that states wanted to attack racial discrimination (Banton, 1996).

CONTEMPORARY STATEMENTS ON RACE AND RACISM IN ANTHROPOLOGY

The AAA

In 1994 the AAA passed a *Statement on "Race" and Intelligence* where the AAA strongly noted their concern about public discussions that implied that intelligence is biologically determined by race. Citing earlier AAA resolutions against racism (1961, 1969, 1971, and 1972) in 1994 the AAA further resolved:

> WHEREAS all human beings are members of one species, *Homo sapiens,*
> WHERAS, differentiating species into biologically defined "races" has proven meaningless and unscientific as a way of explaining variation (whether in intelligence or other traits),
> THEREFORE, the American Anthropological Association urges the academy, our political leaders and our communities to reaffirm, without distraction by mistaken claims of racially determined intelligence, the common stake in assuring equal opportunity, in respecting diversity and in securing a harmonious quality of life for all people (AN, 1995:98).

The most recent statement on race by the AAA was adopted in 1998. The AAA acknowledged the general public's view of race as natural divisions among humans but stated that there is more variation within a population than between populations. They pointed out a 6% difference in genes but did not explicitly state that there were no qualitative differences. They do note that physical characteristics are inherited independent of one another and that knowing the range of one trait does not predict the presence of another trait, discordance. The AAA did an excellent job in outlining the historical contribution to the idea of race. Most notably it is stated that

> ...European-Americans fabricated the cultural/behavioral characteristics associated with each race, linking superior traits with Europeans and negative and inferior ones to blacks and Indians. Numerous arbitrary and fictitious beliefs about the different people were institutionalized and deeply embedded in American thought (AAA, 1998:712).

These myths were spread to the rest of the world and "It became a strategy for dividing, ranking and controlling colonized people used by colonial powers everywhere" (AA, 1999: 712). "The racial worldview was invented to assign some groups to perpetual low status, while others were permitted access to privilege, power and wealth" (AAA, 1998: 713).

The AAA countered racist arguments by stating that cultural behavior is learned and conditioned in infants and that behavior is always subject to modification (AAA, 1998). Although research by Rushton and Herrnstein and Murray have been controversial, the AAA was silent on contemporary examples of scientific racism.

In 1997 the AAA responded to the Office of Management and Budget (OMB) Directive 15 developed in 1978 which described four races (Native American or Alaskan Native; Asian or Pacific Islander; Black and White) and two ethnic categories (Hispanic origin and not of Hispanic origin). Guidelines stated that the racial and ethnic categories should not be interpreted as being biological; both can be considered in terms of social and cultural characteristics as well as ancestry; the distinction between race and ethnicity is not clarified. While the Directive acknowledged the lack of scientific basis for the race concept, it still used it to interpret research findings ranging from biomedical to economic research (OMB, 1978).

The AAA Response to OMB Directive 15 stated that 1) while race is associated with biology and ethnicity with culture, the two concepts are not distinct. Populations of differing physical appearance may have a common identity (in the Caribbean people have origins in Europe, Africa and Asia but are considered, for example, Jamaican) and those of similar physical characteristics may have different ethnicity such as Hutus and Tutsi. 2) The OMB directive ignores the historical evolution of race and ethnicity. Today's ethnicities are yesterday's races. 3) OMB considered categories as fixed while individuals perceive their identities as fluid and changing according to certain situations they find themselves in. 4) People assume certain personal characteristics when they see visible characteristics thought to be associated with a particular race. However, it is not the individual's association with a race or ethnic group that predicts outcomes but the attribution of that relationship by others that influence these outcomes (AAA, 1997).

The AAA suggested that the term race be eliminated from the collection of federal data. As Montagu stated in *Man's Most Dangerous Myth* and the 1950 UNESCO statement, the AAA suggested that ethnic categories better reflect the diversity of the U.S. population. They also recommended that respondents be allowed to identify more than one category in reporting their ancestry (Press Release, AAA 1997). However, Baker (1998a) argued that racial categories rather than ethnic groups are better in terms of identifying and tracking systematic racism that is covert and subtle in contemporary society. Use of racial, not ethnic, classification by the government can provide useful data on disparate outcomes that cannot be sufficiently explained by culture, behavior, class or lack of merit. This stand by the AAA provides a base for those who want a color-blind society that will eliminate social policies such as affirmative action (Baker, 1998a). This type of racelessness could provide a base for subtle forms of racial discrimination.

The AAPA

In 1996 the AAPA adopted a *Statement on Biological Aspects of Race*. In the preamble they stated that since they are scientists who study human variation and evolution, they are obligated to share their understanding of human variation with the general public. They too refer to the history of the race concept but do not provide an historical context for the idea of race. Instead it is simply noted that old racial categories were based on external features such as skin color, facial features, head shape and size and body measurements of the skeleton. In terms of physical traits: "They were often imbued with non-biological attributes, based on social constructions of race" (AAPA, 1996:569). From an historical perspective they acknowledged that scientific traditions of the nineteenth century presumed that these visible features predicted other traits and that such notions were used to support racist doctrines. They wavered on whether or not racism affects quality of life.

> The expression of prejudice may or may not undermine material well-being, but it does involve the mistreatment of people and thus it often is psychologically distressing and socially damaging (AAPA 1996:569).

In the preamble it is stated that "Scientists should try to keep the results of their research from being used in a biased way that would serve discriminatory ends" (AAPA 1996:569). This statement seems to be a revision of the 1950 and 1964 UNESCO statements on race. The lack of discussion of gradients (clinalists) or intergradations (classifiers) is surprising (or not surprising) since these two schools of thought still exist.

The 1996 AAPA *Statement on Biological Aspects of Race* had its inception at the 1989 meeting of the AAAS. The impetus was a presentation by J. Philippe Rushton on racial theory that appalled attendees. Participants at the meeting felt that the AAAS should have consulted the AAPA before providing a platform for Rushton and decided to take a stand against scientific racism. It took seven years to produce the statement (Cartmill, 1998).

Some AAPA members were opposed to any statement on race on philosophical grounds. They felt that the AAPA had no business making such pronouncements and that scientific facts should be sorted out in the scientific literature and not settled by passing resolutions at meetings. Also, if the issues were not fact but politics and morality then physical anthropologists should say nothing with authority. The Statement was rejected at the 1993 AAPA business meeting (Cartmill, 1998).

Among the no-biological race group were the clinalists and forensic anthropologists who argued that racial identification of skeletal remains does not validate the race concept. In providing what St. Hoyme and Iscan (1989) term a "bureaucratic race" that is recognized by law enforcement agencies, forensic anthropologists ..."translate information about biological traits to a culturally constructed labeling system that was likely to have been applied to a missing person" (Sauer, 1992:109). "Bureaucratic race" is simply the imprinting of biological information about ancestry onto categories that the missing person/skeletal remains would have been classified as during his/her life. This does not mean that races occur in nature, only that we label individuals in this way.

Those who defended the concept of race said that human variation was correlated with geography and that average traits represented geographically delimited biological subspecies. "But because such classifications reflect certain facts of human biology, they can also be used justly and fairly to serve benign ends" (Cartmill, 1998:652). There was no discussion of the utility of racial classification or the 'benign ends' that such classification might serve.

CONCLUSIONS

While classifiers continue to dominate the field of physical anthropology, the no-race advocates are predominant among cultural anthropologists. In the 1990s there was a vocal call to study social race by cultural anthropologists such as former President of the AAA Annette Weiner (1995), Johnnetta Cole (1992), Faye V. Harrison (1997, 1998a, 1998b, 2000), Carol Mukhopadhyay and Yolanda Moses (1997), Janis Hutchinson (1997), Lee Baker (1998a, 1998b) and others. Use of the phrase 'social race' acknowledges the social construction of the race concept. Only through the continued examination of social races can we reorient society about human diversity. Social races will always be with us (discussed in concluding chapter) but how we think about them can change.

UPDATE: AFFIRMATIVE ACTION

After examining the concept of race and the repercussions of racism, UNESCO concluded that racism is harmful. It does harm to its victims, corrupts those who participate in it, divides nations internally, and hampers international cooperation. In the United States, affirmative action regulations have been put in place to reduce the destructiveness of racism in the labor market and in higher education. However, the current attack on affirmative action focuses on whether or not such regulation is needed.

There are three arguments for ending affirmative action. Dinesh D'Souza contends that racism has declined since the early 1900s. He argued that while racism continues to exist, it lacks power to prevent minorities from achieving their goals, politically, economically and socially. Instead he asserted that those who have a vested interest in blaming whites for failures among blacks (black civil rights leaders) have created new forms of racism to justify their beliefs (D'Souza, 1995).

The second argument is that the root of the problems among minorities, especially blacks, and is related to their own failures rather than racism. In this argument contemporary discrimination is a reasonable response to "black group traits" that include illegitimacy, criminality, and welfare. D'Souza traces these traits to slavery where he argues that it is understandable that blacks would dislike hard work, have little interest in education, and identify with criminals. However, in a free society, continuation of this culture is dysfunctional and prevents black advancement. According to him, employers who do not hire blacks or offer them mortgages are dealing with the law of averages, not racism (D'Souza, 1995). He seems to be unaware that the labor market has never been an equal opportunity employer. The market in the United States has always benefited from segregation and the disenfranchisement of minorities.

In "Our National Obsession with Race", H. Glynn Custred espoused the third argument. He is in favor of a color-blind society but noted that reverse discrimination toward white Americans is more prevalent than traditional forms of racial discrimination against Latinos and blacks. According to him ...in an attempt to define what is wrong and how to deal with it, we have put our reliance on a reductionist and misguided model based on a national obsession with race"

(1998:17). Custred contended that by being obsessed with race we missed the important class dimension. Assaults on class that whites bear are considered more important than race-specific obstacles of class that racial minorities experience in terms of employment, education, health and accumulation of wealth (Harrison, 1998b, 2000).

In 1978 in the case of Regents of the University of California v. Bakke the Court wavered on Custred's color-blind society. In this case, Allan Bakke, a white man, applied for admission to the medical school at the University of California at Davis in 1972. He was rejected twice. When he learned that 16 of 100 slots in the class were reserved each year for minorities, Bakke, whose academic record was better than those of most of the minority applicants, sued the medical school for racial discrimination (reverse discrimination). In the Supreme Court the Justices were split. Four Justices (William Rehnquist, John Paul Stevens, Potter Stewart and Chief Justice Warren) ruled that the admission policy was unconstitutional. According to them, race can be used to remedy documented discrimination on an individual level, but it could not be used to overcome societal discrimination because the legacy of such discrimination is amorphous and timeless in its reach into the past (Wohl, 2001).

In 1996 California Proposition 209 prevented the state from using race as a factor in admitting students to the University of California system. Two years later Washington followed suite and a year later Florida ended race-based programs in the state's public universities. In Texas in 1996 the U.S. Court of Appeals for the Fifth Circuit in the case of Hopwood v. State of Texas overturned the admissions procedures of the University of Texas law school. The law school had systematically used lower standards for Hispanic and black candidates than whites in their admissions. The Fifth Circuit stated that they violated the Fourteenth Amendment that guaranteed "equal protection of the laws" (which cannot be used to protect minorities against racial profiling). If this decision is supported by the Supreme Court it will end preferential quotas at public universities (Wohl, 2001). The Court did not review Hopwood because the admission program at the University of Texas ended (Riley, 2001).

In "Affirmative Action is Still Needed" Faye V. Harrison (1998b) countered that reverse discrimination is a fallacy. She argued that meritocratic individualism in which deserving individuals should not be oppressed by state regulations that discriminate against the most qualified does not consider that

> ...collective privileges transferred from generations of unequal opportunity are being misrecognized as merely individual achievements gained solely through hard work done on a leveled, colorblind and gender-neutral playing field (1998b:16).

Meritocratic individualism is not subject to systemic inequalities that constrain achievement as among people of color (Harrison, 1998b). Terms such as reverse discrimination, quotas, and maintaining standards implies that remedies for racial inequality will weaken American society as a whole and therefore are part of a new racism (Franklin, 1991). While many believe that structural barriers to black upward mobility no longer exists, studies of black-white mobility indicate that inequities are still based mainly on race (Jaynes and Williams, 1989; Wolpin, 1992; Bowser and Hunt, 1996; Harrison, 1998b).

In the Bakke case, four other Justices (William Brennan, Thurgood Marshall, Harry Blackman, and Byron White) upheld the admission policy (Wohl, 2001; Riley, 2001). The swing vote was Justice Lewis Powell who found common ground by ruling that while the admissions program was illegal, race could be used as a factor in admissions without violating the constitution. Race could be used as a factor such as coming from an underrepresented part of the country because this brings about diversity (Riley, 2001).

Today, college administrators and affirmative action advocates no longer state that affirmative action is needed to overcome the legacy of discrimination but for educational purposes, diversity. Race can be one factor in determining a student's potential to contribute to the diversity without race being the decisive factor. The belief that diversity as a worthy and constitutional goal for institutions of higher education was supported as early as 1954 in Brown v. Board of Education (Wohl, 2001).

In a racially/ethnically diverse society, educators today consider diversity important to creating a learning environment in which all students are prepared to live and work together with people of all races (Bowen and Bok, 1998a). Patricia Gurin reported evidence of a link between education and diversity in a study at the University of Michigan. In particular, she found that diversity helped students to understand differing perspectives, avoid "group" thinking, and appreciate common values. In *The Shape of the River* (1998b) William G. Bowen and Derek Bok (former presidents of Princeton and Harvard, respectively) linked a diverse student body with improved grades and graduation rates.

People assume that if they have high grades and test scores they deserve to be admitted to the university of their choice. Selective colleges do not automatically grant admission for past performance. Rather, using merit means selecting applicants that correspond with the purpose of the organization. This means choosing academically qualified applicants who have the potential to make high grades but who can contribute to the understanding of other students and after graduation contribute to their communities and professions (Bowen and Bok, 1998a, b).

CHAPTER EIGHT

RACE, RACIAL IDENTITIES AND RACISM TODAY

Color is not a human or a personal reality; it is a political reality (James Baldwin)

WHAT IS RACE?

Unlike encounters between physically different people in ancient times, colonization of the New World involved a new form of subjugation, perpetual slavery. With the colonization of the New World, phenotype or color prejudice converged with slavery to make the race concept insidious. Physical appearance was linked with culture, intelligence, and inequality. For Christians, scientific justifications were necessary to provide a rationale for enslavement and acquisition of land and resources outside of Europe. Biological and cultural inferiority of the subjugated was the foundation for this rationale. Subjugation of the biologically inferior for economic gain was considered not only appropriate, but also humane. The development of our current conceptualization of human diversity, races, occurred within this colonial context.

Science followed folk beliefs and provided a scientific rationale for biological inequality and slavery. In so doing, it solidified beliefs about racial groups and justified racial ranking. But does the concept of race have relevance in the modern world? What is that thing called race? Everyone has an answer to that question and everyone can name the race that they belong to. But what is race?

The categories of black, brown, yellow and white are a part of our everyday thinking about people who do not look like us. We think of people in terms of skin color and we associate power or powerlessness, intelligence or lack of intelligence, morality or immorality, criminality or a work ethic with these categories. The roots of these dichotomies have been discussed in previous chapters. Explicit in 'classical' anthropological racial classification is the belief that human variation can be partitioned into discrete categories and that members of these categories possess unique qualities. That is, a particular race is more or less susceptible to specific diseases, criminality, intelligence, promiscuity, et cetera. In other words, we assume that there are fundamental biological differences that produce fundamental social differences between groups and we call these groups races. Three questions are important in determining the relevance of the race concept: 1) Can human variation be partitioned into discrete categories? Or, can a population be biologically separated from other populations; 2) Do populations conform to 'classic' racial traits? 3) Are there qualitative differences between populations?

First, we must determine whether human variability can be partitioned into discrete categories or at least be identified as a separate population. This is central to the race concept for the idea of race implies identifiable biological populations. But, speculation on the origin of races can only demonstrate that a species, *Homo sapiens*, evolved from its predecessor *Homo erectus* about 200,000 years ago in East Africa and spread through Africa, Europe and Asia (Cann, Stoneking, and Wilson, 1987). *Homo sapiens* show great morphological variation but genetic variation between human populations is low. Lewontin (1972), for example, showed that polytypic variation accounts for only 15% of human variability. Of this variation, 6.3% are due to biological diversity while the remaining 8.7% are due to population variation such as nationality.

Mitochondrial DNA (mtDNA) also shows low variation between geographically distant human groups. Using mapping of mtDNA by restriction nucleases, the mean pair-wise difference between human populations is only 0.3%. In other words, the two most divergent humans differ by only two sites in the mtDNA (Stringer and Andrews, 1988). It may be easy to know at a glance that an individual is African, Asian, or Caucasian but the differences dissolve when one scans the genome for DNA hallmarks of race. Based on data from the Human Genome Project, the percentage of genes that reflect the basis for outwardly physical differences between populations account for only .1% of the genome (Angier, 2000). This exemplifies the low level of genetic differentiation within *Homo sapiens*. We are much more similar than different. Low variability within the species prevents the identification of races.

A growing trend among biological anthropologists is the belief in the nonexistence of race as a valid biological category (Livingstone, 1962, 1964; Brace, 1964; Brace, 1982). Analysis of physical variability by clinalists results in identification of overlapping gradients without boundaries between populations (see Figure 8.1). Individual variability overwhelms group differences. For example, there are Caucasians who are darker than some African groups and the same is true for other races (Barnicot, 1964). Since there is greater variation within populations than between them, group differences are very small (Lewontin, 1972).

On the other hand, classifiers believe that, for instance, population B is an intergradation between populations A and C and that there are boundaries between these populations (see Figure 8.1). For them race is the result of adaptation to specific geographical areas, natural selection. But race, a social construct, is inconsistent with evolutionary theory because race is static (three racial groups with associated 'classic' traits) while evolution is an ongoing process (Marshall, 1968; Goodman, 1995). Evolution by natural selection is a slow and ongoing.

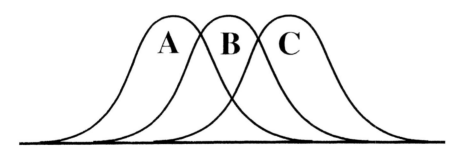

Figure 8.1. Overlapping Distributions

Biological anthropologists are not in agreement over the concept of race. As shown earlier in the chapter on scientific statements, classifiers remain dominant among physical anthropologists while cultural anthropologists lean toward a no-race concept. The difference within biological anthropology lies in the interpretation of overlapping gradients. The Human Genome Project, however, showed that humans have 99.9% of their genes in common. Researchers at the National Institutes of Health have now sequenced the entire human genome and unanimously declared that there is only one race, the human race (Angier, 2000).

Another perspective of race is that it constitutes subspecies within the human species. Ernst Mayr (1982), for instance, stated that a race or subspecies is a geographically localized subdivision of a species that differs from other subdivisions genetically and taxonomically. For him, subspecies occupy a geographical area and are distinguished by physiology, morphology or behavior and must be genetically different from other subspecies. Human races do not conform to these criteria of subspecies. There has always been gene flow between populations so there is no distinct qualitatively different physiology, morphology, or behaviors associated with populations. All characteristics can be found in all populations in varying frequencies.

Templeton (1998) in *Human Races: A Genetic and Evolutionary Perspective* also stated that race is generally used as a synonym for subspecies and that this concept has two meanings. In the traditional definition, subspecies is a population that inhabits a geographically circumscribed area and is genetically differentiated (Smith et al., 1997, Templeton, 1998). The second and modern definition of subspecies is that it is a particular evolutionary line within a species (Shaffer and McKnight, 1996; Templeton, 1998). To examine the traditional subspecies definition of human races, Templeton computed the amount of genetic diversity within and among human populations and found that human genetic diversity was too small to have taxonomic significance. Next, he examined genetic distance measures used to determine if races form distinct evolutionary lineages. He found that "genetic distance analyses strongly and uniformly indicate that human "races" cannot be represented as branches on an evolutionary tree..." (Templeton, 1998:640). Races do not conform to the criterion of subspecies.

Next we must consider if groups conform to 'classic racial' traits. A fundamental belief of racial ideology is that 'classic racial' traits have an original homeland and that the homes of these traits are unique. Such traits found outside the homeland must have gotten there by gene flow or colonization (Keita and Kittles, 1997). But different 'classic racial' traits produce different clinal distributions. Which distribution represents a 'true' race? Is genetic variation for 'classic' racial traits distributed in concordant patterns that correspond to our conception of races as identifiable populations?

What we know is that an individual, for example, can have Asian facial features and an Afro hairstyle or be dark in skin color and have straight hair. When considering blood groups to classify populations, blood type B is more common in African (29%) than European (7-12%) populations but one cannot classify individuals on this basis (Mourant, 1983). These are quantitative differences between populations, not qualitative differences. Examination of blood groups demonstrates that some groups with similar blood type frequencies do not resemble one another in "classical" racial features. For instance, Australian aborigines are similar to American Indians in their low frequencies of the B gene although they are very different in physical characteristics (Zuckerman, 1990).

The bottom line is that "racial traits" are discordant (Molnar, 2002). That is, combinations of "classical" racial traits are not found in all members of a particular racial group because individuals do not conform to group averages. Even a description of races is problematic because all individuals classified in a race will not have all of the racial traits. Human variability is clinal and discordant making racial classification unfeasible and imaginary.

Lastly, are there qualitative differences between populations? As shown earlier, variation within the human species is low and clinal, not discrete. No trait is found in one population that cannot be identified in another population. So there are no qualitative differences between populations. There are only quantitative differences that show a clinal distribution. Different traits will present different distributions. For instance, skin color may have one distribution while tooth size has another. Despite numerous efforts, it has not been demonstrated that characteristics such as intelligence, criminality, promiscuity, or culture are biologically based and that these characteristics conform to racial groupings. These characteristics are exhibited in all populations. Social factors have repeatedly been shown to be better explanations for the frequency and distribution of such traits.

While the term race has been defined and races counted, it is not according to any precise definition or set of rules. It is done any way researchers wish (Lieberman and Reynolds, 1996). Criteria for the identification of races are arbitrary and groups are raced without specifying the reason for the classification. It is simply assumed that biological classification has significant meaning when it is associated with other variables such as disease or intelligence. This goes back to eighteenth century thinking where it was assumed that any variation indicates fundamental differences between populations. The only thing that is evident is that humans vary, not that races exist. Variability does not mean that you have to name races (Gould, 1977). However, we do continue to name races. Why?

RACIAL IDENTITIES

Identity is the way we think about ourselves, the cognitive structure, which gives 'self' unity and social relatedness. Racial identities are the product of learning about 'self' through the enculturation process. Such identities have a number of overlapping social constructions that are fluid and shift with time, vary over space and within differing situational contexts related to power (Omi and Winant, 1994). Power relationships are inherent in the concept of race (Winant, 1994). In particular, since power and capital differentially benefit various sectors of the population around the world (Schiller, 1994), power, or lack of it, is associated with particular races and racial identities.

Racial identities are constructed in at least five ways: 1) through intersections of race, class, gender, and nation; 2) by those in power; 3) in opposition to dominant group ideology; 4) by patterns of sociality; and 5) in everyday experiences. According to Alcoff (1988), identities are constructed relative to your position within a cultural and historical context. This context includes knowledge and discourses related to other people, cultural, political, and economic institutions. Identity, then, is the result of an individual's reconstruction and interpretation of their own history (de Lauretis, 1986). Racial identities, then, are a product of the race concept.

INTERSECTION OF RACE WITH GENDER, CLASS, AND NATION

Gender

Various studies have noted that the intersection of race and gender among whites, for instance females, is nonproblematic in the sense that to be white is to not be concerned about race. However, those who examine whiteness problematicize this intersection. In other words, current research calls for white women to examine their race position and white privilege. As a matter of fact, there has been a general examination of what it means to be white.

On the other hand, race is not problematicized among women of color. It is assumed that they have race consciousness. Paula Stewart Brush (2001) questions this position. Rather, she argues that race consciousness among women of color varies over time, space and contexts. In particular, she examined race consciousness among black women during and after the Civil Rights and Black Power movements. Brush argued that race consciousness developed as a way to resist white oppression. In particular, these movements articulated opposition to a system of racial exclusion. Black people knew how race and racism impacted their lives and how they were victimized and exploited. The "we" was based on race and shared experience of discrimination and oppression (Brush, 2001).

Brush (2001) also contended that responses to racism changed as politics, economies, and domestic relations changed. After the Civil Rights/Black Power movements, the next generation recognized limitation and exclusion as something that others had experienced. It did not apply to them. They had opportunities. Racism became subtle and younger people did not have the strategies developed during the movements to deal with racism. They were caught, for instance, between whites telling them that they were the exception to their race because they were articulate and help that whites offered in terms of school and scholarships. With this dilemma blacks were unsure how to respond. Once again race became problematic.

As Brush (2001) noted, they were "unsure, passive, and polite." They knew that race was an issue but they were unsure how race was an issue. Unlike those in the Civil Rights movement, they did not know how to articulate, resist, and act on their victimization.

Bell hooks (1990) considered racism unproblematic (black women are race conscious) but problematicizes feminism. For example, hooks (1990) argued that black people have a problem denouncing racism simultaneous with black male sexism. Because of white oppression, black women believe that racism is more important than sexism and that the latter must be put on the backburner until white oppression is overcome. Black peoples' connection between racist domination and loss of black manhood is an investment in a sexist ideology (black men should be dominant like white men). As a result, some black people believe that black women's rights cannot be dealt with until the battle against racism is won. Part of the reason for this is that in a white dominated society all women are devalued but white women's bodies are valued more than those of women of color. Fighting color discrimination that affects all members of the race then becomes more important than sexism that affects half of the population (hooks, 1990). The legacy of a racist history and contemporary pervasive racial discrimination contribute to these sentiments between both genders in the black population.

Class

The root of the meshing of race and class can be found in the United States in 1676 with Bacon's Rebellion. In that uprising black servants and poor whites rebelled against the white ruling government. To prevent such coalitions in the future, a divide and conquer strategy was devised where laws were enacted to benefit poor whites and simultaneously restrict the rights of people of color. With the rights of blacks and Native Americans reduced, European ethnic groups coalesced into a white racial identity with high status. Poor whites had privilege by being of European ancestry (Smedley, 1998).

When class and race are examined using class conflict theories, racial conflict is reduced to a form of class conflict either between the ruling class and the proletariat or between two groups of workers. In this model, racism is a function of capitalism and racial oppression is a type of class oppression. The ruling capitalist class, those with power, encourages racism in order to suppress class conflict. In this way the ruling capitalist class controls the working class and increase surplus value from them (Cox, 1948; Wilson, 1996). Since colonialism, employers have benefited from racial conflict in the labor force by eroding labor bargaining power, reducing labor force solidarity, and improving profit margins. White workers also benefit from reduced competition from people of color for higher paying jobs (Baron and Sweezy, 1968; Wilson, 1996).

Michael Reich (1977) provided a similar class conflict theory except the dominant white class benefited and both white and black workers were harmed. For instance, it was the planter class who promoted racist hysteria against the populist movement that promoted racial coalitions between poor black and white farmers. Planters also instituted the debt peonage system, retarded the economic development of the south and contributed to poverty and illiteracy in the south. Such arrangements hurt both poor blacks and whites (Reich, 1981).

Edna Bonacich (1976) examined the relation between race and class using split labor market theory. The split labor market began during slavery and is characterized by low price wage to black laborers compared to the wage of white laborers, holding productivity and efficiency constant. Managers exploit this differential by using blacks as strikebreakers or by substituting cheap black labor for more expensive white labor resulting in aggravated racial tensions.

White workers respond in two ways: either exclude blacks altogether or maintain a racial caste system to prevent employers from hiring cheap black workers for more costly white workers. Both responses subordinate black labor and maintain a racial caste in labor (Wilson, 1996).

Racial conflict is both similar and different from class conflict. There are similarities between the two in terms of racial and class exploitation but racial oppression involves sociopsychogical processes and cultural forms different from class dynamics. For instance, racial prejudice provides an identifiable subordinate group to be a scapegoat for others to feel superior and to release frustrations on (Wilson, 1996).

Nation

Race is based upon shared biological descent and history. The foundation of nationality is also descent and history. Therefore, race and nationality share collections of qualities, both physically and culturally and descendants of races perpetuate these qualities. Nations use race to flourish and identify not only physically but also spiritually. Common biological descent and shared culture form the background for a pseudoscientific belief in the connection between race and nation. It also leads to racism between nations that lead inevitably to racism within nations (Balibar, 1990, 1991).

Another way to investigate the relationship between race and nations is through an examination of the world economic system. Division of labor in the world-economy produced a spatial and racial division of labor. Historically there was an expansion of capitalist world economy from Europe to the United States. Core processes occurred in these areas with peripheral and semiperipheral processes in the rest of the world (corresponding to the Third World) (Wallerstein, 1991). Core processes produce high technology goods for exportation and the core controls operations in the periphery and semiperiphery. Peripheral processes are more labor intensive than the semiperipheral and are associated with primary production such as agriculture and mining. The semiperiphery is intermediate between the periphery and the core. Like core nations the semiperipheral is industrialized and exports goods but like the peripheral nations lacks power and the economic domination of core nations. The interaction between the periphery and core or semiperiphery and core is exploitative where economic relations tend to benefit capitalists in the core at the expense of the other areas (Shannon, 1996). The race concept developed in core nations and focused on these disparate geographical areas and type of economic processes. Races and nations, such as many members of the United Nations, were created to support this world economy (Wallerstein, 1991).

CONSTRUCTION OF RACIAL IDENTITIES BY THOSE IN POWER

Racial ideologies are constructed and made real by those in power (Comaroff and Comaroff, 1991; Omi and Winant, 1994; Sacks, 1994; Smedley, 1998). The dominant population therefore determines racial categories and assigns values to those categories. Formation of racial identity involves institutions such as state activity and policy where the state treats people unequally and aids racial discrimination. Power, then, is an important factor in racial boundaries (Omi and Winant, 1994).

Racial identity developed with the convergence of skin color prejudice, slavery and the power associated with this process in the New World (Drake 1987, 1990). In that context, it emerged as a social category derived from the antagonistic relation of black oppression and white supremacy (Krieger and Bassett, 1986). Race, then, is a sociohistorical concept and racial identities have meaning because of the social relations and historical context embedded in them that can vary over time and space.

The history of slavery is the most illuminating example of the creation of race by a dominant group. Those in power created the concept of race to support the institution of slavery and to expand capitalism. With slavery came the identification of a specific group as biologically inferior and therefore necessitating subjugation. Native Americans experienced the same type of racial configuration related to the acquisition of their land. New World populations were classified as white, black and brown and later yellow, when Chinese were used as cheap laborers. Economics, power and domination interacted to produce racial categories that are imbedded in our psyches today.

Frankenberg (1993) discussed the intersection of race, class and gender by examining white female construction of whiteness. Middle-class white females constructed whiteness in relation to non-whiteness based upon what Frankenberg calls the "colonial discourse." That is, white women constructed whiteness in terms of power gained through colonial exploitation. To be white is to be dominant and to be nonwhite is to lack power. Also, colonial exploitation created an inferior Other, people of African descent. Whites constructed their identity in opposition to the inferior. Lastly, to be white is to lack culture. The 'others' (such as ethnics or minorities) have customs and are culturally distinct. To be white then is not to be a number of other things, that is, not powerless, inferior, or culture-oriented. *Whiteness only has meaning in opposition to others.* These middle-class white women might be expected to be liberal thinkers because of their professed commitments to antiracism and multiculturalism but power, gained through colonialism, is their signifier of whiteness and provides the basis for their racial identity.

Sacks (1994) provided an historical perspective on the construction of race by a dominant group in her article entitled "How Did Jews Become White Folks"? She argued that Jewish whiteness was due to historical timing. But it was also due to U.S. institutions that capitalized on the skills of Jews and thereby assimilated them into the dominant population. For example, during WWII Jews were the only ones from eastern and southern Europe who came from urban, manufacturing and commercial backgrounds, such as the garment industry. Their education and assimilation were related to the government's need for these skills during and after the war. Economic development in the United States was aided by the skills of Jews. This was the backdrop for the whitening of Jews.

Prior to WWII immigrants from southern and eastern Europe were categorized as ethnic whites. After the war, as a response to Nazism and Fascism, there was a more inclusive definition of whiteness. Affirmative action for old and new whites allowed Jews to obtain the best or better jobs, to receive low-interest loans to buy homes in the suburbs, acquire a skilled or college education, and to become a prosperous middle class. Through U.S. government aid Jews gained economic affluence and were reclassified as white. ...."The old white and the newly white masses became middle class" (Sacks, 1994:88).

Accessing power is part of the socialization process among people of European ancestry.

> Despite its uneven development and varying systematization, racism is characterized by an international hierarchy in which wealth, power, and advanced development are associated largely with whiteness or "honorary whiteness" (Harrison, 1995:50).

Through the socialization process and social-psychological development most white Americans learn the superior status of whites relative to people of color (Jones and Wilson, 1996). According to Frankenberg (1993) the enculturation of whites involves learning that they have power because they are dominant and superior.

FORMATION OF RACIAL IDENTITIES IN OPPOSITION TO THOSE IN POWER

Racialized and nonelite groups acquire, contest and transform racial ideologies to form identities in opposition to those in power (Sacks 1988; Sivanandan 1982; Gregory, 1994; Y. Jones, 1997). For example, in contemporary British society cultural and political movements between Afro-Caribbean and Asian youth adopted the term black to express self-identity. Black is a signifier of oppression and refers to all nonwhites (Omi and Winant, 1994).

In New York a subordinated group (African Americans) generated cultural meanings that were in opposition to dominant power relations and ideologies. That is, negative stereotypes presented by white residents, city officials and the media about African Americans were challenged by a black grass-roots organization. While whites perceived black youths to be a threat to the well being of the community, black community activists showed that these youths were not the perpetrators but the victims of that stereotype. In response to negative perceptions by those in power, the grass-roots organization presented positive contributions by these youth in the rebuilding of that community. Black residents resisted the framing of their community in negative stereotypes of the black poor by rearticulating their community as stable and working class (Gregory, 1994).

Y. Jones (1997) also provided an example of racial identity constructed in opposition to those in power. She examined African-American cultural nationalism in Louisville, Kentucky. Here an examination of a local chapter of a scholarly voluntary association organized by African-Americans framed racial identity in a diasporic posture that related Africans and African Americans as the victims of European exploitation. They attempted to undo the negative images created by white Americans and to focus on unrecognized and little discussed contributions by Africans to the development of society. In doing this, African-American Louisvillians developed their own racial identity that was positive amidst numerous negative images by the dominant population.

SOCIALITY

Y. Jones' (1997) article also revealed the social aspect of racial identity. Knowing that negative stereotypes are not representative of African Americans, Kwanzaa and the voluntary associations are celebrations of a positive history and provide group cohesion and solidarity. As Mullings (1978) stated, the symbolic-cognitive part of ethnicity can be utilized to promote social cohesion and resistance to the dominant group. The basis for sociality among African Americans is their commitment to blackness that is rooted in the experiences of Africans in the slave trade and the development of the one-drop rule that posits that anyone of African ancestry is black (R. Jones, 1997). The one-drop rule and racism produced a social and political connection among all people of the African diaspora. This connection is celebrated on special holidays, festivals, and in political, social and economic movements. Black racial identity and solidarity have been in response to the common oppression experienced by people of African descent around the world (Harrison, 1995).

EVERYDAY EXPERIENCES

Everyday experiences also contribute to the formation of racial identity. In the United States race is so ubiquitous that the first thing one notices when meeting a person is their race. When race is identified it is assumed that we know something about the individual. Everyone has preconceived racialized ideas about other races. This can result in, for example, a black man being arrested while jogging through an upper-class-white neighborhood that he lives in. It is assumed that he must be a criminal or that he does not live in that community. We expect differences in skin color to explain non-genetic characteristics (Omi and Winant, 1994).

RACE AND RACIAL IDENTITY

Everyone has a racial identity. But racial identities are not mirror images of racial classifications. The latter have more stability while the former are fluid. Racial identity is fluid because meanings and identities are contested throughout social life. Identities are contested because there is continual conflict over access to economic and political resources (Winant, 1984; Omi and Winant, 1994).

While racial meanings, hierarchies and classification can change, this fluidity is constrained by 'poles of difference' that remain constant: white supremacy and black subordination. This opposition is the stabilizer for a U.S. racialized society (Harrison, 1995). For example, in figure 8.1 consider population A to be black and population C as the white distribution. These poles are considered stable and separate although they overlap. Most instability is between the poles (population B). For instance, racially oppressed immigrants can achieve upward social mobility and intermarry if they reposition themselves above the bottom group(s) (Sanjek, 1994). These 'model minorities' are different from dominant whites but are considered to have transcendable differences, for example, Asian or Egyptian immigrants (Harrison, 1995). Those in power, population C, determine the value and ranking attached to the middle population. This suggests that the hierarchy for racial groups is changeable for some groups but stable for others (black and white at the ends of the poles).

While the poles are stable and those in power determine group position, individual identities are fluid. An individual could have a phenotype that places them in population C but their racial identification is with population A. Twine (1997) provided an excellent example of African-American females who acquired a white cultural identity prior to attending college at UC-Berkeley. Class, in terms of identification with middle- and upper-middle-class segments of segregated suburban U.S. European American communities, was a major factor in black female youths acquiring a white racial identity. Also important was living in a European American environment that was racially and culturally neutral. The main factor in their shift from a white to a black racial identity was the campus socialization process at UC-Berkeley where students of African ancestry pressured them to claim their black racial identity. This study shows that individual racial identity can change during the course of one's life.

There is a wide range of variation, for example, among people classified as Asian that could span, for instance, populations A, B and C (Figure 8.1). They may be able to change their rank between the poles of black and white. Their identity as Asian is not due to biology or to cultural sameness but is related to accessing political and economic power. Pan-ethnicity such as the experiences of Asians or Latinos is a sociopolitical construction that is not based on cultural or biological sameness. Rather, it is an expedient strategy for consolidating effective political power (Harrison, 1995).

According to Omi and Winant (1994) race is central in social relations. It supersedes other identities. As such, we find ways to justify its existence and therefore our existence as racial beings. Although racial identities are fluid, because they are socially constructed, racial identities will always exist in some form as a part of our social lives.

RACISM

Although the biological concept of race is scientifically insignificant, racism as an unscientific spin-off of the race concept is of enormous social significance (Reynolds and Lieberman, 1996). Throughout this book I have argued that scientific justification for the social construction of race changed over time and along with it the rationale for racism. Classic anthropological race is the partitioning of overlapping human variation into discrete categories, called races, for historical, social, political, and economic reasons. It is a social construct that is not found in nature. Racism is the subjugation of a group on the basis of physical appearance or other purported 'natural' or biological differences for the same reasons. The two concepts are permanently related because racism is based on the belief that *Homo sapiens* are composed of distinct groups (races) with different biological characteristics and that races can be ranked. While some scientists (e.g. Kroeber, 1923; Herskovits, 1928; Montagu, 1960, Tobias, 1970; and Gould, 1978) have used the race category without ranking, this volume illustrates many historical (White, 1795; Morton, 1839, 1844; Nott and Glidden, 1854; Ripley, 1899) and contemporary (e.g., Rushton, 1997, 1999; Herrnstein and Murray, 1995) examples of populations being ranked.

Winant (1994) believes that racism is permanent whether or not physical or ideological races exist. According to him race is embedded in our psyche and is not likely to disappear. Sanjek (1994) also noted that race is ingrained in the American psyche. Acknowledging the colonial origin and growth of race in the ... "conquest, dispossession, enforced transportation, and economic exploitation of human beings over five centuries ago"... he believes the legacy of this is the acceptance of ... "inherited racial categories as fixed in nature, and to interpret the systemic inequalities of racist social orders as based on "real" differences among "real" races" (Sanjek, 1994:2). Acceptance of 'real differences among real races' is a way for the dominant group to maintain privilege. Those in power have a vested interest in the race concept, and this, in turn, will maintain racism.

Gilroy (1991) stated that racism is now more subtle and elusive. Blatant racism has been transformed into subtle and complex systematic white preference (Jones and Wilson, 1996). While racial epithets justifying racial oppression may not be evident, new code words are operating to justify racism such as quotas, reverse discrimination, maintaining standards, and cultural fundamentalism. Stolcke (1995) contended that cultural fundamentalism emphasizes differences in cultural heritage. It is assumed that relations between different cultures are naturally hostile because it is human nature to be xenophobic or ethnocentric. In cultural fundamentalism, there is a masking of an uncomfortable topic, race, for something more palatable, culture, class or gender.

Muir (1993) distinguished between "mean racists" and "kind racists." The latter do not mean to hurt although, as a professor of mine once said, their research orientation lends itself to racism. "Kind racists" facilitate the work of "mean racists" who intentionally, and with self-righteousness, search for theories and methodologies that will produce data to support their racist worldview. The end result of both types of racists is the same, racism. It is ugly and results in poorer health status, inequality in housing, education, and occupation for subordinated groups regardless of whether it is "kind" or "mean."

Pervasive racism in the United States is a likely source for the maintenance of the race concept in the scientific community as well as in the general population. Curtin (1960) outlines three schools of racist thought. The first is the teleological view that states that God created humans unequal and that inequalities have a purpose. Blacks were created to serve as laborers for whites who are the managers. Another view is the evolutionary one that all races are in competition and the weaker will ultimately die out to make room for the stronger (social Darwinism). The third view is a combination of the others with elements of Christian tradition added. In this view non-whites are considered barbarians and culturally inferior but they are still deserving of Christian charity. Whites have an obligation to take care of the inferior races. The British Empire was built on the presumption that natives were incapable of governing themselves and needed parental authority by the colonizers (Metress, 1993).

Racism is maintained in American society because it has certain functions. First, is the profit factor where some members of one group benefit economically at the expense of other groups. For example, poor whites profited from better jobs at the expense of poor blacks while wealthy whites profited at the expense of both groups. Second, racism promotes mutual hostility and distrust among the working class and deflects hostility from the ruling class. Third, racism discourages the subordinate group from struggling against their position (internalized racism). Lastly, racism provides a moral justification for systematic disprivilege and exploitation. While racism is built on an invalid biological concept, race, it does not make racism nonexistent. Racism will continue to increase because of economic and political competition between groups (Metress, 1993).

Collective racism is the product of individual racism and both produce institutional and scientific racism. As stated in the introduction, these forms of racism are learned and shared by members of a society. They are a part of the culture of racism and as such are transmitted from one generation to the next. Since race is socially constructed it too will be transmitted from generation to generation in support of racism.

UNLEARNING RACISM

What is evident about racism is that it exists in an environment of unfamiliarity. Unfamiliarity does not mean that people of diverse ancestries do not interact with one another. They may work or attend school together on a daily basis. However, such interaction does not mean they are familiar with one another in terms of culture and social life. If we are to tackle racism and bring about increased understanding we must become familiar with one another outside of work and school. When I attended high school during the first year of integration in Birmingham, I was friends with white students but we never visited one another's homes. For instance, I was in the band and by my senior year it was half black and half white. We were friends and interacted at school and even on band trips, but we never went to one another's homes. It was never discussed. It was just understood. I do not know how it was understood other than the fact that it was not discussed and it was not perceived as a problem. So there was some kind of anonymous friendship or something along that line. Another example is the prom. Even at the prom there was separateness. Blacks danced in a group and whites danced in a separate group. During the prom the two groups sort of merged to some degree and it was a shock. As soon as everyone realized we were dancing together, they immediately began to separate. It was like a no-no, you are not supposed to do that.

How are we to unlearn racism if we do not know one another? I do not think we can. There are two theoretical approaches to reducing prejudice and discrimination. One is conflict theory, which emphasizes that since there are power and value differences between the dominant and subordinate groups, social conflict is a normal consequence of these differences. According to this model, the only way to reduce prejudice and discrimination is to force the dominant group to change through legal measures, such as affirmative action, laws, and protest (McLemore and Romo, 1998). These methods have been used in the United States with some success. However, racism continues although its form has changed from overt racism to subtle and symbolic forms.

The other approach is consensus theory, which emphasizes commonalties between different groups in terms of basic values and norms. In this approach, intergroup contact, vicarious learning (empathize with others through films, books), and education such as classes on racism and workshops are promoted (McLemore and Romo, 1998). People typically discuss diversity workshops.

However, they can only be influential if they are taken on an ongoing basis. That is, we cannot change ourselves overnight. For example, I evaluated an HIV community planning committee and found that there was racial strife within the committee that prevented them from doing the work. We held a diversity workshop that was helpful, but the issues were broader than a single workshop could deal with. For instance, there was a history of distrust because of events prior to the civil rights period, some white participants questioned that they live in all white neighborhoods (does this mean that I'm a racist), and others initially considered themselves exceptions, and not racists, and later began to question this. Participants needed time to absorb what they learned and time to reflect on their lives. Workshops need to take a long-term approach. That is exactly what occurs at the *Center for Racial Healing* in Houston where people examine various aspects and expressions of racism in a ten-week workshop (that are ongoing). I attended it and I know that it widened my perspective and made me more aware of how and why racial antagonisms continue to exist.

Other approaches could increase familiarity outside of work and school, the typical areas of interaction. For instance, communities with predominantly different racial/ethnic groups could become sister communities. In that way, they can understand the issues of the other community and become familiar with their residents. Also, just as people form pen pals with people overseas, this can happen between people of different ancestries in the United States. For instance, this project could take place between elementary schools. Over time, this could result in an exchange similar to cultural exchanges with people abroad where they live with a family for a period of time. In this way, they can learn about another culture within the United States. People in the United States need more than interaction to create understanding, they need familiarity and these are a few ways that it might occur.

Besides the types of exchanges discussed above, billboards, advertisements, and commercials can also be used to allow people to see another perspective of the 'other.' For instance, in commercials people, young and old, could discuss racism. Americans are very visual, so billboards on buses, trains, et cetera could also be used. I think a variety of media sources could be used in a variety of ways such as 'hard hitting' while others are subtle, for example, depicting two people saying "I'm happy we're friends." Just as this country has had a war on poverty and war on drugs, we can have a war on racism.

I am reminded of an episode of *Northern Exposure* in which Marilyn tells Joel the story of Death (supposedly a Native American tale). In the story Death took the Chief's daughter as his wife. The Chief was mean and the wife pretended to be a good wife but she fed him pumpkinseeds. Eventually the pumpkinseeds swelled inside him and made his body explode and pumpkinseeds scattered everywhere. The moral is that good things, pumpkinseeds, can come from bad things, death. While the history of U.S. race relations is a continual cause of anger and shame among Americans, maybe we should concentrate on the pumpkinseeds, diversity and the positive images that go with it within our society, and capitalize on that diversity rather than viewing it in negative terms.

FOOTNOTE

[1]In order to combat racial profiling the ACLU has a website where users can file an electronic Driver Profiling Complaint Form and they can download a "Bustcard", a pocket guideline dealing with police encounters that advise citizens about their rights when stopped by police officers (Beck and Daly, 1999).

REFERENCES

Alcoff, Linda. 1988. "Cultural Feminism versus Post-structuralism: The Identity Crisis in Feminist Theory." In: *The Second Wave: A Reader in Feminist Theory.* Linda Nicholson (ed). Pp 330-55. New York: Routledge.

Alexis, M., Haines, G.H., and L.S. Simon. 1980 *Black Consumer Profiles.* Ann Arbor, Mi: Division of Research, Graduate School of Business Administration, University of Michigan.

Allison, A.C. 1954a. "Protection Afforded by Sickle-Cell Trait Against Malarial Infection." *British Medical Journal* 1:290-294.

————.1954b. "The Distribution of the Sickle-Cell Trait in East Africa and Elsewhere, and Its Apparent Relationship to the Incidence of Subtertian Malaria." *Transactions of the Royal Society of Tropical Medicine and Hygiene* 48:312-318.

————. 1954c. "Notes on Sickle-Cell Polymorphism." *Annals of Human Genetics* 19:39-57.

Alvarez, R. 1994. "Un Chilero en la Academia: Sifting, Shifting, and the Recruitment of Minorities in Anthropology." In: *Race.* S. Gregory and R. Sanjek (eds.). Pp 257-69. New Brunswick, NJ: Rutgers University Press.

American Anthropological Association. 1939. "1938 Resolution on Race." *Science* 89(2298):30.

————.1956. "Resolution to Forgo Meeting in Georgia." *American Anthropological Association Bulletin* 4(2):4.

————.1962. "Resolution: Race (Executive Board)." *American Anthropologist* 64:616-17.

————.1969a. "Resolution: Racial Inferiority." *Anthropology Report,* Pp 39-40.

————. 1969b. "Resolution: Minorities in Anthropology." *Anthropology Report,* P 37.

————.1971. "Theories of Racial, Sexual and Class Inferiority." *Anthropology Report,* Pp 40-41.

————.1972a. "Against the Killings at Southern University." *Anthropology Report,* P 58.

————.1972b. "Against Racist Distortion in Scientific Discourse." *Anthropology Report,* P 59.

————.*1972c.* "A Reply to "Hereditary Reasoning" and Racist Distortion." *Anthropology Report,* P 59.

————.1995. "AAA Resolution on "Race" and Intelligence." *Anthropology Newsletter/January.*

————.1997. "Response to OMB Directive 15: Race and Ethnic Standards for Federal Statistics and Administrative Reporting, Executive Summary." *Chronicle of Higher Education,* Electronic Version.

————.1998. "AAA Statement on Race." *American Anthropologist* 100(3):712-713.

American Association for the Advancement of Science. 1963. "Science and the Race

Problem: A Report of the AAAS Committee on Science in the Promotion of Human Welfare." *Science* 142:558-561.

American Association of Physical Anthropologists. 1962. "American Physical Anthropologists Condemn Racism." *Current Anthropology* 3(4):445.

———.1996. "AAPA Statement on Biological Aspects of Race." *American Journal of Physical Anthropology* 101:569-570.

Anderson, R.M., Giachello, A.L., and L.A. Aday. 1986. "Access of Hispanics to Health Care and Cuts in Services: a State-of-the Art Overview." *Public Health Report* 101:238-252.

Angier, Natalie. 2000." Do Races Differ? Not Really, DNA Shows." *Nytimes.com/library/national/science/082200sci-genetics-race.*

Armelagos, G. 1995. "Race, Reason, and Rationale." *Evolutionary Anthropology* 4:103-109.

Aristotle. 1969. *Politics and Poetic.* Translated by Benjamin Jowett and Thomas Twining. New York: Viking.

Baker, L. 1998a. "Over a Cliff or into a Brick Wall." *Anthropology Newsletter* 39(1):16-17.

Baker, L. 1998b. *From Negro to Savage: Anthropology and the Construction of Race.* Berkeley, Ca: University of California Press.

Baker, Paul T. 1958. "The Biological Adaptation of Man to Hot Deserts." *American Nature* 92:337-357.

——— 1959. "American Negro-White Differences in the Thermal Insulative Aspects of Body Fat." *Human Biology* 31:316-324.

———.1966. "Human Biological Variation as an Adaptive Response to the Environment." *Eugenics Quarterly* 13:81-91.

———.1975. "The Place of Physiological Studies in Anthropology." In: *Physiological Anthropology.* Albert Damon (ed.). Pp 3-12. Oxford: Oxford University Press.

Balibar, Etienne. 1990. " Paradoxes of Universality." In: *Anatomy of Racism.* T. Goldberg (ed.). Pp 283-94. Minneapolis, Mn: University of Minnesota Press.

———.1991. "Is There a 'Neo-Racism'?" In: *Race, Nation, Class: Ambiguous Identities.* Etienne Balibar and Immanuel Wallerstein (eds.). Pp 15-28. New York: Verso.

Banton, M. 1996. *International Action Against Racial Discrimination.* Oxford: Clarendon Press.

Banton, M. and J. Harwood. 1975. *The Race Concept.* London: David and Charles.

Barkan, E. R .1992. *The Retreat of Scientific Racism.* New York: Cambridge University Press.

———.1996. *And Still They Come: Immigrants and American Society, 1920 to the 1990s.* Wheeling, Il: H. Davidson.

Barkow, J.H. 1978. "Culture and Sociobiology." *American Anthropologist* 80:5-20.

Barkow, J.H., Cosmides, L., and J. Tooby. 1992. *The Adapted Mind: Evolutionary Psychology and the Generation of Culture.* New York: Oxford University Press.

Barnicott, N.A. 1964. "Taxonomy and Variation in Modern Man." In: *The Concept of Race.* A. Montagu (ed.). Pp. 180-227. Westport, Ct: Greenwood Press.

Baron, P. And P. Sweezy. 1968. *Monopoly Capital: An Essay on the American Economic and Social Order.* New York: Monthly Review Press.

Barth, F. 1969. *Ethnic Groups and Boundaries: The Social Organization of Culture Difference.* Boston, Ma: Little, Brown and Company.

Beck, P.W. and P.A. Daly. 1999. "State Constitutional Analysis of Pretext Stops: Racial Profiling and Public Policy Concerns." *Temple Law Review* 72:597-618.

Bennett, R.A. 1971. "Africa and the Biblical Period." *Harvard Theological Review* 64:483-500.

Bermer, P. 1998. "The Other and the Almost Same." In: *Blacks and Jews: Alliances and Arguments*. P. Berman (ed.). Pp 1-28. New York: Delacorte Press.

Berlin, I. 1998. *Many Thousands Gone: The First Two Centuries of Slavery in North America*. London: Harvard University Press.

Bernal, M. 1997. "Race in History." In: *Global Convulsions: Race, Ethnicity, and Nationalism at the End of the Twentieth Century*. Winston A. Van Horne (ed.). Pp 75-92. New York: State University of New York Press.

Bitsakis, E. 1987-1988. "For an Evolutionary Epistemology." *Science and Society* 51(4):389-413.

Blakey, M. 1987. "Skull Doctors: Intrinsic Social and Political Bias in the History of American Physical Anthropology; with Special Reference to the Work of Ales Hrdlicka." *Critique of Anthropology* 7(2):7-35.

Blassingame, J.W. 1972. *The Slave Community: Plantation Life in the Antebellum South*. London: Oxford University Press.

Blendon, R.J., Aiken, L.H., Freeman, H.E., and C.R. Corey. 1989. "Access to Medical Care for Black and White Americans. A Matter of Continuing Concern." *Journal of the American Medical Association* 261:278-281.

Blumenbach, Johann Friedrich. 1795 [1969]. *On the Natural Varieties of Mankind*. New York: Bergman Publishers.

Bonacich, E. 1976. "Advanced Capitalism and Black/White Race Relations in the United States: A Split Labor Market Interpretation." *American Sociological Review* 41(February): 34-51.

Boudon, R. And F. Bourricaud. 1989. *A Critical Dictionary of Sociology*. Chicago, Il: University of Chicago Press.

Bowen, William G. and D. Bok. 1998a. "Get In, Get Ahead: Here's Why." *The Washington Post*, September 20.

———— 1998b. *The Shape of the River: Long-Term Consequences of Considering Race in College and University Admissions*. Princeton, NJ: Princeton University Press.

Bowser, B.P. and R.G. Hunt (eds.). 1996. "Preface." In: *Impacts of Racism on White Americans*. Pp ix-xxvii. Thousand Oaks, Ca: Sage Publications.

Boyd, W.C. 1949. "Systematics, Evolution, and Anthropology in the Light of Immunology." *Quarterly Review of Biology* 24(1): 102-108.

Boyd, W.C. 1950. *Genetics and the Races of Man*. Boston, Ma: Little, Brown and Company.

Brace, C. Loring. 1964. On the Concept of Race. *Current Anthropology* 5(4):313-320.

———— .1982a. "Comments on Redefining Race: The Potential Demise of a Concept in Physical Anthropology." *Current Anthropology* 23:648-649.

Brace, C.L., Tracer, D.P., Yaroch, L.A., Robb, J., Brandt, K. and A.R. Nelson. 1993. "Clines and Clusters versus "Race": A Test in Ancient Egypt and the Case of a Death on the Nile" *Yearbook of Physical Anthropology* 36:1-31.

Brandt, A.M. 1978. "Racism and Research: The Case of the Tuskegee Syphilis Study." *The Hastings Center* 8:21-29.

Briggs, L.C. 1960. *Tribes of the Sahara*. Cambridge, Ma: Harvard University Press.

Brinton, Daniel G. 1890. *Race and People: Lectures on the Science of Ethnography*.

New York: N.D.C. Hodges

Brodkin, K. 1997. "Race and Gender in the Construction of Class." *Science and Society* 60(4):471-477.

———— .2001. "Diversity in Anthropological Theory." In: *Cultural Diversity in the United States.* I. Susser and T. Patterson (eds.). Pp 365-388. Malden, Ma: Blackwell.

Brown, Donald E. 1991. *Human Universals.* Philadelphia, Pa: Temple University Press.

Brues, Alice. 1977. *People and Races.* New York: Macmillan Publishing Co., Inc.

Brush, P.S. 2001. "Problematizing the Race Consciousness of Women of Color." *Signs: Journal of Women in Culture and Society* 27:171-99.

Buck, Pem D. 1992. "With Our Heads in the Sand: the Racist Right, Concentration Camps, and the Incarceration of People of Color." *Transforming Anthropology* 3(1): 13-18.

Buffon, Georges Louis Leclerc, Count de Buffon. 1791. *Natural History, General and Particular.* Translated by William Smellie, 2000. Vol. 2. Bristol, England: Thoemmes Press.

Bullard, R.D. 1983. "Solid Waste Sites and the Black Houston Community." *Sociological Inquiry* 53:273-288.

Bureau of Public Affairs. 1988. *Universal Declaration of Human Rights: 40th Anniversary.* United States: Department of State.

Burger, J. 1988. "Indigenous People: New Rights for Old Wrongs". In: *Human Rights.* P. Davies (ed.). Pp 99-110. New York: Routledge.

Buss, D.M. 1989. "Sex Differences in Human Mate Preferences: Evolutionary Hypotheses Tested in 37 Cultures." *Behavioral and Brain Sciences* 12(1):1-49.

———— .1995. "Evolutionary Psychology: A New Paradigm for Psychological Science." *Psychological Inquiry* 6(1):1-30.

Buss, D.M, Abbot, M., Angleitner, A., Asherian, A. et al .1990. "International Preferences in Selecting Mates: A Study of 37 Cultures." *Journal of Cross-Cultural Psychology* 21(1):5-47.

Cancela ,V. De La. 1989. "Minority AIDS Prevention: Moving Beyond Cultural Perspectives Towards Sociopolitical Empowerment." *AIDS Education and Prevention* 1:141-153.

Cann, R.L., Stoneking, M., and A.C. Wilson. 1987. "Mitochondria DNA and Human Evolution." *Nature* 325:31-36.

Caplan, A. L. 1984. "Sociobiology as a Strategy in Science." *The Monist* 67:143-160.

Carlisle, D.M., Leake, B.D., and M.F. Shapiro. 1997. "Racial and Ethnic Disparities in the Use of Cardiovascular Procedures: Associations with Type of Health Insurance." *American Journal of Public Health* 87:263-267.

Carmichael, S. and C.V. Hamilton. 1967. *Black Power.* New York: Random House.

Carson, Clayborne. 1998. "The Politics of Relations Between African-Americans and Jews. In: *Blacks and Jews: Alliances and Arguments.* P. Berman (ed). Pp 131-143. New York: Delacorte Press.

Carter, R.T. and A.L. Goodwin. 1994. "Racial Identity and Education." In: *Review of Research in Education.* L.Darling-Hammond (ed.). Vol. 20, Pp. 291-335. Washington, D.C.: American Educational Research Association.

Cartmill, M. 1998. "The Status of the Race Concept in Physical Anthropology." *American Anthropologist* 100(3):651-660.

Cavalli, Sforza, L.L. and W.F. Bodmer. 1971. *The Genetics of Human Populations.* San Francisco, Ca: W.H. Freeman and Company.

Cell, J.W. 1982. *The Highest Stage of White Supremacy: The Origins of Segregation in South Africa and the American South.* Cambridge, UK: Cambridge University Press.

Chalmers, D.M. 1987. *Hooded Americanism: the History of the Ku Klux Klan.* Durham, NC: Duke University Press.

Chanes, Jerome A. 1997. "Affirmative Action: Jewish Ideals, Jewish Interests." In: *Struggles in the Promised Land: Toward a History of Black-Jewish Relations in the United States.* J. Salzman and C. West (eds.). Pp 295-321. Oxford: Oxford University Press.

Charles, P. 1928. "Les noirs, fils de Cham le maudit." *Nouvelle Revue Theologique* 55:721-739.

Chase, Allan. 1980. *The Legacy of Malthus: The Social Costs of the New Scientific Racism.* Urbana, Il: University of Illinois Press.

Commission for Racial Justices. 1987. *Toxic Wastes and Race in the United States: A National Report on the Racial and Socioeconomic Characteristics of Communities with Hazardous Waste Sites.* New York: United Church of Christ.

Cole, David. 1999. "Discretion and Discrimination Reconsidered: A Response to the New Criminal Justice Scholarship." *Georgia Law Journal* 87: 1059, 1077-78.

Cole, Johnnetta B. 1992. "Foreword: The South in the US and US in the South." In: *African Americans in the South: Issues of Race, Class and Gender.* Hans A. Baer and Yvonne Jones (eds). Pp. Vi-xii. Athens, Ga: University of Georgia Press.

Comaroff, J. and J. Comaroff. 1991. *Of Revelation and Revolution: Christianity, Colonialism, and Consciousness in South Africa.* Vol. 1. Chicago, Il: University of Chicago Press.

Coon, C. S. 1962. *The Origin of Races.* New York: Alfred A. Knopf, Inc.

————.1964. "Comment: On the Race Concept, by C.L. Brace." *Current Anthropology* 5:314.

Cooper, R. 1984. "A Note on the Biologic Concept of Race and its Application in Epidemiologic Research." *American Heart Journal* 108:715-23.

————.1994. "A Case Study in the Use of Race and Ethnicity in Public Health Surveillance." *Public Health Report* 109:46-51.

Cooper, R., Steinhauer, M., Miller, W., David, R., and A. Schatzkin. 1981. "Racism, Society, and Disease: An Exploration of the Social and Biological Mechanisms of Differential Mortality." *International Journal of Health Services* 11(3):389-414.

Cooper, R. And R. David. 1986. "The Biological Concept of Race and its Application to Public Health and Epidemiology." *Journal of Health Politics, Policy and Law* 11(1):97-116.

Copher, C.B. 1986. "3,000 Years of Biblical Interpretation with Reference to Black Peoples." *The Journal of Interdenominational Theological Center* 13(2):225-246.

Cosmides, L., and J. Tooby. 1987. "From Evolution to Behavior: Evolutionary Psychology as the Missing Link." In: *The Latest on the Best on Evolution and Optimality.* J. Dupre (ed.). Pp. 277-306. Cambridge, Ma: MIT Press.

Council on Ethical and Judicial Affairs. 1990. "Black-White Disparities in Health Care." *Journal of the American Medical Association* 263:2344-2346.

Cox, O.C. 1948. *Caste, Class and Race: A Study in Social Dynamics.* New York: Monthly Review Press.

Cravens, H. 1996. "Scientific Racism in Modern America, 1870s-1990s." *Prospects* 21: 471-490.

Curtin, P.D. 1960. "Scientific Racism and the British Theory of Empire." *Historical*

Society of Nigeria 2:40-51.

Custred, G. 1998. "Point-Counterpoint: Our National Obsession with Race." *Anthropology Newsletter* 39(2): 16-17.

Dake, F.J. 1981. *Dake's Annotated Reference Bible.* Lawrenceville, Ga.: Dake Bible Sales, Inc.

Daly, M. and M. Wilson. 1988. *Homicide.* New York: Aldine de Gruyter.

Dart, R.A. 1940. "Recent Discoveries Bearing on Human History in Southern Africa." *Journal of the Royal Anthropological Institute of Great Britain and Ireland* 70(1): 13-27.

Darwin, C. 1871. *Descent of Man.* London: John Murray.

David, R.J. and J.W. Collins. 1997. "Differing Birth Weight Among Infants of U.S.-Born Blacks, African-Born Blacks, and U.S.-Born Whites." *The New England Journal of Medicine* 337(12):1209-14.

Davies, J.D. 1955. *Phrenology: Fad and Science; a 19th –Century American Crusade.* New Haven, CT: Yale University Press.

Davis, D. B. 1966. *The Problem of Slavery in Western Culture.* New York: Cornell University Press.

Dawkins, R. 1976. *The Selfish Gene.* Oxford: Oxford University Press.

Devisse, J. 1979. *The Image of the Black in Western Art.* Vol. 2.1. New York : William Morrow and Company, Inc.

Diamond, S. 1963. "Statement on Racism." *Current Anthropology.* 4(3):323.

Diner, Hasia R. 1998. "Drawn Together by Self-Interest: Jewish Representation of Race and Race Relations in the Early Twentieth Century." In: *African Americans and Jews in the Twentieth Century: Studies in Convergence and Conflict.* Franklin, V.P., Grant, N.L., Kletnick, H.M., and G.R. McNeil (eds). Pp 27-39. Columbia, Mo: University of Missouri Press.

Diop, C. A. 1974. *African Origin of Civilization: Myth or Reality?* Westport, Ct.: Lawrence Hill and Company.

————.1991. *Civilization or Barbarism: An Authentic Anthropology.* Brooklyn, NY: Lawrence Hill Books.

Dobzhansky, T. 1968. "Introduction." In: *Science and the Concept of Race.* Mead, M., Dobzhansky, T., Tobach, E., and R.E. Light (eds.). Pp 77-79. New York: Columbia University Press.

Dover, C. 1950. "U.N.E.S.C.O. on Race." *The Eugenics Review* XLII(3):177-179

Drake, St. Clair. 1987. *Black Folk Here and There: An Essay in History and Anthropology.* Vol. 1. Los Angeles, Ca: Center for Afro-American Studies, University of California.

————.1990. *Black Folk Here and There: An Essay in History and Anthropology.* Vol. 2. Los Angeles, Ca: Center for Afro-American Studies, University of California.

Drescher, S. 1990. "The Ending of the Slave Trade and the Evolution of European Scientific Racism." *Social Science History* 14:3(Fall):415-449.

D'Souza, Dinesh. 1995. *The End of Racism: Principles for a Multiracial Society.* New York: Free Press.

DuBois, W.E.B. 1899. *The Philadelphia Negro: A Social Study.* New York: Schocken Books.

————.1903. *The Souls of Black Folk: Essay and Sketches.* New York: Bantam Books.

————.1935. *Black Reconstruction in America, 1860-1880.* Cleveland, Oh: World Publishing.

Fede, Andrew. 1985. "Legitimized Violent Slave Abuse in the American South, 1619-1865: A Case Study of Law and Social Change in Six Southern States." *American Journal of Legal History* 1985 29(2): 93-150.

Felder, C.A. 1989. *Troubling Biblical Waters: Race, Class, and Family.* New York: Orbis Books.

Ferraro, G., Trevathan, W. and J. Levy. 1994. *Anthropology: An Applied Perspective.* New York: West Publishing Company.

Finkelman, Paul. 1981. *An Imperfect Union: Slavery, Federalism, and Comity.* Chapel Hill, North Carolina: The University of North Carolina Press.

Finkelman, Paul. 1996. *Slavery and the Founders: Race and Liberty in the Age of Jefferson.* Armonk, New York: M.E. Sharpe.

Flanigan, Danield J. 1974. "Criminal Procedure in Slave Trials in the Antebellum South." *The Journal of Southern History* 31(4):537-564.

Fleure, H.J. 1951."U.N.E.S.C.O. on Race" *Man* 16:28-30.

Fogel, R.W. and S.L. Engerman. 1974. *Time on the Cross: The Economics of American Negro Slavery.* Boston, Ma: Little, Brown and Company.

Forman, James. 2001. "The Conservative Case against Racial Profiling: Arrested Development." *The New Republic* 225(11):24-27.

Forstein M. 1984. "The Psychosocial Impact of the Acquired Immunodeficiency Syndrome." *Seminare in Oncology* March:77-83.

Foster, G. and B.G. Anderson. 1978. *Medical Anthropology.* New York: John Wiley and Sons.

Frankenberg, R. 1993. *White Women, Race Matters: The Social Construction of Whiteness.* Minneapolis, Mn: University of Minnesota Press.

Franklin, R.S. 1991. *Shadows of Race and Class.* Minneapolis, Mn: University of Minnesota Press.

Fredrickson, George M. 1981. *White Supremacy: A Comparative Study in American and South African History.* New York: Oxford University Press.

Freese, L. 1994. "The Song of Sociobiology." *Sociological Perspectives* 37(3):337-373.

Fuller, S. 1987. "On Regulating What is Known: A Way to Social Epistemology." *Synthese* 73:145-183.

Fullilove, M.T. 1998." Comment: Abandoning "Race" as a Variable in Public Health Research—An Idea Whose Time has Come." *American Journal of Public Health* 88:1297-1298.

Fulton, J.F. 1927. "The Early Phrenological Societies and their Journals." *Boston Medical and Surgical Journal March* 10:398-400.

Garn, S. 1964. "Comment." *Current Anthropology* 5:316.

Geronimus, A.T. 1992. "The Weathering Hypothesis and the Health of African-American Women and Infants: Evidence and Speculation." *Ethnicity and Disease* 2:207-221.

————.1996. "Black/White Differences in the Relationship of Maternal Age to Birthweight: A Population-Based Test of the Weathering Hypothesis." *Social Science and Medicine* 42 (4):589-97.

Giachello, A.L. 1996. "Latino Women." In: *Race, Gender, and Health.* Bayne- Smith, M. (ed). Pp 121-171. Thousand Oaks, Ca: Sag Publishers.

Gilliam, A. 1992. "Toward a New Direction in the Media "War" Against Drugs." *Transforming Anthropology* 3(1):19-23.

Gilroy, P. 1991. *There Ain't No Black in the Union Jack: The Cultural Politics of Race and Nation.* Chicago, Il: University of Chicago Press.

Glass, B. 1968. "The Genetic Basis of Human Races." In: *Science and the Concept of Race.* M. Mead, T. Dobzhansky, E. Tobach, and R. E. Light (eds). Pp 88-93. New York: Columbia University Press.

Goldenberg, David M. 1997. "The Curse of Ham: A Case of Rabbinic Racism?" In: *Struggles in the Promised Land: Toward a History of Black-Jewish Relations in the United States.* J. Salzman and C. West (eds.). Pp 21-51. Oxford: Oxford University Press.

Goodman, A. 1995. "The Problematics of "Race" in Contemporary Biological Anthropology." In: *Biological Anthropology: The State of the Science.* N.T. Boaz and L.D. Wolfe (eds.). Bend, Or.: International Institute for Human Evolutionary Research by Oregon State University Press.

———.2000. "Why Genes Don't Count (for Racial Differences in Health)." *American Journal of Public Health* 90(11):1699-1701.

———.2001. "Biological Diversity and Cultural Diversity: From Race to Radical Bioculturalism." In: *Cultural Diversity in the United States: A Critical Reader.* I.Susser and T. Patterson (eds.). Pp 29-45. Malden, Ma: Blackwell Publishers.

Goodman, A. and G. J. Armelagos. 1996. "The Resurrection of Race: The Concept of Race in Physical Anthropology in the 1990s." In: *Race and Other Misadventures: Essays in Honor of Ashley Montagu in His Ninetieth Year.* Reynolds, L.T. and L. Lieberman (eds.). Pp 174-186. Dix Hills, NY: General Hall, Inc.

Gossett, Thomas F. 1965. *Race: The History of an Idea in America.* New York: Schocken Books.

Gotanda, N. 2000. "Comparative Racialization: Racial Profiling and the Case of Wen Ho Lee." *UCLA Law Review* 47(6): 1689-1703.

Gould, S.J. .1977. *Ever Since Darwin.* New York: W.W. Norton.

———.1978. "Morton's Ranking of Races by Cranial Capacity: Unconscious Manipulation of Data may be a Scientific Norm." *Science* 200:503-9.

———.1981. *The Mismeasure of Man.* New York: W.W. Norton.

Grant, Madison. 1916. *The Passing of the Great Race or The Racial Basis of European History.* New York: Charles Scribner's Sons.

Graves, R. and R. Patai. 1964. *Hebrew Myths: The Book of Genesis.* Garden City, NY: Doubleday.

Gray, J.P. and L. D. Wolfe. 1982. " Sociobiology and Creationism: Two Ethnosociologies of American Culture." *American Anthropologist* 84:580-94.

Greenberg, Cheryl. 1997. "Negotiating Coalition: Black and Jewish Civil Rights Agencies in the Twentieth Century." In: *Struggles in the Promised Land: Toward a History of Black-Jewish Relations in the United States.* J. Salzman and C. West (eds.). Pp 153-175. Oxford: Oxford University Press.

Gregory, S. 1994. "Race, Rubbish, and Resistance: Empowering Difference in Community Politics." In: *Race.* S. Gregory and R. Sanjek (eds). Rutgers University Press: New Brunswick, New Jersey.

Gutman, H. 1975."Persistent Myths about the Afro-American Family." *Journal of Interdisciplinary History* 6:181-210.

Hackbarth, D.P., Silvestri, B., and W. Cosper. 1995. "Tobacco and Alcohol Billboards in 50 Chicago Neighborhoods: Market Segmentation to Sell Dangerous Products to the Poor." *Journal of Public Health Policy* 16(2):213-230.

Hacker, Andrew. 1998. "Jewish Racism, Black Anti-Semitism." In: *Blacks and Jews:*

Alliances and Arguments. P. Berman (ed.). Pp 154-163. New York: Delacorte Press.

Hahn, R.A. 1992. "The State of Federal Health Statistics on Racial and Ethnic Groups." *Journal of the American Medical Association* 267(2):268-271.

Hahn, R.A. and D. F. Stroup. 1994. "Race and Ethnicity in Public Health Surveillance: Criteria for the Scientific Use of Social Categories." *Public Health Reports* 109(1):7-15.

Hahn R.A., Truman, B.I. and N.D. Barker. 1996. "Identifying Ancestry: The Reliability of Ancestral Identification in the United States by Self, Proxy, Interviewer, and Funeral Director." *Epidemiology* 7:75-80.

Hamilton, W.D. 1964. "The Genetical Evolution of Social Behavior." *Journal of Theoretical Biology* 7:1-32.

————.1972. "Altruism and Related Phenomena, Mainly in Social Insects." *Annual Review of Ecology and Systematics* 3:193-232.

Harpending, H. 1995. "Human Biological Diversity." *Evolutionary Anthropology* 4:99-103.

Harpending, H., Rogers, A., and P. Draper. 1987. "Human Sociobiology." *Yearbook of Physical Anthropology* 30: 127-50.

Harris, M. 1964. *Patterns of Race in the Americas*. New York: Walker.

Harrison, Faye V. 1995. "The Persistent Power of "Race" in the Cultural and Political Economy of Racism." *Annual Review of Anthropology* 24:47-74.

————.1997." Anthropology as an Agent of Transformation: Introductory Comments and Queries." In: *Decolonizing Anthropology: Moving Further toward and Anthropology for Liberation*. Faye V. Harrison (ed.). Pp 1-15. Arlington, VA: American Anthropological Association.

————.1998a. "Introduction: Expanding the Discourse on "Race." *American Anthropologist* 100(3):609-631.

————.1998b. "Point-Counterpoint: Affirmative Action is Still Needed." *Anthropology Newsletter* 39(2): 16-17.

————.2000. "Facing Racism and the Moral Responsibility of Human Rights Knowledge." *Ethics and Anthropology* 925: 45-69.

Hauben, P.J. 1969. *The Spanish Inquisition*. New York: Wiley.

Haynes, M.A. and B.D. Smedley.1999. *The Unequal Burden of Cancer: An Assessment of NIH Research and Programs for Ethnic Minorities and the Medically Underserved*. Washington, DC: National Academy Press.

Held, P.J., Pauly, M.V., Bovbjerg, R.R., Newmann, J., and O. Salvatierra. 1988. "Access to Kidney Transplantation: Has the United States Eliminated Income and Racial Differences." *Archives Internal Medicine* 148:2594-2600.

Herman, A.A. 1996 "Toward a Conceptualization of Race in Epidemiologic Research." *Ethnicity and Disease* 6:7-20.

Herrnstein , R. and C. Murray. 1995. *The Bell Curve: Intelligence and Class Structure in American Life*. New York: Free Press.

Herskovits, M.J. 192. *The American Negro: A Study in Racial Crossing*. Bloomington, Indiana: Indiana University Press.

Hill, W. and C. Osman. 1951. "U.N.E.S.C.O. on Race." *Man* 30-32:16-17.

hooks, bell. 1990. *Yearning: Race, Gender, and Cultural Politics*. Boston, Ma: South End Press.

Horton, James Oliver and Lois E. Horton. 1997. "A Federal Assault: African-Americans and the Impact of the Fugitive Slave Law of 1850." In: *Slavery and the Law*. Paul

174   Footnote and References

Finkelman (ed). Pp 143-160. Madison, WI: Madison House.

Hoyme, L.E. St. and M.Y. Iscan. 1989. "Determination of Sex and Race: Accuracy and Assumptions." In: *Reconstruction of Life from the Skeleton.* M. Y. Iscan and K.A.R. Kennedy (eds). Pp. 53-93. New York: Alan R. Liss.

Hurtado, A. 1932. "Respiratory Adaptation in the Indian Natives of the Peruvian Andes. Studies at High Altitudes." *American Journal of Physical Anthropology* 17:137-165.

Hutchinson, Janis Faye. 1997a. "Introduction." In: *Cultural Portrayals of African Americans:Creating an Ethnic/Racial Identity.* Janis Hutchinson (ed.). Pp 1-4. Westport, Ct.:Bergin and Garvey.

―――. 1997b. "The Resurgence of Genetic Hypotheses to Explain Social Behavior among Ethnic Minorities." In: *Cultural Portrayals of African Americans: Creating an Ethnic/Racial Identity.* Janis Hutchinson (ed.). Pp 5-25. Westport, Ct.:Bergin and Garvey.

Hyde J.S. 1996. *Half the Human Experience: The Psychology of Women.* Madison, Wi: University of Wisconsin.

Jayaratne, T.E. and A.J. Stewart. 1991. "Quantitative and Qualitative Methods in the Social Sciences: Current Feminist Issues and Practical Strategies." In: *Beyond Methodology: Feminist Scholarship as Lived Research.* M.M. Fonow and JA Cook (eds). Pp 85-106. Bloomington, In: Indiana University Press.

Jaynes, G.D. and Williams, R.M., Jr. 1989. *A Common Destiny: Blacks and American Society.* Committee on the Status of Black America. National Research Council. Washington, DC: National Academy Press.

Jenks, C.W. 1968. "The United Nations Covenants on Human Rights Come to Life." In : *Recueil d'Etudes De Droit International by Faculte De Droit De L'Universite De Geneve.* Imprimerie De La Tribune De Geneve.

Jensen, A.R. 1969. "How Much Can We Boost IQ and Scholastic Achievement?" *Harvard Educational Review* 39:1-129.

―――.1972. *Genetics and Education.* London: Methuen.

Jones, J.H. 1993. *Bad Blood: The Tuskegee Syphilis Experiment.* New York: The Free Press.

Jones, EI. 1986. "Closing the Health Status Gap for Blacks and Other Minorities." *Journal of the National Medical Association* 78:485-488.

Jones, C.P., T.A. LaVeist, and M. Lillie-Blanton. 1991. "Race" in the Epidemiologic Literature: An Examination of the American Journal of Epidemiology, 1921-1990." *American Journal of Epidemiology* 134(10):1079-1084.

Jones, J.M. 1972. *Prejudice and Racism.* Reading, Ma: Addison-Wesley.

Jones, J. 1992. *The Dispossessed: America's Underclasses from the Civil War to the Present.* New York: Basic.

Jones, J.M. and R.T. Wilson. 1996. "Racism and White Racial Identity: Merging Realities." In: *Impacts of Racism on White Americans.* Bowser, B.P. and R.G. Hunt (eds.). Thousand Oaks, Ca: Sage Publications.

Jones, Y. 1997. "African-American Cultural Nationalism." In: *Cultural Portrayals of African Americans: Creating an Ethnic/Racial Identity.* J Hutchinson (ed.), Pp 113-137. Westport, Ct: Bergin and Garvey.

Jones, R.S. 1997. "Why Blacks are Committed to Blackness." In: *Cultural Portrayals of African Americans: Creating an Ethnic/Racial Identity.* J Hutchinson (ed.). Pp. 49-73. Westport, Ct: Bergin and Garvey.

Jordan, Winthrop. 1977. *White Over Black: American Attitudes Toward the Negro,*

1550-1812. New York: W.W. Norton and Company.

Kahn, J. 2004. "How a Drug Becomes "Ethnic": Law, Commerce, and the Production of Racial Categories. *Yale Journal of Health Policy, Law, and Ethics* IV (1):1-46.

Kamen, H.A.F. 1965. *The Spanish Inquisition.* London: Weidenfeld and Nicolson.

———. 1985. *Inquisition and Society in Spain: in the Sixteenth and Seventeenth Centuries.* London: Weidenfeld and Nicolson.

Katz-Fishman, W. and Jerome Scott. 1998. "The Increasing Significance of Class: Black-Jewish Conflict in the Postindustrial Global Era." In: *African Americans and Jews in the Twentieth Century: Studies in Convergence and Conflict*, Franklin, V.P., Grant, N.L., Kletnick, H.M., and G.R. McNeil (eds.). Pp 309-345. Columbia, Mo: University of Missouri Press.

Keita, S.O.Y. and R.A. Kittles R.A. 1997. "The Persistence of Racial Thinking and the Myth of Racial Divergence." *American Anthropologist* 99(3):534-544.

Keppel Kenneth G., Pearcy, J.N., and D.K. Wagener. 2002. *Trends in Racial and Ethnic-Specific Rates for the Health Status Indicators: United States, 1990-1998.* Healthy People Statistical Notes, No. 23, Hyattsville, Md: National Center for Health Statistics.

King, G., and D.R. Williams. 1995. "Race and Health: A Multidimensional Approach to African-American Health." In: *Society and Health.* Amick, B.C., Levine, S., Tarlov, A.R. and D.C. Walsh (eds.). Pp. 93-130. New York: Oxford University Press.

Kiple, Kenneth F. and Virginia H. King. 1981. *Another Dimension to the Black Diaspora: Diet, Disease, and Racism.* Cambridge, Ma: Cambridge University Press.

Kjellstrand, C.M. 1988. "Age, Sex, and Race Inequalities in Renal Transplantation." *Archives Internal Medicine* 148:1305-1309.

Klineberg, O. 1935. Negro Intelligence and Selective Migration. New York: Columbia University Press.

———. 1944. *Characteristics of the American Negro.* New York: Harper and Brothers.

———. 1954. "Social Science and Segregation." *The UNESCO Courier* 7(5):24-30.

Knox, Robert. 1850. *The Races of Men.* Philadelphia, Pa: Lea and Blanchard.

Kottak, C.P. 2000. *Anthropology: The Exploration of Human Diversity.* New York: McGraw-Hill, Inc.

Krieger, N. and M. Bassett. 1986. "The Health of Black Folk: Disease, Class and Ideology in Science." *Monthly Review* 38:74-85.

Krieger, N., Rowley, D.L., Herman, A.A., Avery, B., and M.T. Phillips. 1993. "Racism, Sexism, and Social Class: Implications for Studies of Health, Disease, and Well-being." *American Journal of Prevention Medicine* 9 (supplement 2):82-122.

Krober, A.L. 1923. *Anthropology.* New York: Harcourt, Brace and Company Year.

Kuhn, T.S. 1962. *The Structure of Scientific Revolutions.* Chicago, Il: The University of Chicago Press.

Kulikoff, Allan. 1978. "The Origins of Afro-American Society in Tidewater Maryland and Virginia, 1700-1790." *Southern Studies* 16:391-428.

Kushnick, L. 1996. "The Political Economy of White Racism in the United States." In: *Impacts of Racism on White Americans.* B.P. Bowser and R.G. Hunt (eds.). Pp 48-67. Thousand Oaks: Sage Publications.

Landesman S. 1983. *The Haitian Connection: The AIDS Epidemic.* New York: St. Martin's Press.

Lauretis Teresa de. 1986. *Feminist Studies, Critical Studies.* Bloomington: Indiana University Press.

LaVeist, T.A. .1996. "Why We Should Continue to Study Race ... But Do a Better Job: An Essay on Race, Racism and Health." *Ethnicity and Disease* 6:21-29.

Leach, E. 1981. Biology and Social Science: Wedding or Rape? Nature 291:267-268.

Lewontin, R.C. 1972. "The Apportionment of Human Diversity." *Evolutionary Biology* 6:381-398.

Lieberman, L. 1968. "The Debate Over Race: A Study in the Sociology of Knowledge." *Phylon* 29:127-141.

Lieberman, L. and L.T. Reynolds. 1978. "The Debate Over Race Revisited: An Empirical Investigation." *Phylon* 39:333-343.

Lieberman, L. and L.T. Reynolds. 1996. "Race: The Deconstruction of a Scientific Concept." In: *Race and Other Misadventures: Essays in Honor of Ashley Montagu in His Ninetieth Year.* Reynold, L.T. and L. Lieberman (eds.). Pp 142-173. Dix Hills, NY: General Hall, Inc.

Linnaeus, Carolus. 1758.) *Systemae Naturae.* London: London Museum.

Little, K.L. 1951. "U.N.E.S.C.O. on Race." *Man* 30-32:17.

Livingstone, F.B. .1958. "Anthropological Implications of Sickle Cell Gene Distribution in West Africa." *American Anthropologist* 60:533-562.

———— .1962. "On the Non-existence of Human Races." *Current Anthropology* 3(3): 279:281.

———— .1964. "On the Non-existence of Human Races." In: *The Concept of Race.* Ashley Montagu (ed). Pp 46-60. Toronto: The Macmillan Company.

Llorente, J.A. 1967. *The History of the Inquisition of Spain, from the Time of its Establishment to the Reign of Ferdinand VII.* Williamstown, Ma: John Lilburne Company.

MacPherson, C.B. 1962. *The Political Theory of Possessive Individualism.* Oxford: Clarendon Press.

Malik, K. 1996. *The Meaning of Race: Race, History and Culture in Western Society.* New York: New York University Press.

Mandle, J. 1992. *Not Slave, Not Free: The African American Economic Experience.* Durham, NC: Duke University Press.

Mark, V. and L. Ervin. 1970. *Violence and the Brain.* New York: Harper and Row.

Marshall, G.A. 1968. "Racial Classification, Popular and Scientific." In: *Science and the Concept of Race.* Mead, M., Dobzhansky, T., Tobach, E., and R.E. Light (eds.). Pp 149-164. New York: Columbia University Press.

Martenson, J. 1992. "The Preamble of the Universal Declaration of Human Rights and the UN Human Rights Programme." In: *The Universal Declaration of Human Rights.* Eide, A., Alfredsson G., Melander, G., Rehof L.A., and Rosas, A. (eds.). Pp 17-29. Scandinavia: Scandinavian University Press.

Martin, Waldo E. 1997. "Nation Time! Black Nationalism, The Third World, and Jews." In: *Struggles in the Promised Land: Toward a History of Black-Jewish Relations in the United States,*.J. Salzman and C. West (eds.). Pp 341-355. Oxford: Oxford University Press.

Mayr, E. 1982. *The Growth of Biological Thought: Diversity, Evolution, and Inheritance.* Cambridge, Ma: Belknap Press of Harvard University Press.

McBride, D. 1991. *From TB to AIDS: Epidemics Among Urban Blacks Since 1900.* Albany, New York: State University of New York.

McClelland, K.E. and C.J. Auster. 1990. "Public Platitudes and Hidden Tensions: Racial Climates at Predominantly White Liberal Arts Colleges." *Journal of Higher*

Education 61(6):607-42.

McCoy, R.W. 1985. "Phrenology and Popular Gullibility." *The Skeptical Inquirer* 9:261-268.

McGee, W.J. 1899. "The Trend of Human Progress." *American Anthropologist* 1(3):401-447.

McGregor D.K. 1998. *From Midwives to Medicine: The Birth of American Gynecology.* New Brunswick, NJ: Rutgers University Press.

McLaren, A. 1981. "A Prehistory of the Social Sciences: Phrenology in France." *Comparative Study of Society and History* 21:3-22.

McLemore, S. Dale and Harriett D. Romo. 1998. *Racial and Ethnic Relations in America.* Boston, Ma.: Allyn and Bacon.

Mead, M., T. Dobzhansky, E. Tobach, and R.E. Lights (eds) .1968. *Science and the Concept of Race.* New York: Columbia University Press.

Messer, E. 1993. "Anthropology and Human Rights." *Annual Review of Anthropology* 22:221-49.

Metress, S.P. 1993. "Race, Racism and the Human Condition: Ideology and Science in Conflict." *Quarterly Journal of Ideology* 16 (1-2):31-42.

Milic, V. 1984. "Sociology of Knowledge and Sociology of Science." *Social Science Information* 23(2):213-274.

Mitchell, B. And G. Mitchell. 1930. *The Industrial Revolution in the South.* Baltimore, Md: The Johns Hopkins University Press.

Molnar, Stephen. 2002. *Human Variation: Races, Types, and Ethnic Groups.* Upper Saddle River, New Jersey: Prentice Hall.

Monge, C. 1948. *Acclimatization in the Andes.* Baltimore, Md: The Johns Hopkins Press.

Montagu, A. 1942. *Man's Most Dangerous Myth: The Fallacy of Race.* New York: Columbia University Press.

————— .1960 *An Introduction to Physical Anthropology.* Springfield, IL: Thomas.

————— .1961. *Man in Process.* Cleveland, Oh: The World Publishing Company.

————— .1965. *The Idea of Race.* Lincoln, Na: University of Nebraska Press.

————— .1972. *Statement on Race. An Annotated Elaboration and Exposition of the Four Statements on Race Issued by UNESCO.* New York: Oxford University Press.

Morgan, Lewis H. 1878. [1964] *Ancient Society.* Cambridge, Ma: Belknap Press.

Morgan, P.D. 1998. *Slave Counterpoint: Black Culture in the Eighteenth-Century Chesapeake and Low Country.* Chapel Hill, NC: University of North Carolina Press.

Morrison, T. 1993. "On the Backs of Blacks." *Time* 143(21):57.

Morton, S. G. 1839. *Crania Americana.* Philadelphia, Pa: J. Dobson.

————— .1844. *Crania Aegyptica.* Philadelphia, Pa: J. Dobson.

————— .1847. "Hybridity in Animals, Considered in Reference to the Unity of the Human Species." *American Journal of Science* 3:39, 203-212.

Mourant, A.E. 1983. *Blood Relations: Blood Groups and Anthropology.* Oxford, England: Oxford University Press.

Moynihan, D. 1965. "Employment, Income, and the Ordeal of the Negro Family." *Daedalus* 94: 745-770.

Mukhopadhyay, C.C. and Y.T. Moses. 1997. "Reestablishing "Race" in Anthropological Discourse." *American Anthropologist* 99(3):517-533.

Muir, D. 1993. "Race: The Mythic Roots of Racism." *Sociological Inquiry* 63:339-350.

Mullings, Leith. 1978. "Ethnicity and Stratification in the Urban United States." *Annals*

of the New York Academy of Sciences 318: 10-22.
————.1989. "Inequality and African-American Health Status: Policies and Prospects."
   In: *Race: Twentieth Century Dilemmas---Twenty-First Century Prognoses.* Van
   Horne W. (ed.). Pp 155-182. Madison, Wi: University of Wisconsin Institute on Race
   and Ethnicity.
Murray, C. 1984. *Losing Ground: America's Social Policy.* 1950-1980. New York:
   Basic Books.
Myrdal, G. [1948]1975. *An American Dilemma: The Negro Problem and Modern
   Democracy.* Vol. 1. New York: Pantheon.
Nash, M. 1962. "Race and the Ideology of Race." *Current Anthropology* 3:285-288.
Nassi, J.A. and S.I. Abramowitz. 1976. "From Phrenology to Psychosurgery and Back
   Again: Biological Studies of Criminality." *American Journal Orthopsychiatry*
   46(4):591-607.
National Center for Health Statistics. 2002. *Summary Health Statistics for the U.S.
   Population.* National Health Interview Survey, 1997.
Newman, M.T. 1955. "The Relation of Climate and Body Composition in Young
   American Males." *American Journal of Physical Anthropology* 13:386.
————.1960. "Adaptations in the Physique of American Aborigines to Nutritional
   Factors." *Human Biology* 32:288-313.
Newman, M.T. and E.H. Munro. 1955. "The Relation of Climate and Body Size in U.S.
   Males." *American Journal of Physical Anthropology* 13:1-17.
Nott, J.C. and G.R. Gliddon. 1854. *Types of Mankind: or, Ethnological Researches,
   Based upon the Ancient Monuments, Paintings, Sculptures, and Crania of Races, and
   Upon Their Natural, Geographical, Philological, and Biblical History.* Philadelphia,
   Pa: Lippincott, Grambo and Company.
Office of Management and Budget. 1978. "Directive No. 15: Race and Ethnic Standards
   for Federal Statistics and Administrative Reporting." In: *Statistical Policy Handbook.*
   Washington, DC: Office of Federal Statistical Policy and Standards, US Dept of
   Commerce.
Okongwu, A. 1993. "Some Conceptual Issues: Female Single-Parent Families in the
   United States." In: *Where Did all the Men Go? Female-Headed/Female-supported
   Households in Cross-Cultural Perspective.* J. Mencher and A. Okongwu (eds). Pp107-
   29. Boulder, Co: Westview Press.
Oliwenstein, L. 1998. "Dr. Darwin." In: *Understanding and Applying Medical
   Anthropology.* Peter J. Brown (ed.). Pp 34-37. Mountain View, Ca: Mayfield
   Publishing Company.
Oliver, Melvin, Shapiro, L., and M. Thomas. 1999. "Getting Along: Renewing
   America's Commitment to Racial Justice." In: *Rethinking the Color Line*, Charles A.
   Gallagher (ed.) Pp 523-541. Mountain View, Ca: Mayfield Publishing Company.
Omi, Michael and H. Winant. 1994. *Racial Formation in the United States: From the
   1960s to the 1990s.* New York: Routledge.
Osborne, N.G. and M.D. Feit. 1992. "The Use of Race in Medical Research." *Journal of
   the American Medical Association* 267(2):275-279.
Otten, M.W., Teutsch, S.M., Williamson D.F.; and J. Marks. 1990. "The Effect of
   Known Risk Factors on the Excess Mortality of Black Adults in the United States."
   Journal of the American Medical Association 263:845-850.
Ottenberg, R. 1925. "A Classification of Human Races Based on Geographic
   Distribution of the Blood Groups." *Journal of the American Medical Association* 84

(19):1393-95.
Parssinen, T.M. 1974. "Popular Science and Society: The Phrenology Movement in Early Victorian Britain." *Journal of Social History* 7:1-20.
Patterson, J.T. 1995. "Race Relations and the "Underclass" in Modern America: Some Historical Observations." *Qualitative Sociology* 18(2):237-261.
Payne, K.W. and C.A. Ugarte. 1989. "The Office of Minority Health Resource Center : Impacting on Health Related Disparities Among Minority Populations." *Health Education* 20:6-8.
Perbal, A. 1940. "La Race Negre et la Malediction de Cham." *Revue de l 'Universite d'Ottawa* 10:447-453.
Pettigrew, T.F. 1985. "New Black-White Patterns." *Annual Review of Sociology* 11:329-46.
Polakow-Suransky, S. 2001. "Flying While Brown: Must Arab Men be Racially Profiled ? " *American Prospect* 12(20) : 14-16.
Polednak, A.P. 1996. "Trends in US Urban Black Infant Mortality, by Degree of Residential Segregation." *American Journal of Public Health* 86 (5):723-726.
Powell J.W. 1888. "From Barbarism to Civilization." *American Anthropologist.* 1(2):97-123.
——.1899. "Sociology, or the Science of Institutions." *American Anthropologist* 1(3):695-745.
Quadagno, J. 1994. *The Color of Welfare: How Racism Undermined the War on Poverty.* New York: Oxford University Press.
Raper, A.B. 1955. "Malaria and the Sickling Trait." *British Medical Journal* 2:1186-1189.
——.1956. "Sickling in Relation to Morbidity from Malaria and other Diseases." *British Medical Journal* 1:965.
Reed, W.L. 1981. "Suffer the Children: Some Effects of Racism on the Health of Black Infants." In: *The Sociology of Health and Illness: Critical Perspectives.* P. Conrad and R. Kern (eds). Pp. 314-327. New York: St. Martin's Press.
Reich, M. 1977. "The Economics of Racism." In: *Problems in Political Economy: An Urban Perspective.* D. Gordon (ed.). Pp 107-113. Lexington, Ma: D.C. Health.
——.1981. *Racial Inequality: A Political Economic Analysis.* Princeton, NJ: Princeton University Press.
A Report for the Independent Commission on International Humanitarian Issues. 1987. *Indigenous Peoples: A Global Quest for Justice.* London: Zed.
Rice, G. 1972. "The Curse That Never Was (Genesis 9:18-27)." *The Journal of Religious Thought* 29:5-27.
Rice MF, M. Winn. 1990. "Black Health Care in America: a Political Perspective." *Journal of the National Medical Association* 82:429-437.
Riley, Jason L. 2001."The "Diversity" Defense." *Commentary* 111(4):24-27.
Ripley, William Z. 1899. *The Races of Europe: A Sociological Study.* New York: D. Appleton and Company.
Roberts, D.F. 1953. "Body Weight, Race, and Climate." *American Journal of Physical Anthropology* 11:533-558.
——.1973. *Climate and Human Variability.* Addison-Wesley Module in Anthropology, No. 34. Reading, Ma: Addison-Wesley.
Robinson, J. 1984. "Racial Inequality and the Probability of Occupation-Related Injury or Illness." *Milbank Quarterly* 62:567-590.

Rose, A. 1951. *The Roots of Prejudice. The Race Question in Modern Science.* Paris: UNESCO.

Rose, S. 1979. "'It's Only Human Nature: The Sociobiologist's Fairyland." *Race and Class* 20(3):277-287.

Roth, C. 1972. *A History of the Jews: From Earliest Times through the Six-Day War.* New York: Schocken.

Royce, E. 1985. "The Origins of Southern Sharecropping: Explaining Social Change." *Current Perspectives in Social Theory* 6:279-299.

Rushton, J. Philippe. 1985. "Differential K Theory: The Sociobiology of Individual and Group Differences." *Personality and Individual Differences* 6(4): 441-52.

—— .1997. *Race, Evolution, and Behavior: A Life History Perspective.* New Brunswick,
New Jersey: Transaction Publishers.

—— .1999. *Race, Evolution, and Behavior.* New Brunswick, New Jersey: Transaction Publishers.

Sacks, Karen Brodkin .1988. "Gender and Grassroots Leadership." In: *Women and the Politics of Empowerment.* Bookman, Ann and Sandra Morgen (eds.). Pp. 77-94. Philadelphia, Pa: Temple University Press.

—— .1994. "How Did Jews Become White Folks." In: *Race.* S. Gregory and R. Sanjek (eds). Pp. 78-102. New Brunswick, NJ: Rutgers University Press.

Sanders, E.R. 1969. "The Hamitic Hypothesis: Its Origin and Function in time Perspective." *Journal of African History* 10(4):521-532.

Sanjek, R. 1994. "The Enduring Inequalities of Race." In *Race* S. Gregory and R. Sanjek (eds). Pp 1-17. New Brunswick, NJ: Rutgers University Press.

Sauer, N.J. 1992. "Forensic Anthropology and the Concept of Race: If Races Don't Exist, Why are Forensic Anthropologists so Good at Identifying Them?" *Social Science and Medicine* 34(2):107-111.

Savitt, T.L. 1978. *Medicine and Slavery: The Diseases and Health Care of Blacks in Antebellum Virginia.* Urbana, Il: University of Illinois Press.

Schafer, Judith Kelleher. 1987. " Guaranteed Against the Vices and Maladies Prescribed by Law: Consumer Protection, the Law of Slave Sales, and the Supreme Court in Antebellum Louisiana." *American Journal of Legal History* 31:306-321.

Schiller, Nina Glick. 1994. "Introducing Identities: Global Studies in Culture and Power." *Identities* 1(1):1-6.

Schreider, E. 1950. "Geographic Distribution of the Body Weight/Body Surface Ratio." *Nature* 165:286.

—— .1963. *Physiological Anthropology and Climate Variations. Environmental Physiology and Psychology in Arid Conditions.* Reviews of Research. Paris: UNESCO.

Schulman, K.A., Berlin, J.A., Harless, W, J.F. Kerner, et al. 1999. "The Effect of Race and Sex on Physicians' Recommendations for Cardiac Catheterization." *New England Journal of Medicine* 340:618-26.

Seminario, Lee Anne Durham. 1975. *The History of the Blacks, The Jews and the Moors in Spain.* Madrid: Plaza Mayor.

Shaffer, H.B. and M.L. McKnight. 1996. "The Polytypic Species Revisited ---Genetic Differentiation and Molecular Phylogenetics of the Tiger Salamander *Ambystoma tigrinum* (Amphibia, Caudata) Complex." *Evolution* 50:417-433.

Shanklin, E. 1998. "The Profession of the Color Blind: Sociocultural Anthropology and

Racism in the 21st Century." *American Anthropologist* 100(3):669-79.

Shannon, T.R. 1996. *An Introduction to the World-System Perspective*. Boulder, Co.: Westview Press.

Shaw, Theodore M. 1997. "Affirmative Action: African American and Jewish Perspectives." In: *Struggles in the Promised Land: Toward a History of Black-Jewish Relations in the United States*. J. Salzman and C. West (eds.). Pp 323-340. Oxford: Oxford University Press.

Shipman, P. 1994. *The Evolution of Racism: Human Differences and the Use and Abuse of Science*. New York: Simon and Schuster.

Shortland, M. 1985. "Skin Deep: Barthes, Lavater and the Legible Body." *Economy and Society* 14(3):273-312.

Singh, G.K. and S.M. Yu. 1996. "Adverse Pregnancy Outcomes: Differences between US- and Foreign-Born Women in Major US Racial and Ethnic Groups." *American Journal of Public Health* 86(6): 837-43.

Sivanandan, A. 1982. "From Resistance to Rebellion: Asian and Afro-Caribbean Struggles in Britain." *Race and Class* 23(3): 111-152.

Smith, H.M., Chiszar, D. and R.R. Montanucci. 1997. "Subspecies and Classification." *Herpetological Review* 28:13-16.

Smedley, Audrey. 1993. *Race in North America: Origin and Evolution of a Worldview*. Boulder, Colorado: Westview Press.

——.1998. "Race" and the Construction of Human Identity." *American Anthropologist* 100(3) 690-702.

Snowden, F. 1983. *Before Color Prejudice: The Ancient View of Blacks*. Cambridge, Ma: Harvard University Press.

Spencer, Herbert. 1891. *The Principles of Sociology*. Vol. 1. New York: D. Appleton and Company.

Stampp, K. 1961. *The Peculiar Institution: Slavery in the Ante-Bellum South*. New York: Alfred A. Knopf.

Stanton, William. 1960. *The Leopard's Spots*. Chicago: The University of Chicago Press.

Stein, G.J. 1988. "Biological Science and the Roots of Nazism." *American Scientist* 76:50-58.

Stepan, Nancy. 1982. *The Idea of Race in Science: Great Britain 1800-1960*. Hamden, Ct: Archon Books.

Stringer, C.B. and P. Andrews. 1988. "Genetic and Fossil Evidence for the Origin of Modern Humans." *Science* 239:126-239.

Stevenson, Brenda E. 1996. *Life in Black and White: Family and Community in the Slave South*. New York: Oxford University Press.

Stocking, George W. 1968. *Race, Culture, and Evolution: Essays in the History of Anthropology*. New York: The Free Press.

——.1982. *Race, Culture, and Evolution: Essays in the History of Anthropology*. Chicago, Il: The University of Chicago Press.

Stoddard, Lothrop. 1920. *The Rising Tide of Color against White World-Supremacy*. New York: Charles Scribner's Sons.

Stolcke, V. 1995. "Talking Culture: New Boundaries, New Rhetorics of Exclusion in Europe." *Current Anthropology* 102(1): 114-32.

Studd, M.V. and U.E. Gattiker. 1991. "The Evolutionary Psychology of Sexual Harassment in Organizations." *Ethology and Sociobiology* 12:249-290.

Sullivan LW. 1989." Shattuck Lecture--the Health Care Priorities of the Bush
     Administration." *New England Journal Medicine* 321:125-128.
—— .1991. "Effects of Discrimination and Racism on Access to Health Care." *Journal
     of the American Medical Association* 266(19):2674.
Sumner, W.G. and A.G. Keller. 1906. *Folkways: A Study of the Sociological
     Importance of Usages, Manners, Customs, Mores, and Morals*. Boston, Ma: Ginn.
Symons, D. 1979. *The Evolution of Human Sexuality*. New York: Oxford University
     Press.
—— .1987. "An Evolutionary Approach: Can Darwin's View of Life Shed Light on
     Human Sexuality." In: *Theories of Human Sexuality*. J.H. Geer and W.T. O'Donohue
     (eds.). Pp 91-125. New York: Plenum Press.
Takaki, R.T. 1987. *From Different Shores : Perspectives on Race and Ethnicity in
     America*. New York : Oxford University Press.
Tapper, Melbourne. 1999. *In the Blood: Sickle Cell Anemia and the Politics of Race*.
     Philadelphia, Pa: University of Pennsylvania Press.
Templeton, A.R. 1998. "Human Races: A Genetic and Evolutionary Perspective."
     American Anthropologist 100(3):632-650.
Thomas S.B. 2001. "The Color Line: Race Matters in the Elimination of Health
     Disparities." *American Journal of Public Health* 91(7):1046-1048.
Thornhill, N.W. and R. Thronhill. 1990. "An Evolutionary Analysis of Psychological
     Pain Following Rape. 1. The Effects of Victim's Age and Marital Status." *Ethology
     and Sociobiology* 11:155-176.
Tobias, P.V. 1970. "Brain-Size, Gray Matter and Race—Fact or Fiction?" *American
     Journal of Physical Anthropology* 32(1):3-25.
Tooby, J. and L. Cosmides. 1990. "The Past Explains the Present: Emotional
     Adaptations and the Structure of Ancestral Environments." *Ethology and
     Sociobiology* 11:375-424.
Trende S.P. 2000. "Why Modest Proposals Offer the Best Solution for Combating
     Racial Profiling." *Duke Law Journal* 50(1):331-380.
Trivers, R.L. 1971. "The Evolution of Reciprocal Altruism." *Quarterly Review of
     Biology* 46:35-57.
Tucker, R.K. 1991. *The Dragon and the Cross: The Rise and Fall of the Ku Klux Klan in
     Middle America*. Hamden, Ct: Archon Books.
Twine, F.W. 1997. "Brown-Skinned White Girls: Class, Culture, and the Construction of
     White Identity in Suburban Communities." In: *Displacing Whiteness: Essays in Social
     and Cultural Criticism*. Ruth Frankenberg (ed.) Pp 214-243. Durham, N.C.: Duke
     University Press.
United Nations. 1950. *Your Human Rights: The Universal Declaration of Human rights
     Proclaimed by the United Nations*. New York: Ellner Publishers, Inc.
UNESCO. 1945. *Constitution of the United Nations Educational, Scientific and Cultural
     Organization*. United Nations.
——. 1950. *UNESCO Statement on Race*. United Nations
——. 1967. *International Covenants on Human Rights*. United Nations
——. 1969. *International Convention on the elimination of All Forms of Racial
     Discrimination*. London: Her Majesty's Stationery Office. United Nations
——. 1979a. *Four Statements on Race*. Paris: United Nations.
——. 1979b. *Declaration on Race and Racial Prejudice: Adopted by the General
     Conference of UNESCO at its Twentieth Session Paris, 27 November 1978*. Paris:

UNESCO.
——— .1980. *Decade for Action to Combat Racism and Racial Discrimination: The Final Years.* United Nations.
——— .1988. *Programme of Action for the Second Decade to Combat Racism and Racial Discrimination.* Fact Sheet No. 5. United Nations.
——— .1994. *International convention on the Elimination of All Forms of Racial Discrimination.* United Nations.
Van den Berghe, P. 1978. "Race and Ethnicity: A Sociobiological Perspective." *Ethnic and Racial Studies* 1 (4): 401-411.
Vander Zanden, James W. 1983. *American Minority Relations.* New York: Alfred A. Knopf.
Vincent, J. 1974 "The Structuring of Ethnicity." *Human Organization* 33(4): 375-379.
——— . 1993. "Framing the Underclass." *Critique of Anthropology* 13(3):215-179.
Visweswaran, K. 1998. "Race and the Culture of Anthropology." *American Anthropologist* 100(1):70-83.
Wagley, C. and M. Harris. 1958. *Minorities in the New World.* New York: Columbia University Press.
Wallerstein, Immanuel. 1991. "The Construction of Peoplehood: Racism, Nationalism, Ethnicity." In: *Race, Nation, Class: Ambiguous Identities.* Etienne Balibar and Immanuel Wallerstein (eds). New York: Verso.
Waring, Joseph I. 1964. *A History of Medicine in South Carolina, 1825-1900. South Carolina Medical Association.* Columbia: R.L. Bryan Company.
——— .1971. *A History of Medicine in South Carolina, 1900-1970. South Carolina Medical Association.* Columbia: R.L. Bryan Company.
Washburn, S.L. 1978. "Animal Behavior and Social Anthropology." *Society* 15(6):35-41.
Washburn, S.L. and E.R. McCown. 1972. "Evolution of Human Behavior." *Social Biology* 19(2):165-170.
Weiner, A.B. 1995. "Culture and Our Discontents." *American Anthropologist* 97:14-40.
Weiss, Nancy J. 1997. "Long-Distance Runners of the Civil Rights Movement: The Contribution of Jews to the NAACP and the National Urban League in the Early Twentieth Century." In: *Struggles in the Promised Land: Toward a History of Black-Jewish Relations in the United States.* J. Salzman and C. West (eds.). Pp 123-152. Oxford: Oxford University Press.
Wenneker, M.B. and A.M. Epstein. 1989. "Racial Inequalities in the use of Procedures for Patients with Ischemic Heart Disease in Massachusetts" *Journal of the American Medical Association* 261:253-257.
West, Cornel. 1998." On Black-Jewish Relations." In: *Blacks and Jews: Alliances and Arguments.* P. Berman (ed). Pp 144-153. New York: Delacorte Press.
Westermann, C. 1984. *Genesis 1-11: A Commentary.* Minneapolis, Mn: Augsburg Publishing House.
White, Charles. 1795. *An Account of the Regular Gradation in Man, and in Different Animals and Vegetables; and From the Former to the Latter.* London: C. Dilly.
Wiederman, M.W. and E.R. Allgeier. 1992. "Gender Differences in Mate Selection Criteria: Sociobiological or Socioeconomic Explanations." *Ethology and Sociobiology* 13:115-124.
Wiener, A.S. 1946. "Recent Developments in the Knowledge of the Rh-Hr Blood Types; Tests for Rh Sensitization." *American Journal of Clinical Pathology* 16:477-97.

Williams, D.R. 1992. "Social Structure and the Health Behavior of Blacks." In: *Health Behaviors and Health Outcomes*. K.W. Schaie, J.S. House and D. Blazer (eds.). Pp 59-64. Hillsdale, NJ: Erlbaum.

Williams, D.R., Lavizzo-Mourey, R., and R.C. Warren. 1994. "The Concept of Race and Health Status in America." *Public Health Reports* 109(1):26-41.

Williams, J.S., McGrath, J.H., and A. Crighton-Zollar. 1995. "Race and Pistol Access: Variations among Poor Males." *Free Inquiry in Creative Sociology* 23(2):77-83.

Williams, B. 1994. "Babies and Banks: The "Reproductive Underclass" and the Raced Gendered Masking of Debt." In: *Race*. S. Gregory and R. Sanjek (eds). Pp 348-365. New Brunswick, NJ: Rutgers University Press.

———.1996. "Introduction." In: *Women out of Place: The Gender of Agency and the Race of Nationality*. B.F. Williams (ed.). Pp. 1-33. New York: Routledge.

Williamson, J. 1986. *Rage for Order*. Oxford, UK: Oxford University Press.

Wilson, E.O. 1975. *Sociobiology: The New Synthesis*. Cambridge, Ma: Harvard University Press.

Wilson, C.A. 1996. *Racism: From Slavery to Advanced Capitalism*. Thousand Oaks, Ca: Sage Publications.

Wilson, W.J. 1987. *The Truly Disadvantaged: The Inner City the Underclass, and Public Policy*. Chicago, Il: University of Chicago Press.

Wilson, Jay and R. Wallace. 1992. *Black Wallstreet: A Lost Dream*. Tulsa, Ok: Black Wallstreet Publishing Company.

Winant, Howard. 1994. *Racial Conditions: Politics, Theory, Comparisons*. Minneapolis, Mn: University of Minnesota Press.

Wohl, Alexander. 2001. "Diversity on Trial." *American Prospect* 12(8):37-39.

Wolpin, K.I. 1992. "The Determinants of Black-White Differences in Early Employment Careers: Search, Layoffs, Quits, and Endogenous Wage Growth." *Journal of Political Economy* 100(3):535-560.

Wolpoff, M.H., A.G. Thorne, F.H. Smith, D.W. Frayer, and G.G. Pope .1994. "Multiregional Evolution: A World-Wide Source for Modern Human Populations." In: *Origins of Anatomically Modern Humans*. M.H. Nitecki and D.V. Nitecki (eds.). Pp 175-200. New York: Plenum Press.

Yancy, C.W. 2002. "The Role of Race in Heart Failure Therapy." *Current Cardiology Report* 4(3): 218-25.

Zuckerman, M. 1990. "Some Dubious Premises in Research and Theory on Racial Differences." *American Psychologist* 45(12):1297-1303.

Author Biographical Sketch

Janis Faye Hutchinson, Ph.D., M.P.H. is a biological/medical anthropologist in the Department of Anthropology, University of Houston. She received her doctorate from the University of Kansas; and my master's and bachelor degrees from the University of Alabama. Her research interests include condom use, HIV/AIDS, racism and health, and health issues among minority populations. Her publications focus on these topics and African-American identity as shown in *Cultural Portrayals of African Americans: Creating an Ethnic/Racial Identity*, 1997. Currently she is examining the impact of recent DNA information (mapping of the human genome) on health beliefs among Indian/Hindu Americans.

INDEX